FESTIVE FAITH

"This wonderful book shows us why and how celebrating the liturgical calendar isn't just for one hour on Sunday—it's a way of life. *Festive Faith* is a great gift to Catholic domestic and parish churches alike."

Rev. David Michael Moses
Parish priest in Houston, Texas

"Steffani Aquila has solved our too-busy, can't-bother-with-liturgical-living conundrum with *Festive Faith*. She shares practical ideas for bringing rich traditions of Catholic culture into our homes and parishes, tells the story of these traditions, and reminds us that even a little can go a long way in learning our faith by the rhythms of the Church year. Whether you are single or married, young or old, ordained or lay, and whether your household is large or small, this book will live—and be much used—at your kitchen table or office desk alongside your prayer books and calendar, helping you ease your way into celebrating the cycles and seasons of the Catholic year."

Katie Prejean McGrady
Author of *Follow* and host of *The Katie McGrady Show*

"What a treasure trove for liturgical living! Sharing the history of traditions as well as practical applications, this book is sure to promote rich, beautiful, and festive Catholic culture in both homes and parishes. Steffani Aquila's collection will help Catholics in all states of life draw closer to the Lord through their celebration of our liturgical cycles and seasons."

Katherine Bogner
Teacher, blogger, and author of *Through the Year with Jesus*

"We have followed Steffani Aquila on social media for many years. Her insight, simplicity, and deep understanding help us to live liturgically while making our faith and its traditions tangible and acceptable for our children. We are delighted to have her wisdom in book format! Many people will greatly benefit from *Festive Faith*, making every Catholic home a place that lives, knows, and loves the faith—not only in word but also in action."

Jason and Rachel Bulman
National speakers and hosts of *Meet the Bulmans*

FESTIVE FAITH

CATHOLIC CELEBRATIONS THROUGH THE YEAR AND AROUND THE WORLD

A HANDBOOK FOR HOMES AND PARISHES

STEFFANI AQUILA

AVE MARIA PRESS AVE Notre Dame, Indiana

Founded in 1865, Ave Maria Press is a ministry of the United States Province of Holy Cross.

www.avemariapress.com

Paperback: ISBN-13 978-1-64680-336-1

E-book: ISBN-13 978-1-64680-337-8

Cover image © Kortnee Senn, StudioSenn.com.

Cover and text design by Brianna Dombo.

Printed and bound in the United States of America.

Library of Congress Cataloging-in-Publication Data is available.

LOVINGLY DEDICATED TO MY HUSBAND,
DOMINICK.

YOUR INFLUENTIAL FAITH HAS GIVEN
ME THE COURAGE NOT ONLY TO
EXPERIENCE THE WONDER AND MYSTERY
OF EACH SEASON BUT TO SHARE IT.

CONTENTS

ACKNOWLEDGMENTS

My heart is overflowing with appreciation for my husband, who has fervently supported my every dream. When I shared my desire to be a part of bringing Catholic culture back to the world, he said, "Let's do it." When I told him I wanted to start blogging, he shared every post. And when I wanted to open an online market, he packaged every order. Our family, liturgical life, and ministry are enriched with the selfless and encouraging love of a good man and husband.

This book also would not have been possible without the blessing of my family and my husband's family. Each one in their own unique way evokes celebration throughout the year in a manner that is meaningful and authentic. In particular, I want to express my deep gratitude to my cherished grandmother, who shared her Hispanic culture and faith with me and instilled a curiosity to learn more.

To everyone who contributed personal testimonies in this book, I am beyond thankful that they entrusted me with their story, their family, and their very real experiences of faith in the world. Reading the beauty of their lives quite literally brought tears to my eyes, and I believe that without them, this book would be a mere description of activities. They aided me in crafting a book that is truly about the story of God's people still waiting hopefully and joyfully for the Second Coming.

Over the last fifteen years I've worked professionally in Catholic communities across the diverse Archdiocese of Galveston–Houston. I am grateful to those parish and school communities who have treated me like family and shared the unique ways that each culture expresses praise. They taught me about humanity, faith-filled relationships, and what it means to be at the service of God's Church. These wonderful people made it possible for me to know and share what living tradition actually looks like on the ground.

And to my readers, you are the very reason that I wrote this book, because I want you to see that liturgical living is for you too. You deserve a life filled with true festivity! Regardless of the personal season that you might find yourself in, God can still be praised and you can still have joy. Your support has been essential to my ministry, and I am deeply appreciative that you have invited me into your life, family, and community. That is a gift I will cherish always.

INTRODUCTION

Liturgical living has become a trending topic among Catholics on social media, in parish groups, and in households around the world. Although it may seem like a new lifestyle, finding ritual and routine with God in accordance with the seasons is deeply rooted in the life of the Church. In fact, you may have even seen the phrases "sacramental life" and "liturgical life" used in various writings of the Church. The terms may seem loaded, but I have found it incredibly helpful to view them in the more practical light of liturgical living. Essentially, liturgical living or having a liturgical life means fully immersing ourselves in the whole of the Christian life for our own sanctification and as a participation in building the kingdom of God on earth. We are to use the liturgical year as our guide and inspiration for offering festivity and praise to God for the gift of life and for his salvific work. This means that living the liturgical year is not merely undertaking one-off feast-day activities now and then; rather, it is a transformative and ongoing affirmation of God and all God's good creation, which is written into the very core of our being. All of creation reflects God's glory, and when we look to the seasons, both natural and liturgical, we can see a cycle of worship that is undeniably guiding our every day. Experiencing the Church's year should unfold the mysteries of Christ's incarnation in our daily lives and draw us into deeper relationship with him and with one another through the year by way of seasonal cycles and feasts. We are all meant for this!

My husband, Dominick, and I both come from generations of abundant liturgical tradition and culture. I come from Hispanic Catholic roots on my mom's side, and my husband has Italian Catholic heritage from both his mom and his dad. The joining of those traditions under one roof gave our personal lives and married life purpose, devotedness, and community. To say that we have a lively and vibrant family sounds like an understatement in the middle of a crowded home filled with laughter, children running around, adults catching up, grandparents delighting in their family, teens helping to set the table, and amazing food on every counter.

I learned liturgical living in the midst of our extended families, both of which have an open-door policy for neighbors. Catholic festivity has been in my family and in Dominick's for generations, handed down as a rich inheritance and woven into our weeks, months, and seasons with gratitude and enthusiasm for God and for people. To live liturgically alongside family and friends, while holding the memory of those loved ones who have gone before us, makes the mystery of God-with-us always tangible in the Catholic festive traditions that we share throughout the year.

When I decided to share online the inheritance that I had received from Christ and our families, I was introduced to a type of liturgical living that I found difficult to relate to. Most, if not all, of the resources I saw were tailored to children of a certain age range and to young women. Amid resources that seemed unapplicable to me because we don't have children and since my husband wants to have a liturgical life, too, I wondered how many parents of young children were perhaps neglecting their own liturgical lives for the sake of their children's. How many young adult Catholics who aren't married or don't have children are being left out because most liturgical-living guidance and suggestions these last several years seem to be about practices for the home, and most often for families with young children, with no extension or connection to the parish or wider community? How many people perceive that the time of festivity has passed with the growth of their children? How many older Catholics miss the joy, hope, and companionship that regular, repeated festivity brings? How many communities—whether they are rooted in parishes, families, schools, friend groups, neighborhoods, or Catholic workplaces—are left wondering how to practically reclaim and enact our Catholic traditions in large-group environments as they once were practiced? As I began speaking and working with Catholic adults across the country to help them establish a liturgical life through growing a festive Catholic culture in homes, parishes, and neighborhoods, I quickly saw that many people were indeed being left out of the current groundswell of efforts to reclaim Catholic festivity rooted in our liturgical year and calendar.

One evening I was giving a talk at a parish to a large group of adults. After recommending that we celebrate our baptismal anniversaries or name days, one of the women attending raised her hand and said that she didn't know how she and her husband could do that. They were genuinely at a loss for ideas, not only because she didn't know what Catholic liturgical traditions were available to her, but because they struggled to see how they could celebrate the faith as an adult couple. Their children were grown and moved out; how could these two empty nesters live liturgically? After her question came an onslaught of similar inquiries. These very good and valid questions confirmed for me what I had already sensed, which is that Catholics, particularly in America, no longer have larger communities with which to live liturgically. Age-old Catholic familial and cultural traditions have not been passed on, and there are few current resources that articulate how everyone can participate in the life of the Church.

As my husband and I have sought to carry on our inherited traditions, we too have found that there are fewer and fewer people to live them out with. What was once an authentic and communal experience of celebrating God, Mary, and the saints throughout the year has become a more isolated and manicured experience that takes place in each individual home. Distant are the days when people simply gathered somewhere for a feast day or liturgical season over music, singing, dancing, eating, and drinking—when adults in various seasons of life, teens, kids, and babies all gathered in celebration without the pressure of appealing to one age group over another. In light of this realization, I felt a heightened sense of purpose in extending liturgical living as it had been given to me because it is inherently people-centered, organic, and life-giving to anyone in any season. Truly, these elements get to the heart of celebration, not the tasks of gathering and purchasing lots of small activity-based supplies, which can become stressful and run the risk of distracting from genuine festivity.

I want to inspire within your immediate family, extended family, and parish community what I like to call "village Catholicism," which has been the Church's liturgical-living custom for centuries. By "village Catholicism" I mean an interpersonal, story-centered, cultural experience rooted in shared faith and in Catholic festive traditions in the home and in the parish.

I hope you will be encouraged with the resources in this book and on my website to begin or continue to live the Church's liturgical year in your home, but please do not stop there. While liturgical living with your immediate family within your home is good, it is not enough. We must open our doors and hearts to others, to celebrate within our villages—preferably our parish communities and our extended families—and to rebuild our faith and reestablish the Catholic Church as a people who know how to celebrate because God is with us always.

A tip I've learned to trust and rely on when tangibly living out the liturgical year is what I call the "Three A's." These are *accessibility, attainability,* and *authenticity,* and you will be introduced to practical, specific applications of these in the main chapters of this book. A cornerstone of tradition is the ability for all people to participate in it in their own way. This is what I mean by *accessibility* when it comes to experiences of liturgical living. The first step we must take in making liturgical living accessible is embodying and living it for God and ourselves. My maternal grandmother immediately comes to mind in this regard. She exudes love for Jesus, Mary, and her family. You can tell by the way that she cooks, speaks, and celebrates with us that she isn't just doing these things to entertain her children and grandchildren; she is extending to God and her family the joy that she has in her own heart. As I reflect on her generational impact, I realize that a fundamental part of making the liturgical year accessible to everyone who might be present is inviting others into the ways that we ourselves like to celebrate. That's what my grandma does: she invites all of us into her own heart and home, and the impression that it has left inspires me to do as she did. Festive seasonal traditions are made accessible to our large, multigeneration Hispanic family by transcending age-specific catechetics and activities and choosing more authentically cultural celebrations tied not only to our Catholicism but to our Hispanic heritage.

Everyone can do this, no matter where you live in the world or the season of life that you are in, by looking to your faith and family ties. A quote to remind us of the accessibility of liturgical living, or celebrating feasts, comes from Pope Pius XI. Nearly a century ago, he wrote in his 1925 encyclical *Quas Primas,* "Feasts reach them all; the former [official pronouncements of church teaching] speak but once, the latter [feasts] speak every year—in fact, forever. The church's teaching affects the mind primarily; her feasts affect both mind and heart, and have a salutary effect upon the whole of man's nature."[1] This approach to liturgical living doesn't require any extra work or customization but also allows for us to do something more age-specific if we find it helpful and energizing. My rule of thumb is this: if the liturgy is for everyone and with everyone, then a liturgical life must be for everyone and with everyone.

The second of the "Three A's" is *attainability,* or the ability to make liturgical living possible or doable in your current season of life. I think the most prominent deterrent from any attempt at liturgical living is the impression that its primary purpose is to teach and that one must have the wherewithal to teach. This could not be further from the truth. While we do in fact learn about the life of Christ and the Catholic faith from observing the liturgical year, the fundamental reasons for liturgical living are the same as the four ends or purposes of the celebration of the Mass—that is, to give God praise, thanksgiving, sacrifice, and prayer. With this approach we realize that we do not have to take on the role of teacher, but that we can all take on the role of a learner whom God is teaching through the natural and liturgical seasons.

Expand your view of liturgical living, and see it as a positive opportunity for you and your loved ones to praise God in the ways that you can and with the resources that are at your fingertips. You will see in the chapters ahead that this is the way people around the world have lived the Church's year for centuries. Herbs and flowers were blooming outside the windows of the faithful around the Feast of the Assumption, so blessing these seasonal goods and creating herbal Assumption Bundles became a treasured tradition. Like our ancestors in faith, we can learn to celebrate by using what is right outside our windows. To celebrate is to acknowledge and affirm by some words or gestures a thing, person, or experience that bears meaning. Most of the time, particularly in our homes, nothing need be scripted or formal about celebrating the days and seasons of the liturgical year. Instead, let a genuine response of thanksgiving and praise well up from within you, and celebrate with simple words, gestures, or activities that convey what the occasion means for you, acknowledging and affirming that God is present.

The third of the "Three A's" is *authenticity*, which means that you are praising God in a way that is true to who you are as an individual, family, and community. Try as I might to do liturgical-living things that other people are doing, I always seem to come back to my own experiences and nature. We can and should be encouraged to celebrate God in the place we live, with the things we have, and with the people we are with by simply doing what comes authentically to us. In this way, we are writing our own stories of faith, while simultaneously partaking in the stories of our families and communities by giving God thanks and praise through small celebrations of ritual actions throughout the liturgical year. Authentic liturgical living gives ourselves and our families heartfelt experiences to better know and worship God. For some this may be through singing, for others cooking or perhaps praying. Just remember, a feast-day tradition is so much more than just an activity to do. It's a window into a person, a home, a town, a people. We can establish a genuine liturgical lifestyle that is grounded in a sense of grateful appreciation for God and others by celebrating according to our own gifts, talents, cultures, and interests.

USING THIS BOOK

When we observe the celebrations of the liturgical year and enter into an internal disposition of festivity, we incarnate, or embody, the core beliefs of our Catholic faith. Take the season of Advent, for example: we externally express to ourselves and others around us that the celebration of the birth of Christ is such that we not only remember an event of long ago but also strive to make Christ's coming among us in the present tangible year after year in our everyday lives. Throughout the following chapters you will be invited into the homes and communities of people around the world who have sought to do just that: to keep the *invisible* truths of our faith alive in a *visible* way throughout all seasons. This is the sacramental life that the Church summons us to.

Each tradition is shared through the lens of how it came to be and why it is still relevant for us today. Some of the customs you will read about have evolved over time, while others have stayed exactly the same for hundreds of years. This is not a comprehensive list of every faith-filled Catholic practice that stems from our liturgical year; rather, my writing seeks to share popular traditions and pieties that have become commonly practiced. The practices shared throughout this book may not be exclusively undertaken in the country or local community where they originated, but are shared from that perspective because it is helpful to understand the culture within which these traditions were born and developed.

Considering the importance to the Christian life of sharing our lives and our stories, the essence of our Catholic liturgical traditions is most authentically conveyed by those who actively live and cherish them as an integral part of their faith journeys. I invite you to dig into the personal testimonies from Catholics who have either personally engaged in some of the traditions you'll find in this book or who can articulate the beauty and importance of these traditions from the perspective of the cultures that embrace the celebration in focus.

THE FEASTS, FASTS, AND CUSTOMS

This book is organized by the seasons of our liturgical or Church year, sometimes known as the Year of Grace. In each chapter I share what I have learned of the origin stories or histories of popular traditions both old and new across the liturgical calendar and the natural seasons as we experience them, at least in the northern hemisphere where I live. Each chosen day of feasting or fasting was carefully selected because of its preexisting or current rise to popularity, with full knowledge that there are so many more festive traditions and experiences to be discovered for the first time or reclaimed by our Catholic households and parishes. There are simply too many for one book!

Open each chapter and you will find a treasure trove, with each offering something worthy of deepening your faith to help you grow in holiness. This is the enriching experience of living the liturgical year. The schedule or calendar of the secular world was not intended to help us get to heaven, but the liturgical calendar and the natural seasons are formed with that end in mind. As St. Thérèse of Lisieux says, "The world is thy ship, not thy home."[2] The content of this book and the adventurous festivity you can create from it are meant to help you, your family, your parish, and your wider community praise God now and on the voyage home.

"CARRYING ON THE TRADITION" AND "CONSIDER THIS"

Within each spotlighted festive tradition or custom there are subsections entitled "Carrying on the Tradition." Given the sheer number of opportunities and potential ways that you could live out a feast day, I am seeking to offer options that make your liturgical living more authentic to the tradition and to your own life so that you are emboldened to choose what seems to fit into your story and your life. This section is divided up so that a household can discern all of the options for celebrating, and a parish community can do the same. To get you started, I've provided a couple of activities that delve into the essence of the tradition, accompanied by the brainstorming guide labeled "Consider This." This list is my way of acknowledging that every home, family, community, parish staff, and culture is different. To respect this reality, I have listed ways that you might consider maintaining, adapting, changing, or growing the tradition to fit your particular needs and circumstances. Perhaps you might celebrate the tradition as is, but because liturgical living ought to be a natural expression of the heart, it's also okay for you to change it. Make it your own!

Keep in mind that this book is not a list of things to do in entirety. There is no one culture, individual, family, or parish doing everything shared in this book. There's not enough coffee in the world to get you through them all. For both the home and the parish, I encourage you to pick what you find to be most meaningful or simply most intriguing at the outset and give those a try. If you find these help you grow spiritually, learn to do them well.

It is always beneficial to consider your family's or community's cultural makeup. Take this opportunity to learn more about your heritage and those of your fellow parishioners and neighbors. In the parish where I worked as the Director of Liturgical Life, we had three prominent cultural groups: Hispanic, Vietnamese, and Anglo-American. Sometimes with parish dynamics like this, different cultural communities can end up in different silos. To welcome parishioners into a deeper sense of belonging to the parish-wide community, we would do the following. When a feast day or liturgical celebration held special meaning to one of these various groups, we met with some members of that group to discuss how best to serve their community while also creating space for them to lead all of us in sharing their culture's traditions and festivities. Then we made sure to extend the invitation to the entire parish as a way for others to experience union and participation in the Catholic culture of a subgroup within the parish community. When possible, I would also seek to invite surrounding parishes to join us in planning and celebrating. Parishes themselves can end up becoming isolated and overly inward-facing, even seeing one another as competition at times. Collaborating with parishes in your area can help to expand and further impact the liturgical life of your parishioners. This is a prime example of engaging other people's stories that I referenced earlier in the introduction.

Allow festivity to pour out of your heart and into your actions in a way that is organic to you. In all that you do, extend yourself grace within your efforts to praise God through various festive traditions and customs. Remember, your entrance into heaven is not dependent upon how well you pulled off the feast-day treat. If you found something and it became a way to worship God more fully, then you should consider repeating it or making it an annual tradition. But if all it did was bring stress, then adjust your efforts and try it again, perhaps in a simpler way, or do something else from this book next year. If there is a lived experience of Ordinary Time, or any other season mentioned, that you think will positively impact your home or parish, I encourage you to try it.

Keep in mind that most of the traditions presented in this book are communal at the center. They are not meant to be carried out in their entirety alone. No one of us is expected to take on full responsibility for enlivening the faith of our households or our parishes or any community in between. Share this book with your spouse, friend, priest, neighbor, brother, sister, and so on, and tell them that it would mean a lot to you if they would join you in one thing or another. You will see examples of this same sort of collaborative effort when you read the tradition stories; each custom was carried out by the whole. Lean in to those around you to make these things happen and to inspire Catholic culture and tradition in your family and community. Bring the festivity, celebration, and joy of the Catholic faith into your home, your parish, your neighborhood, and the world.

"IN THE HOME" AND "IN THE PARISH"

I have included each of these two sections to facilitate living the liturgical year within both the home and the wider community. There is a shared responsibility here. In order for our liturgical life to thrive and extend out into the world, there must be a synergetic relationship between the life of the parish and the life of the home. Parishes are at the center of liturgical life because they provide the liturgy and sacraments, which we are seeking to extend into our daily lives. Parishes are our Catholic villages and can lead the way in unifying us through our festive customs and rituals. Experiencing these distinctive elements of our faith pulls us out of the mundane and draws us toward seeing the sacred realities of God's presence in all things. Let's rebuild Catholic culture together by using the liturgical year as our model and guide.

The parish sections for each spotlighted tradition are not just meant for clergy and parish employees, but rather they are a call for parishioners, volunteers, and various ministers of the parish to take initiative. Enriching and growing parish festivity rightly belongs to all members. Establish collaborative relationships with parish employees and leaders to make these yearly customs or traditions a reality.

Households, let me be your sister and friend and say that you do not need to wait for a "better" time to live the liturgical year. It doesn't have to be picture-perfect as you might sometimes see online. You don't need to add activities to your already busy lives. Expanding your awareness of and appreciation for the cycles and seasons of our Catholic life is really all you need. You might be surprised by what happens as you do so. Praise God by being who you are and doing things you enjoy with the people you love. The time is now!

"LIVING TRADITION"

The "Living Tradition" sections that are sprinkled throughout the book are a way for you to learn about the life and traditional practice of a particular person, a household or family, and a wider community. It is in their personal testimonies that you can see what liturgical living is about: home, heritage, culture, faith, and love. It is in these accounts that we come to know God through various cycles and seasons of life and how he has made himself known all over the world. Liturgical living is a transcendental, sacred, and personal—but not private—experience of feast days and seasons. These stories will help you see and come to value the intricacies of someone's life: how they encountered God, connected with others, celebrated their heritage, and found solace in the wonders of God's created world. It's a privilege to have these stories and experiences passed on to us, and it's our duty and responsibility to honor their sharing. While I could tell you these stories myself, it's not the same as reading the words from people who live these customs. They are best at sharing their own stories. I am deeply grateful to these faithful believers, nearly all of whom live in or near Houston where I also make my home.

ADDITIONAL CONTENT AVAILABLE ONLINE

Five printable booklets are accessible online to facilitate the implementation of the traditions advocated in this book. Among them, one booklet is tailored to explaining the liturgical calendar, aiding in the comprehension of its cycles and significance. Another booklet serves as a comprehensive guide for embracing the rhythms of feasting and fasting, fostering a deeper engagement with these liturgical and spiritual practices. The remaining trio of booklets are full of practical resources, ranging from recipes to plans, prayers, reflections, tips, and household blessings to assist in the seamless integration of seasonal observances into daily life. Together, these booklets offer a holistic toolkit for individuals seeking to enrich their spiritual journey through tradition and ritual. You can find these companions at www.HisGirlSunday.com/FestiveFaith.

- Booklet One: *Festive Faith Sundays and Essentials Companion*
- Booklet Two: *Festive Faith Rhythms of Fasting and Abstinence Companion*
- Booklet Three: *Festive Faith Advent and Christmas Companion*
- Booklet Four: *Festive Faith Winter Ordinary Time, Lent, and Triduum Companion*
- Booklet Five: *Festive Faith Easter and Summer Ordinary Time Companion*

I welcome you to go through the year and around the world with me and others who are reading this book as we seek to cultivate and live out the heart of village Catholicism. It doesn't matter what time of year you dig in or how often you open and take in the pages of this book. Please come join the celebrations, customs, and traditions of our festive Catholic faith. God is good; let us praise him and give him thanks all the year long!

ONE

LITURGY AND LITURGICAL LIVING

I learned to grasp the foundational purpose and meaning of the word *liturgy* by coming to understand that it is at the most basic level a participatory relationship between God and his people. This relationship is animated and made richer by both offering and receiving (*Catechism of the Catholic Church* [*CCC*], 1069–70). A more precise doctrinal definition of liturgy is derived from the Greek origin of the word, which is *leitourgia*. This word loosely translated means "the public work of the people." The work that is being referred to is our communal prayer, worship, and celebration of God. The Church tells us that this is what we humans are created to do. Interestingly, that is not the only dynamic at play. The liturgy is also Christ working on our behalf by offering himself to us as the sacrificial lamb since we cannot attain salvation on our own. In the liturgy, we participate in God's own work by imitating his love and sacrifice in our worship.

The liturgy is not a single celebration or act of worship, but instead encompasses all of the prescribed public worship of the Church. Because liturgy is our communal and public worship, it is regulated, with prescribed words and actions making up the various ritual celebrations. In this important way, liturgical celebration is different from the Church's devotional prayer. Devotions can be prayed by individuals or in groups, but are not regulated in the way that liturgical celebration is. Devotions are more fluid and easily adaptable to particular circumstances—whether for groups or individuals. Liturgical prayer and devotional prayer ideally exist in harmony within the Church.

Under the umbrella term *liturgy* is included the celebration of the Mass and all the other sacraments, the Liturgy of the Hours, particular rites (a single celebration made up of several ritual elements), and official Church blessings used to mark special days and events in the life of the People of God. Some of these liturgical celebrations are taken up by the universal Church, such as the Celebration of the Lord's Passion on Good Friday—the only day of the year when Mass is not celebrated. Others are celebrated on a quite local level and only rarely, such as the Dedication of a Church or an Altar. At its most basic level, liturgy is ritual celebration. We express in the present through repeated gestures, words, and communal experiences what we believe to be eternally true. Through these celebrations we come to know who we are and how we are to live as God's people here on earth. We develop continuity, a sense of belonging, and an increasingly clearer understanding and deeper embrace of the sacred mysteries of our faith. In other words, by participating in the liturgy (the public worship of the Church), we continuously reaffirm the eternal truths of our Catholic faith by expressing worship and praise in the particular time and place where we gather.

FESTIVITY IN THE LIFE OF THE CHURCH

Ritualizing seems to be inherent for human beings. We naturally and regularly engage in ritual actions—large at times, but mostly small. We greet other people when we encounter them, wear our favorite team's jersey when they are playing, and have a cup of coffee in the morning to get our day started. We pick up or learn the specific ways of these ritual interactions, but the impetus to do these things seems to be inborn in us as humans. Ritualizing the liturgical year is what prompts us toward more routine celebration. And when those celebratory actions within a household or community are directed to God's goodness we can come to understand true festivity.

It is human to celebrate. Celebration or festivity is a distinct part of our drive to understand life, create and grasp meaning, express emotion, and reinforce our need for social and cultural connection. In today's world, celebration is often more plainly understood as partying, but from the richness of our Catholic theology and traditions we can see that while celebration or festivity is indeed an expression of excitement, it also lends itself to so much more. *Festivity* is a multilayered term that I have adopted from Josef Pieper's book

In Tune with the World: A Theory on Festivity. For our exploration of liturgical living, it means to mark significant events in the life of Christ, our own Christian lives, and that of the whole Church here on earth and in heaven—the Communion of Saints. Distinct from marking time, or doing something for the sake of passing time, the Church year prompts us to holistically engage in important milestones so that our human experience is elevated and connected to the larger context of Christ's saving actions. In essence, true Christian festivity, or celebration, is a living affirmation of God and of his life in which we share. This means that not every celebration is undertaken to recognize and affirm a happy or pleasant event, and not every expression of celebration is one of festive indulgence.

Take, for example, celebrations such as All Souls' Day, Good Friday, the beheading of St. John the Baptist, the Feast of the Holy Innocents, or the funeral of a loved one. These are not days upon which we withhold our festivity—in fact, just the opposite. The Church is drawing us out of ourselves to use even grief, tragedy, and death as a way to celebrate, proclaim, and affirm everlasting life. When given the opportunity, the liturgical year can mold our humanity into a Christ-centered lifestyle of ritual and personal connection that is applicable to all life's seasons and circumstances.

OUR WAY OF KEEPING TIME

The liturgical calendar's feast days, solemnities, octaves, days of fasting, monthly dedications, and rhythms are universal invitations to make our faith incarnational, lived, and sacramental, as visible signs to our household and community of the invisible grace that dwells within us. As the phrase suggests, *liturgical living* means to live out the liturgy. I believe that liturgical living can be made more timeless, personal, and attainable if we better comprehend what the liturgy is and how it is our primary means of being formed in our Catholic faith. The liturgy establishes our identity as the Body of Christ and as God's pilgrim Church. We are both Christ's living presence here and now and a people aiming for heaven. Most essential to this twofold identity is the worship we participate in every time we go to Mass. Let's take a step closer and examine four primary ends, or purposes, of participating in the Mass: adoration, thanksgiving, atonement, and petition.

The Holy Mass, particularly Sunday Mass when the whole community is called to worship together, is a profound act of **adoration.** In this reverent offering of praise the faithful, from newborns to the elderly, and everyone in between, join together to give God the glory that he so deserves. Mass is where we derive not only the language but the actions of festivity in our everyday living. In the Mass, we are affirming God as the source of all goodness by offering thanks and praise for all of creation. When we leave Mass, we are sent out to extend our affirmation of God and life's goodness by allowing both the liturgical and natural seasons to prompt and inspire a spirit of festivity. Our authentic expression of daily adoration (i.e., praise, festivity, and worship) is our personal and communal way of positively responding to God's salvific work.

It is no coincidence that the rhythms and cycles of the year stir a sense of holy curiosity within us to discover and relate to God, since each of them retell the great story of our salvation in Christ. Just as the natural seasons die and are reborn, so too the liturgical seasons usher us into the Death and Resurrection of Our Lord. Taking this a step further, both the natural and liturgical seasons show us the resurrected life that we too are meant to live. If we pay attention with the eyes of faith, we can see this. The cycles and season of the liturgical year anchor us in the great mysteries of our faith: the Incarnation, Christ's Death and Resurrection, Christ's ongoing presence in the sacraments—particularly the Eucharist—and the Holy Spirit who dwells among us and animates the Church. Each time we participate in the Mass, we bow down in adoration of God, who heals, saves, and restores all things back to the goodness of creation. God is worthy of our living in harmony with the rhythms, seasons, feasts and fasts of each year. The Church, in her wisdom, has aligned the cycles and seasons such that we might more readily attune our everyday lives to God's action on our behalf through all of time.

The second end, or purpose, of the liturgy is **thanksgiving**. In the Mass, this is most evident through the sacrificial offering of Christ's Body and Blood, fully present in the Eucharist. The term *Eucharist* finds its origins in the Greek form *eucharistia*, which means "thanksgiving." The liturgy, most often defined as the work of the people, can also be explained as the redemptive work that God is doing on our behalf, in which the People of God participate. What is revealed to us in this subtle yet invaluable nuance is that Christ generously extends to us that which we cannot accomplish for ourselves: salvation. This truth is made real again every time we go to Mass. The Passion, Death, and Resurrection of Christ, which we both physically and spiritually enter into through the Eucharist, is the divine work of Christ in which we receive and actively participate. Thanksgiving is the natural participatory response, not only within the context of Mass, but every day. Liturgical living, as it extends from Mass, ushers us into daily experiences and moments of gratitude. We can practice thanksgiving in the most uncomplicated of ways by keeping a gratitude journal or expressing thankfulness in our prayers, or more elaborately by sharing in feast-day parties or communal liturgical rituals.

Oftentimes habits of gratitude, or thanksgiving, are what form the basis for cultivating the virtue of joy. Joy is an interior disposition that can be sustained regardless of how we are feeling or the circumstances that we may be living in. Just as Christ amid great persecution gives generously of his life for our sake, we, too, can give generously of ourselves for his sake and for the sake of Christianizing our homes and societies. Your liturgical-living efforts are life-giving expressions of gratitude.

Atonement is the third end of the Mass, a term that indicates that we are in need of reparation because we are poor sinners. Often understated, the sacrifice of the Mass is the same sacrifice of Jesus on the Cross, offered on our behalf and made present to us for the forgiveness of our sins and to free us from all that would keep us from eternal life with him in heaven. Christ submitted himself completely for us on the Cross as a living sacrifice. Through his Passion, Death, and Resurrection we were freed from our sins, and the power of death itself was taken away. The liturgy is a re-presentation of both the sacrifice of Jesus's Crucifixion and the hope that comes forth from his Resurrection.

While there is undoubtedly more attention given to discussing the fun ways that we can live the liturgical year, reparation for our sins and the sins of others is an essential and irreplaceable part of our daily faith lives. What most don't know is that the penitential opportunities provided by the liturgical calendar go far beyond Ash Wednesday, Good Friday, and the Fridays during Lent. For a more in-depth explanation of all the possibilities, check out the online *Festive Faith Rhythms of Fasting and Abstinence Companion*. If you have never practiced days of penance and reparation before, begin with what the Church recommends, and then grow from there. We can refine our spiritual character by offering sacrifices to God throughout the year in imitation of Christ's sacrifice on the Cross and the sacrifice of the Mass.

The fourth and final end of the Mass is **petition**. Mass is the most powerful and highest form of prayer that the Church can offer. During the Mass there are many avenues of prayer happening all at once; we lift up our prayers to God, Jesus intercedes and acts on our behalf to the Father, and the entire Communion of Saints is united together in asking for God's aid and comfort. By placing ourselves in a posture of petition, we recognize how dependent we are on God to hear and provide for us in our need. Let this also be the approach that we take when striving to live liturgically. We might feel that we must provide all that is needed to offer praise on a feast day or throughout a season, and in this way, we might miss out on what God is offering that is right before us in nature or among our neighbors. By reminding ourselves that we are dependent upon God, we can turn our attention back to the resources that are more authentic to us and to our locale than perhaps to the experiences of others. When we seek to prioritize venerating God in accord with what the seasons offer, and what our larger communities can or are able to do, we are given an avenue of celebration that is more organic. Our minds can be alleviated by knowing that our liturgical-living efforts do not solely rest upon our own abilities, but that God will provide what we need to praise him in any given season, and we can do that together.

Infusing the four ends or purposes of Mass into all of our liturgical living can give our customs a sense of purpose while simultaneously offering the breadth and flexibility that is required to welcome Catholic individuals from diverse corners of the world into this way of life. It can be easy to forget this, especially since many of us only see liturgical living within the context of our own homes, but there are Catholics from vast arrays of villages, cities, cultures, and time periods who are also called to know Christ through the liturgical year. And while the traditions may remain, grow, or adapt, the underlying mission of them remains the same, which is to relate to God and one another through shared experiences of adoration, thanksgiving, atonement, and petition.

VILLAGE CATHOLICISM

With these elements in full view, I warmly welcome you into a way of liturgical living that I call village Catholicism. Village Catholicism is my way of creating imagery-rich inspiration for living the Church year in an interpersonal, story-centered, local, festive, and cultural way. It's an approach to liturgical life that embraces and goes beyond one-time feast-day experiences in the home to establish daily living, timeless tradition, and an ongoing appreciation for God's people. On a smaller scale our liturgical living should embrace the village that is our family, not just those who share our dwelling or even our immediate families, but our families of origin with whom we no longer live and our extended families.

Our more central or local villages are our parishes and people we go to church with. Parish communities have the unique ability and responsibility to lead liturgical experiences as they flow directly from the liturgy and sacraments. Their very existence is meant to establish the kingdom of God on earth.

In both our households and parishes, we can and should live the Church year as a way of encountering God anew and praising him for all that is good.

The benefits to approaching liturgical life as it has been throughout the history of the Church, as a village, are innumerable. To name a few, it gives people a sense of cultural and social connection, it offers the security of living our faith with other like-minded people, it establishes a sense of belonging, it shows us how interdependent we are upon one another, and it encourages us toward mutual support in spiritual growth. It's been shown that living as a village, or a community, is a more fulfilling and beneficial way of life because it draws us out of isolation and into a lifestyle of appreciation. To live liturgically like this is certainly a culture shift for our households and parishes, especially in our American society, but is one that will stir up a sense of heartfelt heritage that I see we are so deeply longing for.

Use the history, stories, and examples of liturgical traditions showcased in the following chapters to help you visualize what you would like to see in your own home, your parish, your extended family or friend group, and perhaps even your neighborhood. Then you can become a more active and integral part of sacramentalizing the world. This means that you can help others around you come to see and embrace the sacred in the ordinary, and for those ready to receive the mystery, you can help them encounter Christ present in all the world.

TWO

ADVENT

The life of an authentic Catholic
[person] is also a liturgical life.
It is through the liturgical life
that God transforms his people,
enabling them to participate in divine life.
—St. Teresa Benedicta of the Cross

Begins: Four Sundays before Christmas Day
Ends: Sundown on Christmas Eve
Natural Seasons: Fall and Winter
Advent Disciplines: Penance, Preparation, and Anticipation
Seasonal Prayers: O Antiphons and St. Andrew Christmas
Novena (Christmas Anticipation Prayer)
Liturgical Colors: Violet and Rose
*For Nativity Scene and Christmas tree traditions that begin
during the Advent season, please refer to pages 43 and 47
respectively.*

Advent is the beginning of the liturgical year, and while most of the world thinks that the Christmas season has already started, for Catholics we just are not there yet. Instead of rushing into the celebration, we begin with a period of anticipation and waiting. In the northern hemisphere where Christianity was born and where I live, the natural seasons of late fall and early winter assist our waiting with shortened days and growing cold as the Church calls us to embrace with quiet anticipation the coming of Christ. This is such a beautiful example of the way in which grace builds on nature and how the work of God is so vividly made present in everything around us!

Our yearning for light during Advent is twofold: as the leaves fall and temperatures drop, our days grow shorter and colder. And as the darkness of day lengthens, so too does our desire for warmth, the company of loved ones, and the coming celebration of the birth of Christ. Jesus came as a light to the nations, and in a profound sense our physical longings become reminders of our spiritual desire for Christ, our Light.

By beginning the Church year with this particular season, we are afforded many opportunities to refocus ourselves and reflect with hopeful anticipation on the birth of Jesus. This is the most obvious meaning of the preparatory weeks of Advent, but there is also another theological meaning to explore here. Advent actually focuses us on two comings of Christ. I try to remind myself of this as I am going through these Advent days because, as we all know, it can be very easy to get distracted by the more material preparations of Christmas. The first purpose of the Advent season is preparing for the great feast of Christmas, which commemorates God becoming human in Christ Jesus. But we are also called to be ready for the Second Coming of Christ, and Advent is a time for us to be focused on this calling.

It's no coincidence that Advent starts the liturgical year because it truly speaks to how we should be waiting vigilantly, always. This season sets the tone for the entire year. Christ came to us at his birth in Bethlehem, and he remains with us, being born anew in us every single day until one day when he will come to us in glory at the end of time. Advent is an annual reminder to live every moment with a sense of expectant desire, so that we live each day as an opportunity to grow in holiness as we await the Second Coming of Our Lord.

Advent also invites and challenges us to cultivate gratitude and rejoicing, which are expressed in the traditions of our Catholic culture and community. This profound Advent gladness can be seen all over the world through customs such as the Advent wreath, Las Posadas, the Feast of Seven Fishes, and St. Lucy treats and choirs. As St. John Paul II says, "The liturgy of Advent . . . helps us to fully understand the value and meaning of the mystery of Christmas. It is not just about commemorating the historical event, which occurred some two thousand years ago in a little village of Judea. Instead, it is necessary to understand that the whole of our life must be 'advent,' a vigilant awaiting of the final coming of Christ."[1]

THE ADVENT WREATH

EACH WEEK OF ADVENT

THE STORY

The most common tradition of the season that is practiced in parishes and homes around the world is the Advent wreath or the *Adventskranz,* in German. Pre-Christian Germanic people were known for using wreaths adorned with candles during the challenging winter days. The practical reason is clear, given that December brings the winter solstice, the darkest and coldest days of the year. Yet even for these non-Christians the wreath bore greater symbolic meanings. The light and warmth of candles expressed hope that winter, and the difficulties that it brought, would pass and the brighter days of spring would come.

Out of cultural folklore developed the more formal practice of the Advent wreath by the Lutheran Johann Wichern, who created and directed a home for young orphans. Much like an Advent calendar in which we count down days to Christmas, he sought to teach the children how to prepare by counting down the days with candles. He took an old cart wheel and adorned it with four white candles, one for each Sunday before Christmas, and nineteen small red candles were required for each of the other days of the weeks. Traditionally, there will be six red candles between each white candle if there is a full twenty-eight-day cycle of Advent, but in the year that it was created he needed nineteen. This physical representation of the four weeks before Christmas taught their community hopeful anticipation as they awaited the birth of Jesus. This overlap of Germanic custom with Christian meaning immediately connected with people, and the practice spread as a tradition transfigured by the Christian faith.

By the late 1800s the Advent wreath became common practice in Germany with the use of an evergreen wreath and four red candles. Catholic Christians then adopted this practice with caution when they learned about it through evangelizing the German people. America didn't see this tradition until immigrants from Germany brought it with them in the 1900s. In the well-known 1955 book *Around the Year with the Trapp Family* (of *The Sound of Music* fame), Austrian-born Maria von Trapp explains how confused she was when she came to America in 1938, saying, "Nobody seemed to know what an Advent wreath is." For her family, "it was not a question of whether or not we would have an Advent wreath. The wreath was a must. Advent would be unthinkable without it."[2]

THE TRADITION

Over time the practice of using the evergreen Advent wreath has kept its symbolic meaning of light and counting down the weeks until Christmas with four candles, while developing in other ways. Take, for example, the color of the candles. While most of us know them to be purple and rose, it was not always the case. Initially individuals and families were using natural beeswax or white candles. If you were to see a traditional German Advent wreath, the candles would be red. This color symbolizes the blood of Christ that was shed for us and our sins. In Catholic tradition, we have three purple candles and one rose: purple for prayer, penance, and sacrifice, and rose for the joy and hope of what is to come. These same colors are used for priests' vestments at Mass during Advent, with rose reserved for Gaudete Sunday, which ushers in the third week of Advent. *Gaudete* means "rejoice," and this Sunday reflects a lighter tone as the celebration of Christmas draws near.

It is customary now for many Catholics to incorporate the Advent wreath into their daily religious routines during the weeks of Advent. Often done in the evening around dinner time or shortly thereafter, a member of the family will light the appropriate candle or candles of the wreath, and a prayer will be prayed. Some people pray the Rosary, offer up their intentions, or sing a Marian hymn. I encouraged you to cherish this time with family, friends, or neighbors around an Advent wreath. Slow down, be more present to the current moment, and let this tradition lead you more fully into the joyful spirit of waiting that Advent brings. You may want to learn this playful little German poem that goes along with the Advent wreath:

> *Advent, Advent, ein Licht-*
> *lein brennt.*
> *Erst eins, dann zwei, dann*
> *drei, dann vier,*
> *und dann steht Christkind*
> *vor der Tür!*

> *Advent, Advent, a little*
> *light is burning.*
> *First one, then two, then*
> *three, then four,*
> *and then the Christ Child*
> *at the door!*[3]

You might even set it to a simple melody and sing it at each lighting of your wreath!

CARRYING ON THE TRADITION

AT HOME

The essentials of creating an Advent wreath are quite basic. Place an evergreen wreath (faux or real) in the center of your dining-room table or another prominent place in your domestic church. Place four pillar candles inside the inner part of the wreath or four taper candles in the built-in candleholders that some wreaths come with. See the notes on candle colors below for guidance.

Consider This

- Think carefully about where you will place your wreath. If others will be praying with you, is there room enough to gather around the wreath?
- Do you want to protect the surface where your wreath will be placed with a seasonal cloth or perhaps a tray to keep candle wax off furniture?
- Choose between naturally colored beeswax, white, red, three purple and one rose-colored, or four purple candles. If you have other candles at home you'd like to use, rather than buying new ones, feel free! There's really no right or wrong way to do this. Perhaps add three purple ribbons and one rose to link home and parish church.
- Bless your Advent wreath or try to have your local priest bless your wreath and candles before using it.
- Each Sunday of Advent, light one additional candle. Continue lighting these each day of that week. If you are using three purple and one rose, light the rose candle for the third week.
- Plan a time during each day when you will light that week's candle, perhaps during breakfast, dinner, or daily prayer time.
- Is there a prayer or song that you'd like to say when using your Advent wreath? Print that ahead of time and store it somewhere that you will remember.

IN THE PARISH

It is customary to place a large evergreen wreath (faux or real) in a prominent place in the parish church in preparation for the first Mass of Advent. In some places one rose and three purple candles are placed in the wreath and lit progressively on each Sunday in the following order: purple, purple, rose, purple. In other places, four white candles are used, with purple and rose ribbons to adorn the wreath. The wreath should be blessed according to the rubrics and prayers found in *The Book of Blessings*. And the Advent wreath is customarily lit at all Masses celebrated in that space.

Consider This

- Place the parish Advent wreath in a prominent place, and bless it when the parish community gathers for the Saturday night vigil Mass for the First Sunday of Advent.
- In the weeks before Advent, invite your parishioners to bring their Advent wreath and candles to one designated Mass, or all of the Masses, so the parish priest can bless them.
- While Advent is also a time of prayer, preparation, and fasting, the Third Sunday, also called Gaudete Sunday, is a special time to rejoice. Offer a special hospitality Sunday.
- Provide a weekly Advent reflection and holy hour, and light the Advent wreath candle(s) as a part of your prayer experience.

Resource

You can find "An Advent Wreath Blessing" in the *Festive Faith Advent and Christmas Companion* at www.HisGirlSunday.com/FestiveFaith.

A LIVING TRADITION

I grew up in a rural nondenominational Protestant church. We didn't have many traditions in my family or in my church, but the one I most remember from growing up was during the time before Christmas, what I now know as Advent. I loved decorating the tree with my family and still cherish the ornaments I have from my years growing up. When I converted to Catholicism as a young adult, I was introduced to the liturgical seasons. Initially I was overwhelmed, but the one seasonal tradition that seemed to fit with what I already knew—the tradition of decorating a tree at Christmas—was lighting and praying around an Advent wreath.

I began putting an Advent wreath in my home when my children were little. In that wreath I used three purple candles and one pink candle. Over the years I've made some additions to my Advent wreath, like adding a white "Christ" candle in the middle of the wreath that is molded into the shape of an angel. Our family tradition is also to add a red cardinal bird and holly berries. The red is intentionally used to symbolize Christ's sacrifice.

For our family, handing down Christmas decorations to our children is dear to my heart. There is something very special about my daughter holding ornaments I made as a child. Similarly, my adult daughter has an Advent wreath with a white "Christ" candle, red ribbons, and a red cardinal. She lights it with her children during the Advent and Christmas seasons. The fact that she's specifically chosen to incorporate white and red, like the wreath she saw lit every Advent growing up, reminds me that the traditions we hold fast to and the things we bring into our homes not only contribute to the current culture of the home for our children, but form our family for generations, even if it is something that seems as insignificant as the color of a bow on the Advent wreath. The Advent wreath reminds us to believe in the promise of the Messiah. The colors, the candles, and the smells of the Advent wreath all beautifully communicate the wonder of Christmas in a tangible way for all of us.

Melynda Ludwick

ST. NICHOLAS DAY SHOE TRADITION

DECEMBER 6

THE STORY

"All the stockings were hung by the chimney with care, in hopes that St. Nicholas soon would be there." We all know these familiar lines from the famous poem, "A Visit from St. Nicholas" by Clement Clarke Moore, but many do not know the origins of the Christmas stocking or shoe tradition. The festive custom of putting a gift in someone's shoe on December 6 has its roots in the story of St. Nicholas, the bishop of Myra in the Roman Empire at the end of the third century. Nicholas is famous for helping a poor family by secretly dropping bags of gold coins into their house under cover of night, thereby providing the father with a dowry for each of his three daughters and so saving the man from having to sell his daughters into prostitution. With these stories in mind, St. Nicholas was named the patron of children and of unmarried girls along with several other titles.

THE TRADITION

In the Netherlands and in Dutch communities elsewhere, the custom of leaving gifts in the shoes of family members on the Feast of St. Nicholas has been practiced for more than seven hundred years. They call him Sinterklaas, which means St. Nicholas, and his story carried on from generation to generation through Catholics who sought to imitate this saint in their homes. Children would put their clogs by the window and leave a carrot for the saint's horse with hopes that he would stop by and leave them candy, a trinket, or a riddle. Parents would then place little gifts in their children's shoes on the eve of St. Nicholas's feast day. The following day, December 6, the children would wake up to find these special treats and would know that Sinterklaas had come by to visit.

There is also a communal celebration of this feast day that takes place on December 5 with great cheerfulness. It is said that the physical representation of Sinterklaas came to be around 1873 when a couple of wealthy farmers paid a man to dress up as the saint and distribute sweets and candy to the poor children in their town. Of course, everyone enjoyed this, and people would wait out in the streets to see and greet him. Over time this custom grew, and now some of these celebrations go on for days. One might find parades filled with people singing traditional Sinterklaas songs, enjoying food and drinks, and waiting to wave hello to St. Nicholas or get a picture with him. Many shops in the Netherlands will even close early, and everyone will anticipate the arrival of Sinterklaas riding his white horse and carrying a bag of treats for those looking on. The parade is now a broadcast event in the Netherlands.

The tradition that most Americans who celebrate St. Nicholas Day seem to follow is to place chocolate gold-foil-wrapped coins, oranges, and small religious gifts in the shoes of their children or loved ones. The gold coins remind us of the financial gift that St. Nicholas made to families in need. The tradition of gifting oranges has at least two interpretations attached to it. The first is that oranges used to be more challenging to obtain, not like now when grocery stores are always stocked full of them. To receive an orange was a real treat and something to be delighted in. Second, in many depictions and icons of St. Nicholas, the gold coin pouch that he is seen carrying resembles an orange. As people tried to emulate what they saw in these images, oranges became a natural offering. In fact, many parishes will even offer a special blessing of oranges before the Feast of St. Nicholas. Worth noting is another variation of this custom, which is done in Spain on the Solemnity of the Epiphany of the Lord. Children will leave their shoes out overnight, and the three kings are said to come by and drop gifts in their shoes; adults will enjoy the exchanging of small gifts too.

Another traditional custom associated with this St. Nicholas Day is the Sinterklaas cookie, also known as *speculaas*, a treat made on this feast day. These are spiced shortbread cookies typically made with springerle cookie molds, carved wooden boards, or rolling pins, and they are enjoyed after the children have opened the treats from their shoes.

Whether it be leaving a gift in a friend or loved one's shoe, or making *speculaas* cookies, there is a place for everyone in the traditions surrounding St. Nicholas Day if you only allow yourself the time and wonder to join in. Although the legend and customs of Sinterklaas have evolved over time and transformed into the widely recognized figure of Santa Claus, it's important to remember that the origins of this celebration trace back to Catholic liturgical culture and tradition.

CARRYING ON THE TRADITION

AT HOME

On the eve of St. Nicholas's feast day, December 5, ask your loved ones to leave their shoes out. When everyone has gone to bed, place an orange, chocolate coins, and/or a small religious gift in their shoes. On the day of his feast, bake your favorite cookies, traditional *speculaas,* or check out recipes for this feast day in the *Festive Faith Advent and Christmas Companion* at www.HisGirlSunday.com/FestiveFaith.

Consider This

- Consider your household dynamic! If you have children, remind them to put their shoes out. If you are married without children, or have children who have moved out, invite your spouse to participate so you can exchange gifts together. Maybe drop St. Nicholas stockings (rather than shoes) on friends' or neighbors' porches in the dark of night. Or treat your coworkers to cookies and oranges the morning of December 6.
- Plan ahead by buying oranges or gold coins online or in your local grocery store before this feast day.
- Bring Catholic culture into your home. Many Catholic shops, artists, and artisans have St. Nicholas specialty gifts and goods for you to use instead of or along with your Santa Claus products.
- Host a St. Nicholas gathering with friends and/or family. Serve the *speculaas* cookies that you made with a warm beverage, and watch a seasonal movie. Have your Advent wreath lit as a sign of your Catholic faith.

IN THE PARISH

Now is a great time to show our Catholic identity in the midst of a predominantly secular Christmas season. Host a St. Nicholas Meet and Greet. A small ministry team or group of volunteers can provide cookies and candy canes, hot chocolate, a St. Nicholas book read-aloud, crafts, and pictures with St. Nicholas.

Consider This

- Extend the invitation for surrounding parishes to meet St. Nicholas.
- See if a ministry in the parish will support this event.
- Share the story of St. Nicholas with the entire parish before this event.
- Ask the parish priest to offer a blessing of oranges and/or candy canes at the event.
- Pair this event with your annual angel-tree or donation-tree efforts.

OUR LADY OF GUADALUPE TRIBUTE

DECEMBER 11 (VIGIL) AND DECEMBER 12 (FEAST DAY)

THE STORY

It's hard to believe that Our Lady of Guadalupe appeared almost five hundred years ago, in 1531. The impression she left on the people of Mexico is so full of life and color that it feels as if it might have happened more recently. The devotion is so prominent that in 1945 Pope Pius XII gave her the title "Empress of the Americas" and then in 1999 St. John Paul II declared her title as "Patroness of the Americas." The apparition site of Our Lady of Guadalupe to St. Juan Diego is said to be one of the most visited Catholic sites in the world. The devotion to her is simply unrivaled, and many pilgrims travel from far-off distances just to be near the image that Our Lady painted of herself with miraculous roses on a humble tilma. The tilma itself is imbued with mystery and miracle, a reality that is not overlooked by those who love Our Lady of Guadalupe and St. Juan Diego. Reports hold that some eight to ten million pilgrims visit the Basilica of Guadalupe in Mexico City leading up to her feast day each year on December 12 to honor and wonder at this miracle.

THE TRADITION

In Mexico, Our Lady of Guadalupe is celebrated for days leading up to her feast. On December 3 a novena begins, a prayer that is said for nine consecutive days in devotion to her. Faithful Catholics and parishes throughout Mexico do this together as a way to contemplate the apparition, emulate her virtue, and invoke her aid. On December 11, the eve of her feast, a serenade to Our Lady—what some call the *tribute*—begins. This usually lasts hours as a countdown to midnight, which is when things really liven up!

Choirs sing and live music is played outside the doors of the Basilica of Our Lady of Guadalupe and near the tilma where pilgrims and the local community honor Our Lady with their gifts and offerings. This is usually accompanied by scripture readings, prayers dedicated to peace in their community, the Rosary, and folk dancing. At midnight visitors can witness the singing of "Las Mañanitas" (The Little Mornings) to Our Lady of Guadalupe, followed by other traditional Mexican hymns. For those who are not familiar, "Las Mañanitas" is a traditional Mexican birthday song that is often joyfully sung at midnight or dawn to wake up a loved one on their special day. It can also be sung on their name day or patron saint's day.

There are also dances performed by the *matachines*, native folk dancers, who are typically dressed in traditional Aztec clothing. These performances are very meaningful because each dance expresses the integration of ancestral tradition with total devotion to the Catholic faith. The annual procession is an inspiring one as hundreds of people fill the streets to travel through the town praying, singing, dancing, and carrying a prominent statue of Our Lady.

All this celebration and joy communicates to the larger community the love and closeness to Mary and Jesus that Catholics delight in. It is truly a proclamation of faith to the world. Once everyone is back in the square, they have Mass and a blessing of roses, a fitting liturgical experience for this apparition. Everyone brings, or is given, a rose, then the priest confers a blessing upon them. There are also readings from the account of the apparition where Our Lady tells St. Juan Diego to go find flowers and take them to the bishop. The remainder of the early hours of the morning is filled with various Masses, praying of the Rosary, more dancing, socializing, and, of course, food. Typical on the menu are sweet breads, tamales, tacos, tostadas, pozole, Mexican hot chocolate, and warm coffee.

Such wondrous festivity calls to mind the abundant life that Our Lady speaks of by expressing trust in her power to bring us closer to her son. "I am your mother" is what Our Lady of Guadalupe told St. Juan Diego, and she says it to us too. Confidently approach her motherly protection as we see the Mexican community do, and let that be your inspiration on her feast day.

CARRYING ON THE TRADITION

AT HOME

Host a Guadalupe gathering with friends and family. Try attending Mass together, then go to someone's house to share in a feast-day party filled with music, dancing, Mexican food, and the praying of a Rosary.

Consider This

- Locate online a copy of the Our Lady of Guadalupe Novena and pray it in preparation for her feast day.
- Make Mexican food and traditional hot chocolate, or encourage a potluck. Integrate prayer, singing, dancing, and scripture readings.
- Decorate your home with roses, and ask your priest to bless them beforehand.
- Pray the Rosary on this Marian feast day.
- Read or share the story of St. Juan Diego and Our Lady of Guadalupe.
- At your Guadalupe gathering, play a trivia game about the tilma or the apparition.

IN THE PARISH

Since Our Lady of Guadalupe is Patroness of the Americas, this would be a fitting celebration opportunity within Advent for all of us, but especially if you have a Hispanic community within your parish. Encourage the Hispanic community to lead the parish in cultural devotion to Our Lady. Provide the opportunity for a special Mass and Rosary followed by a celebration at your parish community center with traditional music, dancing, and Mexican food.

Consider This

- Form a committee to lead and organize the festivities and raise money if needed for food, music, decorations, and so on.
- Place an image of Our Lady of Guadalupe near the sanctuary, and arrange bright and colorful flowers in front of her.
- Prompt your community to start the Our Lady of Guadalupe Novena, and provide them with resources to pray.

- See if a group can play traditional Mexican hymns or if *matachines* can perform for the community.
- Try incorporating a procession around your parish as they do at the Basilica of Our Lady of Guadalupe.

Resource
You can find my Mexican Hot Chocolate recipe and a "Prayer to Our Lady of Our Lady of Guadalupe" in the *Festive Faith Advent and Christmas Companion* at www.HisGirlSunday.com/FestiveFaith

ST. LUCIA DAY, FESTIVAL OF LIGHT

DECEMBER 13

THE STORY

From Sweden we have a tradition that highlights again the desire for light amid the darkness of late fall and early winter in the northern hemisphere. St. Lucy of Syracuse was a consecrated virgin and martyr living in what is now Sicily during the early centuries of Christianity. During the worst persecution under Emperor Diocletian, she was martyred for refusing to worship an idol of the emperor. Lucy comes from the Latin word for "light," which is appropriate for a woman who was said to have had a visible glow of love for her spouse, Christ. She was known for bringing supplies and food to the poor Christians in the darkness of the catacombs and would wear a wreath of candles so that she could see more clearly.

St. Lucia Day, also known as the Festival of Light, is celebrated on December 13. On this day we commemorate our beloved St. Lucy by imitating her acts of charity and service to others. St. Lucia Day is a day of celebration that dates back as early as the fourth century. In the old Julian calendar, St. Lucia Day marked the longest and darkest night in the year, with the shift toward light when the days finally begin to get longer. The devotion to St. Lucy is celebrated with great pride in Sweden, and many customs have been handed down through generations surrounding her feast day. It is said that around

AD 1100, Catholic monks brought the story of St. Lucy to the Swedish people, and the traditions surrounding her feast day have been a significant part of Swedish culture ever since.

THE TRADITION

On December 13, the eldest daughter wakes the household with St. Lucia buns, coffee, and treats while wearing a wreath of candles, a white gown, and a red sash. These two colors hold great symbolic meaning: the white represents the purity of Lucy's baptism, and the red sash reminds us of her martyrdom. The oldest daughter might also be accompanied by small brothers known as "Star Boys," who wear white gowns and cone-shaped hats decorated with stars and who carry a star-tipped wand. St. Lucia buns are commonly served on this day and are better known as *lussekatter*, which translates to "Lucia cat." This is a saffron bread that is typically shaped like a curled-up cat and often is served with mulled wine or coffee.

This is also a day of great festivity in Sweden where everyone can participate in the most enchanting community celebrations. One of the more prominent expressions of faith happens with a candlelit St. Lucy choir procession. Though this particular element is not done anymore, a "Lucia of Sweden" used to be selected through a competition that ran on television and in newspapers where locals could cast their vote for one candidate or another. There are many Santa Lucia songs in Swedish culture, and the more well-known pieces can be sung by heart in many local communities. The most commonly used song throughout Scandinavia was actually a Neapolitan folk song. This is an extract from the official song of the Lucia celebrations; it is called "Santa Lucia" and dates back to 1835 from the Italian composer Teodoro Cottrau:

> *The night treads heavily*
> *around the yards and dwellings.*
> *In places unreached by the sun,*
> *the shadows brood.*
> *Into our dark house she comes bearing lighted candles,*
> *Saint Lucia, Saint Lucia!*

Light in the darkness is a very fitting theme for the Feast of St. Lucy in the darkness of a Swedish winter. The human desires of body and heart are united and expressed in the hopeful expectation that Christ will come again as light to the nations. Through the Incarnation, Christ shattered the darkness of sin and division, and all creation rejoiced at the coming of our God. Don't let this feast day go by without trying your hand at making St. Lucia buns, and offer them to a friend or neighbor as a small act of charity and service as St. Lucy would want us to do.

CARRYING ON THE TRADITION

AT HOME

If this fits your family situation, ask your eldest daughter to help with the festivities on St. Lucia Day. Help her dress up as St. Lucy and serve St. Lucia buns, treats, and coffee in the darkness of this mid-December morning. If she has brothers, invite them to dress up as star boys to help her serve the family. If these traditions do not fit your household exactly, make whatever adaptations seem suited to your home. Or transfer whatever elements of this festive tradition you can to a wider circle of family, friends, neighbors, or coworkers. Try your hand at baking *lussekatter*. I have the perfect recipe for you, which you can find in the *Festive Faith Advent and Christmas Companion* at www. HisGirlSunday.com/FestiveFaith. Light candles on this day, as many as you want! Focus on the hope and promise that Christ, our Light, brings us.

Consider This
- St. Lucy's name means "light." Consider waiting to put some of your Christmas lights up until her feast day.
- Try making and sharing St. Lucy saffron buns. You can find my recipe in the *Festive Faith Advent and Christmas Companion* at www.HisGirlSunday. com/FestiveFaith.
- Pray by candlelight this evening, and ask for St. Lucy's intercession.
- St. Lucy served and cared deeply for the poor. Offer an act of service this week or on her feast day.
- Make a wreath of candles for your oldest daughter or someone (or everyone) else to wear. Perhaps you could use battery-operated candles, or if you are crafty, you could make pretend candles out of felt, heavy card stock, or cardboard.

IN THE PARISH

Last year, at the parish where I worked, we hosted a special candlelight Eucharistic adoration, with a traditional St. Lucy choir, for our community and surrounding parishes. During this unique holy hour, we turned off all lights in the church and flooded the entire sanctuary and main aisle of the parish with the gentle light of candles. The choir sang traditional St. Lucy hymns, each member carrying a candle, and St. Lucia led the choir in her white robe, red sash, and customary candlelit headdress. Afterward, we served St. Lucia buns and coffee for our guests as they were leaving.

Consider This
- Offer a traditional St. Lucy choir with an additional opportunity for Eucharistic Adoration.
- For candlelight adoration, purchase votive candles beforehand and assemble a volunteer team for setting up and tearing down.
- You can't have a St. Lucy choir without St. Lucy represented by one lead choir member! Purchase or have someone make the sash and a battery-operated wreath crown in advance.
- Arrange a hospitality team that can bring saffron or cinnamon buns, brew a pot of coffee, and offer other hot drinks for this cold winter-evening experience of prayer and festivity.
- Invite the other nearby parishes, invite the neighbors, whether church-goers or not!

What a great feast on which to share a bit of our festive faith!

LAS POSADAS
DECEMBER 16–24

THE STORY

Las Posadas is a Mexican cultural tradition that reenacts the journey of the Holy Family to Bethlehem. The celebration not only invites but *requires* the involvement of multiple people and several homes. I especially like this custom because in a time when most religious customs are practiced privately, this is one that includes a public display of the journey to Bethlehem. *Las Posadas* translates to "the inns," and it is essentially a living novena that extends for nine days beginning on December 16 and ending on December 24, Christmas Eve.

It is believed that the custom originated through the Augustinian friars of San Agustín de Acolman who were in Mexico to evangelize the indigenous people. In 1586 one of the friars received a papal bull from Pope Sixtus V that encouraged priests to celebrate *Misas de Aguinaldo* or the "Christmas Bonus

Masses" from December 16 to December 24. Around this time of year, the winter solstice, the Aztecs had a tradition of honoring one of their gods, and the friars saw this as a natural way to pivot their understanding toward our Catholic faith and to direct them to the one, true God. This custom originated in churches with Mass each day, for nine days, leading up to Christmas. Gradually the example of the liturgy was imitated in the homes of the community in each neighborhood.

THE TRADITION

Tradition tells us that beginning each day of the celebration at sundown, multigenerational groups would go door to door singing *Canto Para Pedir Posada* while seeking to be invited into the house they were visiting. Those outside represented the Holy Family and sang, "In the name of heaven I ask you for shelter, for my beloved wife can go no farther." Those inside would sing, "This is not an inn; get on with you; I cannot open the door; you might be a robber." This call-and-response would be sung up to five times with varying verses at different houses. The travelers were turned away at each home until they reached the final destination, where those inside, realizing that it was Joseph, Mary, and baby Jesus at their door, would invite the Holy Family into the home. This final house then hosted an evening of food or a potluck, with prayer and celebratory time with their community spent in anticipation of the great feast of Christmas. This festive neighborhood journey would take place every evening until December 24, when the whole group attended Midnight Mass together and shared in a big, festive meal afterward.

Today, Las Posadas in the United States doesn't always manifest in the same way, since living tradition can often change according to the circumstances of different parishes, individuals, and generations. Commonly some customs include Mass, a Rosary, Eucharistic Adoration, food, dancing, and even piñatas. In fact, it is said that the piñata originated out of the Las Posadas custom. A seven-pointed star was created out of paper-mâché or pottery and filled with candy as a way to catechize the indigenous people on the seven deadly sins. Breaking the candy from the piñata was a representation of the reward and joy of conquering those sins.

However one carries out Las Posadas, the pillars of this practice should remain as prayer, song, community, and the reenactment of the Holy Family searching for an inn. This tradition became so popular, and such a testament to the power of friendship and awaiting the birth of Christ, that in many regions of Mexico even non-Catholics practice Las Posadas. This is the power that festivity and togetherness can have on a community.

CARRYING ON THE TRADITION

AT HOME
Invite a group of individuals and families to join you in hosting Las Posadas. Be ready to sing the traditional songs and act as inn owners as the Holy Family does the door-to-door reenactment. Plan a potluck dinner with friends, and spend some time together in prayer after the Holy Family's journey. If the group is willing and able, follow the traditional custom of celebrating Las Posadas for several, if not all, of the evenings between December 16 and December 24.

Consider This
- If you can't do all nine days, condense this into a couple of nights or one night.
- Ask your neighbors or Catholic families nearby to join in with you.
- Print out the songs in advance so everyone can sing along.
- Incorporate costumes for the Holy Family.
- Arrange for a family's or individual's home to be the last or only house that the Holy Family will be invited into. This is traditionally where dinner and prayer will be shared.
- Create a sign-up sheet for dinner, desserts, and drinks to help the host.

IN THE PARISH
Schedule a special Mass for the parish during the traditional days of Las Posadas. Encourage and equip a group of volunteers or a ministry within your parish to arrange the celebration by using the classrooms of the faith-formation building as the inns or perhaps makeshift inns in the parish hall, or even outdoors if weather permits. After visiting each inn, follow the tradition by gathering in a communal space for a meal or simple refreshments, prayer, and fellowship.

Consider This
- Print out the songs for participants to sing along.
- Ask a volunteer, a parish cantor, the parish choir, or other music ministry to lead the singing.
- Encourage parishioners of all ages to get involved.
- Try to provide food and drinks by arranging a sign-up ahead of time.

- Teach the tradition beforehand and explain what a novena is so that the nine stops or inns of Las Posadas make more sense, thereby encouraging a more robust participation.

A LIVING TRADITION

I remember around the holidays my parents would often reminisce about their childhood. My dad told me stories of the town in Mexico that he grew up in. He recounted every year how all his neighbors gathered together and celebrated the last nine days of Advent as a community. I always thought it was such a beautiful and sentimental way to celebrate the anticipation of the birth of Christ. Growing up, Las Posadas was not something that I had personally experienced, but because of the impact I could see that it left on my dad's life, it became a tradition that I really desired to carry on in my own family and community. In 2021, my husband and I hosted and revived my dad's tradition of Las Posadas in our home. It was a small gathering, but we had all the key elements, prayer, singing, and good food. Our family goal is to continue to host one of the nine nights at our home and then to celebrate the other days with our parish community and school. It has meant so much to me to give this piece of my parents' childhood to our family and friends.

Danielle Mondragon

SIMBANG GABI
DECEMBER 16–24

THE STORY

Simbang Gabi is a Filipino Advent tradition that is another example of a novena of sorts, heightening the sense of expectation in the final days of Advent and ushering us into the great feast of Christmas. *Simbang Gabi* translates to "Night Mass" and is celebrated in preparation for the coming of baby Jesus and in honor of Our Blessed Mother. Interestingly, you might hear some refer to this as the "Misa de gallo," which from Spanish translates to the "Mass of the rooster." This cultural tradition has a Spanish title because it is believed to have started around AD 1668, when Spanish missionaries arrived in the Philippines. The Spanish priests would hold predawn Masses around 4:00 a.m.

to accommodate the fishermen and farmers who began work so early in the morning that they woke with the roosters. By doing so, the priests made it a priority to ensure that workers and families could still participate in the Catholic liturgy and receive the Eucharist together. The missionaries also shared with the Filipino people the devotional practice of a Christmas novena. With these things combined, along with a growing devotion to Mary and the faith, we see the development of Simbang Gabi, a distinct Catholic cultural tradition.

THE TRADITION

Traditionally each day begins early in the morning with a Rosary followed by Mass beginning on December 16 and ending on December 24. As this custom has evolved in the United States, practical reasons have led some parishes to offer the Masses in the late evening or to celebrate at a different parish across a region or diocese each day as a community. This is a great example of a tradition that has evolved to fit current circumstances of life while still embodying the devotion and meaning of the season.

Many Catholics who participate in this novena are holding special intentions on their hearts in hopeful prayer that God will grant their request. Another notable custom that is often tied to the special Simbang Gabi novena is a Filipino ornament called a *paról*, a star-shaped lantern, that is used to adorn homes and celebratory spaces. This stunning piece of décor is adapted from the Hispanic word *farol*, or "lantern," and was originally carried as a simple source of light during that nine-day Christmas novena. In the darkness of those early morning walks to church, these colorful lanterns would help guide the way and also became symbolic of the star of Bethlehem. Following the Masses are spirited family or community gatherings filled with delicious foods like whole-roasted pig, steamed rice cakes, sticky rice, egg rolls, sweet bread, noodles mixed with vegetables and meat, and ginger tea, to name a few. I've even attended a few celebrations where there is karaoke, dancing, and lively games with door prizes and comradery.

These are sacred memories and traditions that are looked forward to with excited anticipation. For this community it is about offering a gift to God; it's not about themselves, but about self-gift. The tradition is the vehicle for giving God praise for all that he has done and will continue to do. The people involved combine their time, energy, and resources together to offer God all that they can in prayer and celebration. This profound yes to God's gifts proclaims not only affirmation of God, but affirmation of the gift of life, and that gets to a very core principle of liturgical living.

CARRYING ON THE TRADITION

AT HOME
Go to Mass for the nine consecutive days leading up to Christmas, and collaborate with a friend or two to host a Simbang Gabi community get-together after Mass on the last day.

Consider This
- If you can't do all nine days, condense this into a couple of days or even just one.
- Consider serving some of the traditional foods that were mentioned above.
- Decorate with the traditional *paról*, a star-shaped lantern.
- Coordinate games or activities that your community will appreciate doing together.
- Don't forget to pray with one another during your celebration.
- Invite your friends to go to Mass with you all nine days.

IN THE PARISH
Simbang Gabi is a joyous occasion within Advent that can unite the entire parish family, but especially if you have a Filipino community this is a prime opportunity to share the richness of Filipino cultural heritage. Provide the opportunity for a special Mass followed by a celebration at your parish community center with traditional Filipino music and food, decoration, dancing, and games.

Consider This
- Form a committee to lead and organize the festivities and raise money if needed for food, music, decorations, and so on.
- Communicate the tradition in advance, and teach your community about this living novena.
- Equip the Filipino community within the parish to take the lead and share traditions through the planning process.
- If there isn't a Filipino community present, you can still offer a series of Masses leading up to Christmas Day and arrange a festive gathering afterward. You might connect with other parishes nearby to make this successful.

LA VIGILIA OR THE
FEAST OF SEVEN FISHES

DECEMBER 24

THE STORY

Christmas Eve customs are alive and well, especially among Catholics from various cultures. From baking cookies to watching movies, opening gifts, or going to Midnight Mass, the most common practices of them all revolve around food. Most families on Christmas Eve come together for a big meal in hopeful anticipation and waiting for the birth of Christ. It's no surprise to see this because of the way that a good meal can bring people of any age, culture, or social status together across various seasons of life. This is exemplified beautifully in a tradition that comes from southern Italy and is commonly known as *La Vigilia di Natale*, "the vigil of the Nativity," or the "midnight birth of Christ."

Through a combination of shifting political circumstances, poverty, and changes in family and culture, we see the development of what is now often called the "Feast of Seven Fishes." Before 1861 Italy was composed of varying regions, each with its own governmental authority. When these governments unified, many of the resources were distributed to northern Italy, and the southern region remained the poorest area in the country. Although the people of the region faced poverty and crime, they were also situated so close to the ocean that fish was an easily accessible and bountiful resource.

THE TRADITION

Until the 1983 Code of Canon Law, the season of Advent included the disciplines of fasting and abstinence on Christmas Eve until Midnight Mass. Now, one might ask, "If we are supposed to be fasting, then why did the Italians feast on seven different kinds of fish?" And to this we can say one of three things. First, they could have considered this their full meal for the day. Second, this could have also been their double collation, two small snack-size meals, which according to the 1962 law of fasting could be had on Christmas Eve. Third, it could also simply be that Italian food culture is very strong; this community is known for making lots of food to feed lots of people, and perhaps this amount fed their family and friends. This leads us to the number of fish, and there doesn't seem to be consensus on why seven fishes are made, but we could of course connect that with the seven sacraments, seven gifts of the Holy Spirit, or seven as it signifies perfection, and let me be the first to say that this meal truly is perfection.

There is no set menu for the evening, and you may see it vary from family to family or region to region. Some do the meal as a buffet, while others serve their fish dishes in specific courses. There does, however, seem to be a typical lineup that could be used as a springboard for other ideas: cod, calamari, shrimp, clams, crab, whitefish, and mussels or oysters. Don't forget your antipasto, sides, and dessert for this meal as would be the custom for an Italian table on Christmas Eve.

Interestingly, Italians aren't the only culture to have a long menu for this vigil. In France the menu usually involves oysters and foie gras. A traditional Catholic Polish and Ukrainian dinner serves up to twelve meatless dishes. If you were to visit a Ukrainian family this evening, you might even see them throw a spoonful of kutia—a sweet wheat berry pudding—onto the ceiling. If it sticks, then that means good fortune for the upcoming year. This last bit isn't necessarily Catholic, but it's a lively part of dinner that I couldn't leave out, and one that I think your guests might enjoy experiencing too.

CARRYING ON THE TRADITION

AT HOME

Transform your Christmas Eve dinner into a Feast of Seven Fishes. Plan ahead so you don't have any doubles, and when you're done eating, head off to Midnight Mass together.

Consider This
- Make all the dishes yourself, or arrange the meal as a potluck.
- Consider sharing the story of where the tradition came from during your dinner.
- Invite your parish priest to come, so he can bless your dinner and enjoy time with dear friends before going back for Mass.
- Encourage "around the table" affirmations that can be shared. This is a lovely addition to a special dinner.
- Ask your family or friends to attend Midnight Mass with you.
- Adding printed menus with the variety of fish being served can bring a little pizzazz to your Christmas Eve tablescape.

IN THE PARISH

Several years ago, I held a Seven Fishes appreciation dinner for a parish liturgy committee, and it was talked about in high regard for years afterward. This dinner certainly can be done as a large-scale potluck for the entire parish with proper planning, but I believe it best serves as an opportunity to offer your staff, pastoral council, avid volunteers, or liturgy committee a gorgeous dinner before an intensely busy work and volunteer season.

Consider This
- Have the meal catered, or arrange for those attending to provide a dish.
- Provide wine or champagne to elevate your dinner.
- Host this at the parish community center or at one of your volunteer's homes.
- Ask your parish priest to open the evening in prayer.
- Prepare a thank-you speech for the dinner to let your staff and trusted committee members know that you appreciate them.
- Share the tradition so they know its meaning.
- Incorporate a Christmas game or gift exchange to lighten the mood and bring out more laughter.

Resource
Try or adapt my recommended Seven Fishes Menu, which can be found in the *Festive Faith Advent and Christmas Companion* at www.HisGirlSunday. com/FestiveFaith.

A LIVING TRADITION

When I was growing up, I remember going to my uncle's house on Christmas Eve. He didn't do all seven fishes, but he did do some, and I believe this is my first memory of the tradition. My husband's Italian family also enjoyed this tradition, so it was only natural that when we got married and began to live more liturgically, we would implement the Feast of Seven Fishes into our family life. This dinner custom is supposed to be done on Christmas Eve because it stems from our Catholic belief that you should avoid meat during certain days of the year as a way to prepare yourself for our most holy days.

In the Aquila family, we make all seven fishes, and as our family has grown it has become a bigger and more festive meal than even Christmas. We gather with our eleven children, their spouses, and our grandchildren for what never fails to be an amazing meal. The menu has changed over time, especially now that we have in-laws who participate in the cooking, so they bring in their own dishes too. This is what our menu has grown to look like.

1. Chilean Sea Bass in a Lemon Butter Sauce
2. Crabmeat and Asparagus in a Lemon Butter Sauce
3. Mussels with Tomato and Pancetta
4. Shrimp Creole
5. Fried Calamari
6. Seared Scallops
7. Spaghetti Scoglio: This is an Italian seafood stew with clams, shrimp, calamari, and mussels in a tomato base.

As you can see, there are seven delicious reasons why we love our fish dinner!

Diane Aquila

LEAVING A CHAIR OPEN
DECEMBER 24

THE STORY

Creating a place at the table for family and friends is a gesture of hospitality that is nearly universal across cultures and through generations. The Advent and Christmas seasons usually see the number of times we gather in the kitchen increase exponentially for baking, drinking, storytelling, or just being with loved ones. Setting each place around the dining-room table may seem like a small gesture, but it communicates a sense of welcome and home to your guests. It is an act of charity that says, "We anticipated you coming, and you belong here." As Catholics we can appreciate this double meaning as it echoes the hopeful waiting that we experience in Advent for the coming of Christ. It also harkens back to the image of Christ's invitation to the banquet feast where a place is set for all of us. From the charming Polish heritage, we receive a tradition that illuminates this beautiful sentiment: leaving a chair open at the Christmas Eve dinner table.

There seems to be some discrepancy regarding how this tradition came to be, but like many other traditions that have been "baptized," so to speak, it is said that this one may have come from pagan practices before the conversion of Poland in AD 966. One of the pre-Christian rituals was for a dinner guest to sweep, or clear, the empty seat before sitting down to ensure that the soul of their ancestor was excused before they used that chair. After everyone had finished eating, the table would remain as it was for several hours so that their deceased family members could also have their share of the feast at table.

THE TRADITION

Some Polish cultural scholars believe that this tradition developed and took on new meaning and importance after Poland's conversion to the Catholic faith. The custom is to leave a chair and place setting empty at the table during the Christmas Eve dinner. The dinner host is supposed to prepare an extra chair and plate at the table in case an unexpected visitor arrives. In the occurrence that someone does come by, we should invite that individual in and host them as if they were meant to be there. This ritual is closely tied to the spirit of Christmas and the Holy Family. As the story goes, Mary and Joseph traveled to Bethlehem but were turned away from the inn because there was no room, until they eventually found a humble stable for Jesus to be born. The Polish community reminds us through their hospitality that we should welcome in the stranger, just as we all wish the Holy Family had encountered on that cold and dark night. In fact, there is a Polish phrase that stems from this tradition that I think we could all emulate, which states, "A guest at home is God at home."[4]

At a time when isolation and avoidance are so common in our society, this tradition is a much-needed reminder for all of us to be better innkeepers than those whom Joseph and Mary met. And by being more attentive to a potentially unexpected guest we, in turn, develop a warmth and readiness in our hearts and homes. The vulnerability from which this tradition arises is profound when we consider how open we are when we invite others into our home. We show them where we dwell, feed them, and treat them with a tenderness that speaks of God's own embrace. This is typically done for those we know, but contemplate the possibility of taking in an unexpected guest, possibly someone you know, and maybe someone you don't. This hospitality echoes clearly the teachings of Jesus in his public ministry to treat all people as if they were Christ. "Amen, I say to you, whatever you did for one of these least brothers of mine, you did for me" (Mt 25:40). When setting your Christmas Eve table, remember the empty chair and that simple Polish phrase from above, "A guest at home is God at home."

CARRYING ON THE TRADITION

AT HOME

At your Christmas Eve dinner, leave a chair open at your family table in memory of a beloved deceased family member, or in anticipation of an unexpected guest.

Consider This

- Pray for the souls of the faithful departed with your Catholic meal blessing.
- Allow your guests the opportunity to bring one of their friends to Christmas Eve dinner at your house.
- Consider ways you can be more hospitable to the guests whom you are having over. Are you treating them like Christ in your home?
- Share the phrase "A guest at home is God at home." Explain to your family and friends what this means as inspiration for their lives too.
- If you lost a loved one within the last year or two, serve their favorite dish at this Christmas Eve dinner.

IN THE PARISH

Christmastime has become a family-focused season, and for many who have lost someone special to them during the last year it can be particularly challenging to grieve while also maintaining joyfulness. As parish communities we should strive to be aware and sensitive to this reality. Try one of the following to let your parishioners know that you see their sorrow.

Consider This

- Put a notice in the bulletin, on the parish website, or in whatever regular correspondence goes out to the households of your parish about family struggles that can be felt even more deeply during the holiday season, and include some direction about how to attend to these matters.
- Add a special petition to your Mass prayers for those who have lost a loved one over the last year.
- If you schedule special liturgical celebrations during Advent, such as the Liturgy of the Hours or a holy hour, devote one of them to the souls of the faithful departed and to those who are grieving.
- Encourage your bereavement committee or grief ministry to host a holiday gathering for extra support and pastoral care.

Resource
You can find a traditional "Catholic Meal Blessing" and the "Eternal Rest Prayer" in the *Festive Faith Advent and Christmas Companion* found at www. HisGirlSunday.com/FestiveFaith.

THREE

CHRISTMAS

Be not lax in celebrating.
Be not lazy in the festive service of God.
Be ablaze with enthusiasm.
Let us be an alive, burning offering before the altar of God.
—St. Hildegard of Bingen

Begins: December 25
Ends: Feast of the Baptism of the Lord
Natural Season: Winter
Christmas Disciplines: Joy and Hope
Seasonal Prayers: Te Deum and Nativity Sermon of St. Isaac
the Syrian
Both prayers can be found in the Festive Faith Advent
and Christmas Companion *at www.HisGirlSunday.com/
FestiveFaith.*
Liturgical Color: White

Catholic homes around the world are brimming with the warmth of Christmas décor, Nativity Scenes, family gatherings, and seasonal dishes. *It's a Wonderful Life* plays in the background of many living rooms while trees are lit up, dried orange slices dangle whimsically in front of the windows, and every mug gets filled with fragrant coffee, cider, or cocoa. We are comfortably situated in a season of fullness, the same sort of fullness that we hope envelops a home when a new baby arrives.

It is important that we see this moment in the life of Christ and the Holy Family as our own. We shouldn't just read it through the lens of the past, but as an immortal truth that impacts our life and our salvation today and every day. God divinely willed this plan, that Mary would give her life over to the child Jesus and suffer the pain of watching his eventual death upon the Cross. The Father sent his Son to redeem all the world through Mary's yes and Joseph's faithful care. Through this act of immense mercy and love—God becoming flesh in Jesus—each and every one of us receives the profound gift of welcoming that very Christ child, Jesus the Lord.

It can be easy to take this salvific action for granted by thinking about Christmas more secularly or as an oversimplification of the season by only remembering that Jesus was born. Yet, the invisible God being made visible in Jesus is a personal and intimate gift for each of us. This is why we take the entire season of Advent to prepare our hearts and homes to celebrate a moment so profound that it has lived on for thousands of years. Advent has to prepare us to openly receive Jesus in our hearts as Mary and Joseph did. It is to our spiritual benefit to make good use of our time during this Christmas season as well, as we see and contemplate the mystery of the distance between the Heavenly Father and humanity grow shorter and shorter.

As John's gospel states,

> And the Word became flesh and made his dwelling among us, and we saw his glory, and the glory as of the Father's only Son, full of grace and truth. (Jn 1:14)

Jesus's birth is the fulfillment of the Incarnation promised by God, and the Church wisely sets aside several weeks to unfold and ponder the truths of this great mystery. Salvation history has prepared us for this. The birth of Jesus took place in human history, and our recalling and honoring it year after year marks God's keeping of the promise to save us from the slavery of sin and evil in which our world is so entrenched. God becomes like us in our human existence, so that we can learn to be more like God, and more like who we were meant to be from the beginning of creation. Christ's birth reveals to us that we also are God's beloved children, created out of love, to offer praise and thanksgiving. And on the tender occasion of Christmas when we recall and celebrate the birth of God's Son, we are drawn into Christ Jesus and through him to the Father as adopted children.

This incarnational faith of ours is observed not only through the divine babe, but through all those surrounding Jesus who outwardly expressed their affirmation of all that God had done. Mary and Joseph powerfully lived out their *fiat* (their yes) even before Jesus was born. Their actions of faith as individuals and as a couple were courageously carried out in spite of all difficulty, and both have worthily become models for what true devotion to God looks like. The offering of the Magi also prompts us to recognize the importance of extending our gifts in worship. We witness three men who traveled from far-off distances to follow the star that led them to Our Lord. Upon finding the Christ child, they too expressed their faith outwardly by offering the baby kingly gifts and worshipping him. The shepherds gave honor and adoration through their loyal presence and humble gaze of trust. They came with their animals and show us in their simple gestures how every part of creation will be restored through Jesus. We can rest peacefully in this very moment, by recognizing that all of creation is in harmony.

The same incarnational experience that we are familiar with at the manger can be seen and heard across the world through the gift of Christmas customs and traditions. Catholics through the years have waited up for Midnight Mass, celebrated with a slice of King Cake, and blessed their front doors on the Solemnity of the Epiphany of the Lord. These faith-filled efforts are worth noting especially during a time when it can be so easy to get distracted by shopping, deadlines, cleaning, and to-dos.

Sadly, of course, there are towns and cities that carry on as if Christmas, the day itself and the season, isn't happening at all. We drive around or walk outside, and it looks the same as it always does. And to this dreary sight we must respond with steadfast and festive faith, reminding ourselves that if we believe that God became man, then we must live out this truth with exultation. The blessing is that there is plenty of time to learn to maintain our high spirits because Christmas has only just begun. Don't be quick to take down the lights and the tree, but instead settle into these upcoming weeks by partaking in one or a few of the following liturgical traditions.

MIDNIGHT MASS
LITURGICAL OBSERVANCES

DECEMBER 25

THE STORY

Midnight Mass is one of the oldest traditions that remains popular in many places, and it dates back to around AD 385! Early Christians in Jerusalem are credited with a Nativity custom that began in Bethlehem, the birthplace of Jesus, with a solemn celebration of the Lord's Supper or what we now call Mass. Afterward, everyone would process to Jerusalem by the light of torch and candle. This pilgrimage usually concluded just before the sun would rise and another liturgical celebration of readings and a blessing would begin.

Traditional accounts tell us that news of this beautiful ritual came to spread through Christian regions because of a woman named Egeria, a Christian from Rome, who had experienced many of these awe-inspiring liturgical traditions throughout the year. It impacted her so deeply that toward the end of her journey she described and documented her travels in a work that translators have compiled into a book called *The Pilgrimage of Etheria (Egeria)*. This writing was invaluable to the spread of customs from the Holy Land and the development of the liturgical year, which began to take more shape during the fourth century. Her precise accounts of practices, observances, and services that were being implemented throughout the liturgical seasons in Jerusalem are unique and unrivaled.

In 440, not long after Egeria shared the midnight Nativity tradition observed in the East, Pope Sixtus III implemented a version of this in Rome. He had a small chapel built at St. Mary Major where relics of the true manger are kept and began to say Mass at midnight on December 25 in keeping with the long-standing tradition that Jesus was born at midnight. By this time, the Solemnity of Christmas had become its own observance after having been commemorated on January 6 for the first centuries of Christianity along with the Solemnity of the Epiphany, the Baptism of the Lord, and the Wedding at Cana. These three feasts are also known as the three Epiphanies. Many regions in the late fourth century had already made Christmas and Epiphany distinct feasts from each other, and in 567 the Council of Tours officially set December

25 as the Solemnity of the Nativity of the Lord and January 6 as the Solemnity of the Epiphany of the Lord.

THE TRADITION

The tradition of Christmas Eve Midnight Mass has only grown in its attraction and devotion for the faithful through the centuries. In fact, you may have noticed in several instances from the chapter on Advent that many cultures have integrated elaborate meals and family gatherings on Christmas Eve just before going to Midnight Mass together. There is no obligation or rule compelling us to attend Midnight Mass and yet the moving power of the experience is witnessed by the large numbers of those who attend every year! It certainly speaks volumes, when we put into perspective all that has happened in our world between the fourth century and now, that this quiet and solemn act of going to Mass at midnight remains. We bundle up, warm our cars, drive to our parish churches, and walk into a church newly decorated and now filled with other faithful Catholics who are also awaiting the Savior of the world. It's as if we are at the manger with the Holy Family, and all of creation is in harmony again.

While it is commonly referred to as "Midnight Mass," the *Roman Missal* (the liturgical book containing all the prayer texts needed by priests for Masses) actually titles it "Mass during the Night." This liturgy can be celebrated at any time between vespers on December 24 and dawn on December 25. The Church discourages the faithful from attending more than one Mass in a day, and priests from offering more than three Masses in a day, to avoid overfamiliarity or carelessness toward the sacraments. The unmatched joy of Christmas is an exception to this. We now have four distinct Masses for Christmas: the Vigil Mass, Mass during the Night, Mass at Dawn, and Mass during the Day. Each liturgy has a unique focus to help the Church contemplate the mystery of the Nativity. The Vigil Mass emphasizes the genealogy of Jesus, Mass during the Night recalls the birth of Jesus and the glad tidings of the angels, the Mass at Dawn shares the story of the Good News proclaimed to the shepherds, and the Mass during the Day articulates the divinity of the Christ child. All the faithful, including our clergy, are permitted to participate in all four of these, so great is our joy!

While attending Midnight Mass might not come with ease for every person or family, there are certainly many reasons to experience it at least once. Maybe you can make it a part of your personal or family customs through a manner of planning that echoes the cultures we have learned about. Perhaps have late Christmas Eve dinner, a lively arrangement of games, a white-elephant gift exchange, a Christmas movie viewing, or the recitation of a Rosary as everyone works to stay awake while waiting for the late Mass to start. Don't hesitate to extend the invitation for your family to join you or to have your friends meet you at church, so together you might celebrate the birth of Christ joined with the angels, with Mary and Joseph, and with all the saints in heaven and here on earth, in the middle of a cold winter night.

CARRYING ON THE TRADITION

AT HOME
Make Christmas Eve an evening of high anticipation as you wait up with your family and friends for Midnight Mass. While this may not be for every family, those who do prefer this liturgical practice can try out these ideas.

Consider This
- Try serving your Christmas Eve dinner spread a bit later in the evening. This can help the time to go by with a sense of ease as everyone stays up later for Midnight Mass.
- Incorporate a family Rosary between dinner and Mass.
- Pick Christmas movies to watch while you wait to leave, or allow for one gift to be opened by each person present.
- Read Christmas stories aloud to one another.
- Explain the tradition of Midnight Mass to your family and children.
- Plan to take a Christmas family picture together that evening.

IN THE PARISH
Offer Mass during the Night, and make an effort to have beautiful music and a full team of ministers to show the importance of this liturgy. Publicize this Mass and share resources with parishioners to help them understand and engage with the mystery and beauty of this liturgy.

Consider This
- Think about whether you will begin exactly at midnight or slightly earlier.
- Ask the choir to offer an additional set of Christmas hymns before Mass begins for parishioners to appreciate.
- Change out the candles in your Advent wreath for all white candles, or place one white candle in the center of the wreath.

- Create and distribute a handout or website notice that explains how each Mass for Christmas unfolds the mystery of the birth of Christ (see the explanation in the section above).
- Sing the Christmas Proclamation that is said right before the start of Mass during the Night. The text can be found in Appendix I of the *Roman Missal.*

=== *A LIVING TRADITION* ===

When I was a child, the anticipation of Christmas morning was too much for me to bear. As I grew older, I discovered Midnight Mass and convinced my family to attend. What began as the perfect solution to my excited Christmas Eve insomnia soon turned into one of my most treasured Christmas memories. There is something so special about venturing out into the still, dark night and leaving behind the busyness and external trappings of the Christmas season. Midnight Mass invites us to receive the Christ child with an open heart. As the meaning of Christmas is so often obscured by consumerism today, this tradition is a beautiful opportunity to experience true Christmas joy.

Laura Rivera

NATIVITY SCENE PRACTICES

ADVENT THROUGH THE CHRISTMAS SEASON

THE STORY

Establishing meaningful, holy customs is a hallmark of Catholic life in homes and communities alike. One of the many forms in which we see this is the Nativity Scene, a well-known staple of the Christmas season whose popularity is attributed to St. Francis of Assisi, who created the first crèche for Christmas Eve in 1223. A crèche is a model that depicts the manger scene of Jesus's birth and can be found gloriously showcased in homes, churches, and even in many public areas. The origin of the Nativity Scene by St. Francis was witnessed and recorded by Thomas of Celano, a Franciscan who was near the age of St. Francis and knew the saint personally. Thomas was tasked by Pope Gregory IX to write the biography of St. Francis on the occasion of his canonization, and from this text we have the story of the Christmas Eve manger scene. You can find this firsthand account and more in *The First Life of St. Francis* by Thomas of Celano.

It was St. Francis's principal desire to give the utmost honor to Our Lord at his birth and to inspire the hearts of the faithful with fervor and zeal. To achieve this, he sought to re-create the manger scene in the town of Greccio and did so with the help of a beloved friend and ex-soldier named John. A couple of weeks before Christmas, St. Francis had John go out and collect animals, hay, and a manger to display on Christmas Eve for all those gathered to physically witness the trials and unpleasant conditions through which Our Lord was born into the world. He also believed that if the townspeople personally witnessed this scene, their hearts would be enkindled with a more fervent love for God. "For I would make a memorial of that Child who was born in Bethlehem, and in some sort behold with bodily eyes his infant hardships; how he lay in a manger on the hay, with the ox and the ass standing by."[1] When Christmas evening came, all of those in the town gathered together by firelight to experience the re-creation of the Nativity Scene of Bethlehem in Greccio. Tradition tells us that those who attended were able to embrace the humble, reverent, and joyous occasion of Mass, and the people were filled with exceeding charity and joy.

Tradition holds that the hay used for Francis's manger was blessed by God and made holy, giving it the power to heal. The disease-ridden animals of the town that ate of the hay were cured, and people suffering various ailments and illnesses were healed by placing the hay over their bodies. Since this had become a sacred place, the people of Greccio made an altar where the manger had been and eventually built and dedicated a church there. They believed that if the animals that had eaten of the hay had been healed in this place, then men and women could also find healing through the supremely divine food of the Body and Blood of Christ in the Eucharist.

THE TRADITION

Nativity Scenes are now a common sight during this festive season, but there is one iteration that stands out as particularly interesting because of its uniquely petite size. The French are known for their precious ceramic nativities called *fèves*. This term means "fava bean," which is what was originally used in the center of a King Cake to represent the child Jesus. These miniature heirloom nativities are a blending of two traditions in France. First, following the French Revolution when religious displays were outlawed, the faithful Catholics in France decided they would simply shrink their nativities to an easily hidden size. This allowed them the opportunity to display their faith at Christmas, while also making it simpler to protect themselves and their families if needed. The second tradition is to hide a small prize in a King Cake on the Solemnity of the Epiphany of the Lord. Oftentimes the trinkets placed inside the cake were these tiny ceramic nativity figurines. Some families in France have pieced together their cherished miniature nativities over the years by acquiring the figures in their slices of cake. It is not only a festive Advent tradition, but a custom that ties Christmas seamlessly to the Epiphany.

In many churches, following Midnight Mass, the faithful are invited to reverently kiss the baby Jesus figurine, and then he is the last piece to be placed in the crèche. This custom is addressed and detailed in the *Directory on Popular Piety and the Liturgy*, "At Midnight Mass, an event of major liturgical significance and of strong resonance in popular piety, the following could be given prominence: . . . at the end of Mass, the faithful could be invited to kiss the image of the Child Jesus, which is then placed in a crib erected in the church or somewhere nearby."[2]

Many homes have echoed this practice by setting their Nativity Scene out during the Advent season and waiting to place baby Jesus in the manger on Christmas Day. Even the act of placing the little Jesus in the manger has a range of customs: some have their children do it together, others have the head of the household take the lead, and some leave it to the eldest child. Whichever way it is done, it's clear that for many it is important to wait until December 25 to celebrate the birth of Jesus with this special festive ritual.

Others even take this a step further by waiting to set out the Magi or wise men figurines near the manger. Instead, they have the three statues travel around the house until the Solemnity of the Epiphany of the Lord. On this day they reach the crèche with their gifts of gold, frankincense, and myrrh. Another practice more pronounced in American Catholic culture is the act of small children acquiring more hay for baby Jesus through good deeds. The more acts of virtue they exhibit during the Advent season, the more hay there is for Jesus to be comfortably laid upon when his birth is celebrated on Christmas Day. Regardless of your family dynamic or the multitude of cultures you find in your community, there is plenty of room to purposefully integrate the Nativity Scene into Christmastide. Ultimately it speaks for itself. Much as the awestruck crowd gathered around St. Francis of Assisi, there is not one of us who can look at the setting of Jesus's birth and not be moved by its modest and delicate nature. The way that you choose to take part in this affirmation can only add to and enhance your understanding that God humbled himself to become human out of pure and tremendous love for us.

CARRYING ON THE TRADITION

AT HOME
In a prominent place within your home, set out a Nativity Scene, but wait until Christmas to place baby Jesus in the manger, and wait until the Solemnity of the Epiphany of the Lord to place the Magi in the scene.

Consider This
- Ask your parish priest, another priest, or a deacon to come over and bless your Nativity Scene during the Christmas season.
- Incorporate the Te Deum or the seventh-century Nativity Sermon of St. Isaac the Syrian by saying that prayer in front of your Nativity Scene as a family during dinner or before bed.
- If you have small children, think about encouraging them toward acts of virtue by having them add straw to the manger every time they exhibit a good deed.
- Leave your Nativity Scene up throughout the entire Christmas season.

IN THE PARISH
Place a parish Nativity Scene in an area of prominence, but wait until Midnight Mass to put out the Christ child, and wait until the Solemnity of the Epiphany of the Lord to place the Magi in the scene. You could also try the tradition of Bambinelli Sunday on the Third Sunday of Advent.

Consider This
- On the Third Sunday of Advent, Gaudete Sunday, you can carry on the tradition started by St. Pope John Paul II called Bambinelli Sunday. Invite families to bring the baby Jesus from their Nativity Scenes to Mass with them this Sunday. Have one member of the family come to the altar with their baby Jesus to be blessed by the parish priest.
- At the end of Midnight Mass, invite your parishioners to process forward to kiss the statue of the infant Jesus before placing him in the manger.
- Explain why you waited to place the infant Jesus and the Magi in the Nativity Scene so they can develop a further sense of the liturgical year.
- Have the children of the parish sign up to put on a Nativity play just before Christmas or during the Christmas season.

You can find the Blessing of a Nativity Scene in the *Festive Faith Advent and Christmas Companion* at www.HisGirlSunday.com/FestiveFaith.

THE CHRISTMAS TREE AND TREE BLESSING
ADVENT THROUGH THE CHRISTMAS SEASON

THE STORY

The custom of Christmas trees seems to take root (pun intended) in two different versions of a story that—while notably distinct—bring us to the same ending point: a lasting and ubiquitous Christmas tradition in many countries of the world. To begin with the earliest of the inspirations, we can look at the episcopacy of St. Boniface in the early eighth century and his time spent ministering to the Germanic peoples. His evangelization, successful ministry, and travels there were so remarkable that he became known as the Apostle to the Germans. Pope Gregory II sent him from Rome to bring the Gospel to central Germany. While there, Boniface made extraordinary achievements in establishing monasteries, building up the Catholic Church, and converting pagans. When Pope Gregory II heard news of the effectiveness of Boniface's missionary work, he called Boniface back to Rome to report on all that he had done. The Pope then consecrated Boniface as archbishop of Germany East of the Rhine and sent him back there to continue his work.

After returning from Rome, St. Boniface became aware that pagan idolatry was still being practiced to celebrate the winter solstice in the village of Geismar in the German state of Thuringia. The villagers would gather around a vast oak tree known as "Thunder Oak," a tree dedicated to the god Thor, which acted as an altar for human and animal sacrifice. One year on the night of this pagan ritual, St. Boniface and his followers arrived in time to interrupt the forthcoming child sacrifice. Filled with holy anger, he took an ax and chopped down the Thunder Oak. The German villagers stood in utter shock as St. Boniface proclaimed the truth of the Gospel to them while using the example of a small fir tree, which stood behind the broken oak. From "The Oak of Geismar" by Henry van Dyke we have this very popular quote that is attributed to St.

Boniface from that night, "This little tree, a young child of the forest, shall be your holy tree tonight. It is the wood of peace . . . it is the sign of an endless life, for its leaves are evergreen. See how it points upward to heaven. Let this be called the tree of the Christ-child; gather about it, not in the wild wood, but in your own homes; there it will shelter no deeds of blood, but loving gifts and rites of kindness."[3]

In this story, St. Boniface draws upon the practice of offering sacrifices to the gods on the wood of a tree by linking it to the sacrifice of Christ on the wooden cross, a symbol of everlasting life. In turn, the ritual use of the tree was sanctified and redirected toward the true God of all creation.

While that story is often credited as the main inspiration behind the development of the Christmas tree, many, including the United States Conference of Catholic Bishops (USCCB), attribute the modern actualization of the Christmas tree, with its lights and decorations as we know it, to medieval religious plays. These performances, also known as mystery plays, were almost entirely religious in genre and were meant to teach the illiterate about Christianity. It was believed that if ordinary people could simply act out moral truths, Christian principles, and biblical stories, then those who were not able to read could still learn to practice and live out the tenets of our faith. These plays became common throughout Europe, but especially a performance that was celebrated on Christmas Eve known as the Paradise Play. The purpose of this play was to depict the story of creation, Adam and Eve, original sin, and their banishment from the Garden of Eden or paradise. It concluded with the dramatization of the promised Messiah and the birth of Jesus on Christmas. The focal point of the play was a tall evergreen tree that was used to symbolize the Tree of the Knowledge of Good and Evil, and on its branches were fresh red apples.

Imitating this depiction, people began placing an evergreen tree in their homes as a way to honor Adam and Eve and the birth of Christ at Christmas. Families would put apples in the branches as a reminder of our first parents, and as a way to represent Jesus and the Eucharist they would also adorn the tree with white wafers made in special molds. It also became customary to embellish the tree with candles to symbolize Christ as a light to the world in the midst of a dark and cold season. It didn't take long for the popularity of the Christmas tree to spread throughout Europe and into other parts of the world.

THE TRADITION

Putting up the Christmas tree and decorating it with lights and ornaments, many of which are family heirlooms, is the yearly activity that most prominently begins the preparation for Christmas in many homes. As early as the day after Thanksgiving, most of us can drive down our streets and notice that romantic winter twinkle of a Christmas tree through the front windows of our neighbors' homes. And if not that early, we can certainly count on admiring them all through the Advent season. As Christmas trees are put up earlier and earlier each year, there has been much attention, particularly in Catholic spheres, to the appropriate timing of when the tree goes up and when the tree comes down. While not a simple answer, I think we can take as our guiding principle the season itself to teach us the balance and tension between the solemn time of purifying preparation that is Advent and the exuberant rejoicing that comes with Christmas.

Many Catholics try to wait until as close to Christmas as they practically can to put up their trees, or they wait to finish decorating it until just before Christmas. Some decorate the tree and their houses in small steps all throughout Advent, linking those tasks with the spiritual work of quiet anticipation. While each family and culture have different circumstances, there have emerged several different days in the Advent season that are associated with putting up the tree. First is St. Lucia Day, because of the meaning of her name and the inherent connection to light that her feast day brings. Another is Gaudete Sunday, which begins the third week of Advent when the liturgical focus turns to joyful hope. Tree decorating seems to fit the festivity of this Sunday and the week. And still others wait entirely until Christmas Eve or Christmas Day to add to the festivity of the household.

Taking the tree down also seems to bring about lively discussions with, again, legitimate variation in practice. What is perhaps the clearest variance in the long tradition comes from which liturgical calendar one follows. For those following the current calendar, the Christmas season ends with the Feast of the Baptism of the Lord, the date of which varies a bit from year to year in the dioceses of the United States. Some choose to mark the day by taking down the Christmas tree. Others may choose the traditional day of Epiphany, January 6, and still others opt for the Feast of the Presentation or Candlemas, the last of the Christmas feasts of light, on February 2, as the day to take the tree down.

For my eyes have seen your salvation,
which you prepared in sight of all the peoples,

a light for revelation to the Gentiles,
and glory for your people Israel. (Lk 2:30–32)

Whether you take the tree down on a specific feast day, remove the decorations and finally the tree in stages, or simply take it down when the tree dies, it is clear that Catholics around the world are striving to maintain their Christmas festivity until the very end of the season.

Decorating itself can be a great way to bring your loved ones together in cheerful Christmas spirit, especially if everyone assumes an attitude of festivity, rather than letting the stress of too little time (or too many decorations) win the day. Ornaments themselves are often treasure troves of sentimental value, which some collect from their travels, give as anniversary gifts, or receive from their children covered in drip-dried glue and craft supplies. When my husband and I were betrothed, a beloved friend of ours arranged a reception, and to our delight she asked that everyone bring an ornament for us to put on the first Christmas tree of our marriage. We still hang all of those from year to year while we reminisce on both the special and the endearingly ordinary days of our married life.

Anyone can grow to appreciate this custom of decorating a tree and other parts of one's home because even if it is not already within your tradition, it is practical and attainable enough to adopt. The decorative rituals don't end with the lights and ornaments of course. Some string popcorn, others place battery-operated candles on the branches, and almost everyone has a particular way to top the tree and choice of person who will go about making this final adornment. Watching this iconic symbol of Christmas come together as people work in harmony is nothing short of inspiring because through this practice we experience the spirit of Christmas, with its profound sense of being welcomed home and belonging there.

However, there is one important element that is often neglected. It is the one thing recommended by the USCCB that we do with our trees on Christmas Day, and that is to bless them. As Catholics, we don't put up a tree only for the sake of ornamentation or sheer sentimentality, but also because it stands as a reminder to us of God's promise. Look back to the words attributed to St. Boniface: the wood stands for peace, the evergreen communicates eternal life, and its height and shape direct our gaze upward to heaven. We bless our Christmas trees so that we can set them apart as distinct from the rest of our Christmas décor. When we look at our trees, we should be prompted to remember the Incarnation, promised to us by God in response to the Fall, and to consider his

Second Coming. If you would like to bless your Christmas tree this year and in years to come, you can find the "Christmas Tree Blessing" in the *Festive Faith Advent and Christmas Companion* at www.HisGirlSunday.com/FestiveFaith.

CARRYING ON THE TRADITION

AT HOME

Put up your Christmas tree and decorate it with lights and ornaments that mean something special to you. These might be family treasures, or they can simply follow a color scheme or particular style that you love. Decorate your tree in a way that helps you feel festive, draws you into beauty, and brings you and those who gather with you around the tree closer to the hope and joy of the season. Try to keep your tree up this year throughout all of Christmastide, keeping in mind that there are differences deep within Catholic tradition for just when the season draws to a close. Be creative!

Consider This

- If you use a fresh-cut Christmas tree, you may have to put it out a little later in the Advent season so that it will last through the Christmas season. You can lengthen the freshness by drilling holes in the bottom of the trunk and putting the trunk into a bucket of water outside until you are ready to decorate it. But be mindful of a freeze in colder places!
- Make your tree decorating an entire family affair, or gather friends or neighbors. Every year our entire family goes to my in-laws' home to decorate the family tree. We eat treats, sing songs, and everyone hangs ornaments. This makes for cherished family memories.
- Every year since my husband and I got married, we have purchased one or two ornaments that symbolize one of our treasured experiences from that year. Our tree is gradually being filled with these symbols of memories we hold dear in our hearts. You can adopt this tradition as well by adding an ornament each year that signifies something meaningful to you. If you live with others, perhaps each person can do so, sharing the story behind the ornament before adding it to the tree.
- Bless your Christmas tree as a symbol of our Catholic faith.

IN THE PARISH

Host a Christmas tree lighting ceremony. Invite everyone to join the blessing of the parish Christmas tree and enjoy hot drinks, Christmas cookies, and maybe even caroling through the neighborhood, spreading Christmas cheer.

Consider This

- Put up a large Christmas tree in the parish courtyard, community center, or the narthex of your church. Arrange for volunteers to decorate it.
- Invite parishioners to gather for a blessing of the Christmas tree and simple party.
- Consider making this gathering a lighting celebration where everyone can gather to see the Christmas tree glow for the first time this season, then participate in the blessing of the tree.
- Serve refreshments, and have someone well-rehearsed to read or tell the legendary story of St. Boniface and the Christmas tree.
- Serve refreshments, and maybe go caroling after the main events.
- Provide printed copies of the Christmas Tree Blessing for use in parish homes.

Resource

Bless your Christmas tree with the Christmas Tree Blessing found in the *Festive Faith Advent and Christmas Companion* at www.HisGirlSunday.com/FestiveFaith.

ST. STEPHEN'S DAY AND WREN FOLKLORE

DECEMBER 26

THE STORY

In pre-Christian Ireland, the day after Christmas, December 26, was known as Wren Day, pronounced "wran" to those native to Ireland. The ritual of Wren Day is believed to be so ancient that it developed when Celtic Druids reigned, high-ranking priests, teachers, and judges who viewed the wren as the king among all birds. With the coming of Christianity to Ireland the observance has taken on a new meaning, while maintaining many of the cultural expressions authentic to the Irish. The wren had long been a highly esteemed bird in Ireland because of its wit, cleverness, and lovely winter song. Wrens also provided helpful assistance in keeping the crops well by eating harmful insects from the soil. Most important to the story of Wren Day is the Druids' perception of this little creature as a mystical bird, deeply connected to the divine.

It was believed that if you heard the songs of this respected bird, then you would have good luck in future endeavors, but if you ever disturbed a wren's nest, it was considered a bad omen. There is a story that endures in Irish folklore that highlights the cunning nature of the wren, and it goes like this: One day there was a flying contest in the kingdom of birds to see who could reach the highest heights. The strong and determined eagle soared upward into the sky, leaving all other birds behind him, except for that little wren. The wren in its wisdom tucked itself under the eagle's wing without him knowing, and when the eagle tired and could ascend no further, he looked around and saw there weren't any other birds. In gladness and pride, he shouted, "I am the king of all birds!" The wren then released itself from under the wing and flew up a few feet higher, proclaiming, "I am the king of all birds!" When every bird had landed from their competition, the wren was awarded the title "King of the Birds"!

No one would have ever considered harming the wren during prosperous times, but when harsh winters became too difficult to endure, ancient Celts would hunt a wren and offer it as a sacrifice to their gods. A proper sacrifice, especially during the dark and bleak winter months, would surely convince the sun to come out sooner and provide more warmth and light to help their cause.

The practice of catching wrens remained popular even after the Druids died out, and the hunters of these little songbirds became known as wren boys. These men began their hunt days before December 26 clothed in straw and with painted faces. Catching a wren was no easy task, and it very much became a days-long procedure to find one in the hedges or roof eaves, kill the bird, and then tie it to a staff to parade around the streets. The meaning behind this was to show that the debt to nature had been paid in hopes that the people would be looked upon favorably by the gods.

This ritual continued until Catholicism reached the areas of Ireland where it was commonly practiced and the Church reoriented the pagan ceremony in dedication to the Feast of St. Stephen. With December 26 given a renewed focus on St. Stephen rather than the pre-Christian Wren Day, we see the lore of the wren story transform into a Christmas tale about a great saint. As with other cultural stories that we have explored in this book, old habits and customs can be challenging to uproot and would often begin to merge together. This is the case with Wren Day morphing into St. Stephen's Day, and unfortunately for the wren, it maintained its reputation as being the bird of sacrifice. In this transition the Druidic ritual became Christianized with a different story, which tells how the wren is to blame for the death of St. Stephen as opposed to it being a sacrificial offering to the gods. Oral tradition tells us that when St. Stephen was hiding behind a bush from the authorities who were seeking to kill him, a chirping wren that was in the bush gave notice to the authorities that he was hiding there. The wren was blamed for having betrayed St. Stephen, the first Christian martyr, and this is why the wren boys were justified in hunting, and sometimes stoning, the bird.

THE TRADITION

There are certainly not as many places in Ireland today where you will find Wren Day as elaborately participated in as in years past, but many rural towns still enjoy this day as a major event. The Wren Day tradition has spread to parts of Scotland, England, and France over the centuries, though it is not as universally practiced in these cultures. Under the influence of Christianity, sacrificing an actual wren has since yielded to a more humane version of the tradition that spares the wren any harm. Some will still catch a wren but will keep it alive, while others will use a stuffed animal or an effigy to parade around on St. Stephen's Day. This is now a purely symbolic act of what their ancestors had done, while also maintaining the story of St. Stephen's supposed betrayal. In connection with earlier times, some people in Ireland have birdhouses near their gardens in hopes that the wren will come and dwell there and eat the insects, thereby protecting their flowers, herbs, and vegetables as the wren is believed to have done in the days of the Druids.

In some Irish counties, St. Stephen's Day is marked by a full-day festival with lots of merriment, parades, dancing, Irish folk music, and the annual door-to-door wren boy routine. For those involved in the merrymaking, the wren boys, also known as straw boys or mummers, are certainly a sight to see! They continue the custom of dressing up in straw costumes and masks, some with their faces painted, and holding a staff with a holly bush or an evergreen wreath tied to it along with a fake wren. The wren boys start the festival day by joining in the day's parade early in the morning, and then later that day they go door to door to sing a traditional song and dance for the home dwellers while asking for money. The donations are spiritedly asked for in honor of giving the wren a proper burial, but practically speaking they go to funding the festivities and giving to a local charity. The song has taken various forms at different times and places, but when I had the privilege of hearing a personal account of Wren Day from Irish-born Bishop Edmond Carmody, he sang it to me like this:

> *The wren the wren the king of all birds*
> *St. Stephen's Day was caught in the furze*
> *Her clothes were all torn, her shoes were all worn*
> *Up with the kettle and down with the pan*
> *Give us a penny to bury the "wran"*
> *If you haven't a penny, a halfpenny will do*
> *If you haven't a halfpenny, God bless you!*

There are two important lessons I have learned from the Wren Day tradition. First, it is another example of how human customs and rituals can be transformed by an encounter with Christian beliefs so that they become enhanced and reoriented to a higher purpose. Second, Wren Day is a distinctive observance because of the essential involvement of boys and men from the community. One of the struggles I have witnessed emerging with the contemporary renaissance in liturgical living is that boys and men often seem not to have a realistic place carved out for them. In fact, one of the more commonly asked questions that I've received in my work from women is "How do I get the guys in my life involved?" I think the St. Stephen and Wren Day tradition holds part of the answer. The activities in this celebration tend to appeal to boys and men. They are not limited in scope, but rather invite everyone in the community into the festivities in different capacities.

Are the liturgical-living activities you are practicing at home accessible to everyone in your house? What about in your parish and neighborhood? Have you talked about the deeper meaning of liturgical living with all the key players you want to involve in Catholic festive traditions? Men, women, children, youth, young adults?

I believe there are two prominent factors that largely contribute to a lack of male involvement in anticipating, planning, and facilitating liturgical life celebrations. First, broadly speaking, that liturgical customs, specifically in America, don't manifest as organic communal expressions of faith, cultural heritage, and patriotism as they once did within Catholicism. Festive traditions have skipped over generations, and have come to change as cultures blend and adapt to the ways of our American sensibilities. By becoming more aware of the ways in which we revive traditions in our country that were once formed in more village-oriented locales, we can seek to encourage the involvement of men in the liturgical life of their homes and communities. While the loss of heritage and cultural customs is a tragedy, the renewed interest in the liturgical year is a hopeful opportunity to refashion old customs that still hold meaning and to grow new ones that reflect our current circumstances as faithful expressions of the joy of the Gospel.

The second layer of the struggle to ensure that festivity is truly accessible and welcoming to *everyone* is the overemphasis on curated activities that do not give clear invitation for boys and men about how to comfortably participate. When these activities are the total sum of the liturgical-living experience, the whole notion and intent of living liturgically begins to lose its deeper significance and innate appeal. In the celebration of St. Stephen's Day combined with ancient Celtic Wren Day lore and festivity, we see that boys and men not only participate but lead the entertainment with their gifts. This day especially can be a model of encouragement and inspiration for all of us as we remember that liturgical life belongs to every Catholic.

CARRYING ON THE TRADITION

AT HOME

It's easy to run out of steam the day after Christmas, but what this feast day has taught me is to learn how to pace my energy according to each season. Make room for Advent to be a place of waiting and calm, then let Christmas be for greater rejoicing. For the Irish, this is a day that is often celebrated with even more exuberance than Christmas. Now that we are actually in the Christmas season, this is a good time to up the ante!

Consider This
- Be mindful to ask for St. Stephen's intercession today.
- Prepare an Irish-inspired dinner or drink to make your mealtime a festive opportunity to share the history of Wren Day, and don't forget its merging with St. Stephen's Day.
- Make thank-you cards or write a thank-you email to the deacons in your parish in honor of St. Stephen, who was the first deacon.
- Try a family or friend-group service project to aid the poor like the saint we honor today. Make and share a holiday meal, or put together care bags to give to your local shelter or to hand out when you see someone on the street corner.
- If the traditional Irish celebrations that you read about speak to you, collaborate with local friends and neighbors to begin a modest take on the parades and parties that are held in Ireland.

IN THE PARISH

Especially after all the Advent and Christmas celebrations, we can certainly feel drained by the time we reach December 26. I encourage you to model Irish Catholic Christmas spirit by honoring St. Stephen today, even if it's in more simple terms.

Consider This

- Share this Irish tradition of St. Stephen's Day through one of your communication methods.
- After Mass, extend time for hospitality with Irish treats and folk music.
- If you have an Irish population at your parish, ask them if they are familiar with this tradition and if they'd like to coordinate a St. Stephen's Day and Wren Day party.
- St. Stephen was the first deacon; perhaps you could make this a deacon appreciation day.
- Imitate St. Stephen's efforts to care for the poor by giving parishioners the opportunity to come to church today and make blessing bags or care kits to be handed out to people in need or taken to a shelter.

A LIVING TRADITION

Culture is a very important aspect of our life. It's the feeling, thinking, acting, and speaking that differentiate one group from another. Cultural norms and behaviors are handed down from the mother—that's why we talk about the "mother tongue"—and the only way you can get rid of a person's culture is to deliberately try to change it. St. Stephen's Day is different in Ireland than in any other country. In England it's called Boxing Day, and even from person to person there are variations in how they tell the story. Some will say it's the day they collect charity boxes for Christmas; others will say that it is a tradition of having a boxing match the day after Christmas. In Ireland, when I was growing up, St. Stephen's Day was famous for the wren boys. The festivities began on the vigil of St. Stephen, the night of Christmas Day, and you could hear the drums, the tambourine, and the bodhran from miles away. The wren boys were, even then, an old tradition of children and men who go around singing songs and playing tambourines, bodhrans, and accordions to entertain the people from house to house. I remember them coming to my house; they would walk in and go to our fireplace to heat up the goat skin of the bodhran by the fire to get a better sound on it while doing a little step dance. Especially as kids we absolutely loved it when they would come to our home. I was one of thirteen children, and we had a really good time. After the penance we engaged in throughout Advent, we were now in a time of rejoicing.

When I got older, as a seminarian, I would go out with about ten to twelve men and walk along with them as they would go to the houses. If a family member from the house we visited had died within the last year, we wouldn't play any music. One of the most impressionable parts about this was the immense respect that was given to those who have lost loved ones.

The practice of this feast is compelling because although in some ways the tradition is about begging to get money for a party, everyone enjoyed this community celebration, and it truly built excitement around Christmas and the Feast of St. Stephen. The custom of the wren boys still happens today, but they don't go from house to house anymore; they typically just walk around town in the style of a parade. While very little actually had to do with St. Stephen specifically, it was still a way for us to grow closer together through our Irish roots and the joyfulness of the Christmas season.

I fondly remember my mother going out a couple of weeks before Christmas to get raisins for raisin bread, lemon peel for baking, and candles that stood three feet tall, which we would put in our windows. Every window would have one, and it would represent that Christ was welcome here. During the time that Catholic priests were persecuted and on the run, they would see a candle in the window and know that they were welcome here too. In fact, before candle stands were created for candles this large within the home, we would cut out the center of a rutabaga and set the candle in the center of it.

The importance in carrying this on is so that we can remember our history. You have to consider the country, too, including the Irish Catholic persecution and how it all ties in together. We have to remember our roots, why we did things in the past, but to also be aware that what we do today is remembered in the future. Our traditions connect to our faith, so we have to remember Stephen as the first martyr, what he did, and the way he followed the ways of the Lord. This is about keeping the Lord in our midst. And you have to recognize joy; we are supposed to be joyful people in the time of Christmas when Our Lord was born in this world.

Bishop Edmond Carmody, Diocese of Corpus Christi

ST. JOHN'S DAY WINE BLESSING

DECEMBER 27

THE STORY

On December 27, we celebrate the Feast of St. John the Apostle and Evangelist. John is also known as the brother of St. James the Greater, to whom the Camino de Santiago—a network of pilgrimage trails in southern France and Spain—is attributed, and the two of them hold the unforgettable title of "sons of thunder." It is believed that St. John and his brother, St. James, were originally disciples of John the Baptist, who directed them to the Lamb of God, and from there they became followers of Jesus. St. John holds a special place in the Gospel of John. Jesus grants him the manifold blessings of observing the raising of Jairus's daughter, the Transfiguration, and the agony in the garden and also the honor of sitting next to Jesus at the Last Supper. St. John is also known for being with Jesus at the foot of the Cross, and there Jesus commended his mother to John, who represents the whole Church. Throughout the Gospel of John, it is commonly accepted that he is the "one whom Jesus loved." St. John is the only apostle not to have suffered martyrdom, but we are about to learn how he did have a close call.

For those of you who enjoy indulging responsibly in a glass of wine, have a heavenly friendship with the apostle John, or are particularly drawn to the eccentricities of our faith that give it character, this will be a captivating legend to know and pass along to others. There are multiple sources and variations of this story as is common with oral history and tradition. Most online resources today tell a simplified version of one particular account: St. John was offered a chalice of poisoned wine, and when he blessed the wine, the poison rose up out of the cup in the form of a snake or a dragon.

Now, this version of the story is credited to *The Golden Legend: Readings on the Saints* collected by Jacobus de Voragine, archbishop of Genoa around AD 1275. This relatively late version of the story is easily related to the origin of the traditional blessing since it includes John being offered a chalice of wine. The influence of this version is evident in the rubrics of a blessing of St. John's wine found in the *Roman Ritual* of 1964. The rubrics or instructions read: "The priest . . . blesses the wine brought by the people. This is done in memory and in honor of St. John, who drank without any ill effects the poisoned wine offered to him by his enemies."

While many pious stories are a part of the history of this blessing and the traditions surrounding it, I would like to focus on the earliest recounting. I believe this earlier version has a profound depth of symbolism and offers us a startling depiction of St. John's utter faith in Christ and his redemptive chalice. Here is an overview of the poisoned cup story that we receive from the apocryphal writing (early Christian texts not gathered in the Bible) called the Acts of John. In this work, we find a collection of writings about St. John the Apostle that began circulating in written form during the second century AD.

We enter the scene with St. John standing before the Roman Emperor Domitian. In an attempt to test the unbreakable faith of St. John, the emperor demanded he prove that Jesus is the true and eternal King as the apostle had claimed. To do this St. John asked that a goblet of deadly poison be brought to him. Mixing the poison with water, he blessed it loudly in Jesus's name, asking the Holy Spirit to mingle with the poison and let it act as nourishment for body and soul. Then he took a confident drink. These actions call to mind Mark 16:17–18, which reads: "These signs will accompany those who believe: in my name they will drive out demons, they will speak new languages. They will pick up serpents [with their hands], and if they drink any deadly thing, it will not harm them. They will lay hands on the sick, and they will recover."

Everyone watched, waiting for St. John to drop dead on the ground, and yet there he stood before them in gladness and good health. As you would imagine, Domitian was infuriated and believed that his servants had brought something other than poison to spare John's life. When St. John realized that this didn't stand as enough validation, he orchestrated another trial. Taking the same poison that had been given to him, he asked that a condemned criminal be brought down to drink from the cup. The poison proved itself on the prisoner, who died immediately. But St. John, who is not a murderer, went to Domitian that evening to discuss the death of the prisoner. When the emperor ordered the body to be thrown away, St. John resurrected him through the power of Christ. For this, and all the works he had shown that day, he was exiled to the island of Patmos.

Whether it was wine, water, or both that was given to St. John, the connection to Christ's chalice is abundantly clear. The symbolism and practice of this blessing communicates the incredible power of true faith in Christ, the unmatched love God has for his creatures, and the goodness of the created world.

THE TRADITION

The custom of blessing wine for the Feast of St. John dates back as early as the fifth or sixth century with initial observances found in Catholic regions of Germany and Austria. By the sixteenth century most of Christendom took part in this devotion. The account of St. John's miracle has inspired many artists to portray their version of the events. Early Christian artwork depicted St. John the Evangelist's triumph over the deadly chalice, often showing a snake or a dragon rising out of the cup, to visually convey the victory over the poison of sin. The snake and dragon can be understood as signs of something evil or deadly, which St. John conquered through his steadfast faith in Christ.

As this miraculous trial from the life of the apostle John was shared throughout the early Church, the wine blessed on St. John's feast day became known as the "Love of St. John." It was seen as a symbol of the unique love that Jesus had for his beloved disciple and the fullness of heart with which St. John reciprocated Our Lord's love in deed and devotion. The wine is still referred to in those terms, and it has been used in the homes of ardent Catholics for more than a thousand years now as a special wine, blessed and set apart, so that the blessing and drinking of it becomes an occasion of celebrating God's grace in daily life. The blessed wine is traditionally sipped and served on special occasions such as solemnities, special feast days, and sacramental anniversaries.

The actual Rite for the Blessing of Wine on the Feast of St. John the Evangelist has been a part of the liturgical books of the Church for centuries. It can be found in many places, but the authoritative texts are recorded in the *Rituale Romanum* (*Roman Ritual*), which is a multi-volume collection of all the liturgical services not contained in the other liturgical books such as the *Roman Missal*. The *Roman Ritual* contains two versions of the blessing, which are both very similar. These blessings are a part of the history of the Church and have not been invalidated. There is also a much newer blessing of wine found in the *Book of Blessings* that can be used. Though this is not specifically for the Feast of St. John, it can be adapted by a priest or deacon for the occasion.

On December 27, the Feast of St. John, in many Catholic parishes the congregation is invited to bring to church all the wine they intend to use for St. John's feast day and for the New Year so that a priest or deacon can bless it. If your parish is not hosting such a blessing, you can ask your priest to bless your family's wine, either using an older form of the blessing to invoke St. John, or the more recent version of the blessing. Having the wine blessed is believed to bestow the same divine help that came to St. John by aiding the sick, safeguarding next year's harvest, offering assistance to the dying, and giving protection for new marriages.

An important part of Catholic blessings is the attitude or disposition of the faithful who receive the sacramentals that have been blessed. Sacramentals are sacred signs (material things, gestures, or acts) that are blessed by the Church and used to direct our holiness and worship of God. To consume this wine excessively or to indulge in drunkenness is an obvious affront to the blessing and God's grace. I encourage you to participate in the blessing of wine with an open heart, and let it be a reminder of the blessings of God and the healing of all creation, and, yes, a "cheer to the soul."

Within the last century or so, many Catholics offer the following toast when consuming their blessed wine at home, especially when toasting the New Year. A head of the household raises their glass toward the person sitting next to them at the dinner table and says, "I drink to you the love of St. John." The person who was just toasted then replies back by saying, "I thank you for the love of St. John" and takes a drink. Then that same person turns to the person on the other side of them and begins the call-and-response again. It should go around the table until each participant has been toasted.[4] As we move forward to honor Our Lady, I extend my glass to you and wish you the graces of God upon your year: "I drink to you the love of St. John." You can access the toast in the *Festive Faith Advent and Christmas Companion* at www.HisGirlSunday. com/FestiveFaith.

CARRYING ON THE TRADITION

AT HOME
Take the wine you intend to use for the year to your parish to have it blessed. Then pour a glass for dinner on the Feast of St. John the Evangelist, and toast one another in the traditional way described above.

Consider This
- Ask your parish priest if he can bless several bottles of wine for you.
- Save the wine you had blessed for sacramental anniversaries, feast-day celebrations, and other special liturgical observances throughout the coming year.
- If you can't buy and bring a year's worth of wine at once, have just a couple of bottles blessed, and save one to pour into others that you buy throughout the year.

- Write out or print the toast so that the entire family knows what to say at dinner.

IN THE PARISH
Extend an invitation to your parishioners to have them bring bottles of wine to be blessed for use throughout the year on special liturgical occasions.

Consider This
- Explain the importance of this blessing and why it's done on the Feast of St. John the Evangelist.
- Create a handout or website post with the toast so parishioners can take it home and use it during dinner time on December 27 and on other special occasions.
- Tell the story of the miracle that is associated with this blessing in a homily or on one of the parish digital communication platforms.
- Use this feast as an opportunity to emphasize the Eucharistic miracle we witness every Sunday and the importance of the Blood of Christ in our Catholic faith.

THE SOLEMNITY OF MARY, MOTHER OF GOD AND NEW YEAR CELEBRATIONS
DECEMBER 31 AND JANUARY 1

THE STORY

New Year's Eve and New Year's Day are by no stretch of the imagination a liturgical calendar observance, but no matter where you find yourself in the world, it is a culturally anticipated time of entertainment and countdowns. It's also common to see collections of friends and loved ones enjoying food, drinks, and fireworks while promising that they'll finally make good on that gym membership this year! Even with all its secular dressings and extravagances, this point in the year has a remarkable ability to encourage a positive outlook and inspire the receptivity of new blessings in the hearts of people worldwide.

While embracing the experience of the coming year, Catholics are also called to pivot our attention to the Solemnity of Mary, Mother of God, on January 1. We often find ourselves here, situated right in the middle of the sacred—anticipating an upcoming solemnity—and the secular—enjoying the close of a calendar year. And through the wisdom of the Church, we get an aerial view of what New Year's truly expresses about our human nature: the very physical need to rejoice with loved ones over a year gone by, and the very spiritual need for renewed holiness to which the liturgical year beckons us. By holding these two realities before us, we can see how the passing of an ordinary year to a new one points to the deep truth of who we are as mortal and immortal beings. We are jewels of God's created order and yet destined for heaven.

Celebrating Mary as the Mother of God at the start of a New Year is not accidental. In fact, this Marian title is as old as the feast of the Nativity itself. However, the location of this feast day on the liturgical calendar is a relatively recent and intriguing development. The earliest written form of Mary's title as Mother of God can be found in the writings of Origen (AD 185–254), who referred to her with the title of *Theotokos,* which from Greek means "God-bearer." However, Origen notes that this phrase was in use even before his time. As Catholics we assent to the truth that Mary is the woman who physically carried the child Jesus in her womb, and that she also provided Jesus the genetic material needed to form his human body with the aid of the Holy Spirit. We also believe that Jesus is not just man but God-man. We read in Romans 1:3 that Jesus is God's "Son, descended from David according to the flesh." Therefore, we must logically conclude that Mary is the Mother of God. In this way, Mary's divine motherhood becomes a fundamental part of our Christological beliefs. "Mary is truly 'Mother of God' since she is the mother of the eternal Son of God made man, who is God himself" (*CCC,* 509). It was only a couple of centuries after Origen that this very title of *Theotokos* would be called into question by Nestorius but in response was officially made a dogmatic declaration by the Church at the Council of Ephesus in AD 431.

Although our understanding of Mary's role in salvation history has never changed, I can't say the same for the placement of this feast on the calendar. Honoring Mary's maternity has long been an enduring discipline—this is irrefutable—but finding which date when the universal Church was going to do that all together has quite a circuitous story. Beginning as early as the fifth century, various regions around the world were unofficially observing the feast on dates ranging from October to December to January. Even through the seventh century, January 1 emphasized the octave of Christmas with the primary focus being on the extended Solemnity of the Nativity of the Lord. Perhaps there might have been a Mass on this day in dedication to Our Lady, as she was never forgotten, but the Nativity of Our Lord was central. The Christmas octave was the most prominent observance until the turn of the fourteenth century. Then January 1, while still remaining the last day of the octave, was appointed as the Circumcision of Our Lord. It remained this way until 1960, just before the start of the Second Vatican Council, when St. John XXIII changed it back to the octave of the Nativity and removed the feast day for the Circumcision from the day it had been celebrated on for more than five hundred years. In 1974, after the close of Vatican II, Pope Paul VI declared January 1 as the Solemnity of Mary, Mother of God. His purpose for establishing the solemnity was a desire for the Church to know not only how connected we are to Mary in her role as mother of Christ and the Church, but also how deeply interwoven we are with one another. He declared, "This will also bring the faithful to a deeper realization of the brotherhood which unites all of them as sons and daughters of the Virgin Mary, 'who with a mother's love has cooperated in their rebirth and spiritual formation,' and as sons and daughters of the Church, since 'we are born from the Church's womb we are nurtured by the Church's milk, we are given life by the Church's Spirit.'"[5]

Living together throughout the year, and celebrating its conclusion and culmination, unites us in praising God and seeking holiness. Still, with the cultural emphasis on January 1 being about New Year's Day and not much about Our Lady, there's room for growth in celebrating and asking for Mary's intercession at the beginning of each New Year.

THE TRADITION

It's fair to say that practicing Catholics are just as desiring of a lively New Year's party as the next person, but many are tired of the typical shenanigans that usually involve overindulging and objectionable revelry. Due to the relative newness of this solemnity, it's clear that tradition has not yet solidified around its celebration. In fact, I've encountered parish communications that miss entirely the opportunity to mention the solemnity, instead only wishing people a Happy New Year. While extending well wishes for the New Year is certainly not problematic, it is a missed opportunity to remind the faithful to celebrate the Solemnity of Mary, Mother of God. We have an opportunity here to sanctify what is already a celebratory two-day occasion in our culture and to align the festivity more closely with our Catholic faith and traditions. This is low-hanging fruit; we just need to grab the secular holiday and make it Catholic like we've done time and again, as we're exploring in this book (think back to Wren Day/St. Stephen's Day).

Celebrating a New Year has already been ingrained in us, with the traditions of fireworks, parades, evening gatherings, champagne, kissing your loved one at midnight, watching a countdown, sharing good food, and enjoying liveliness in the streets. We don't have to uproot all of that; we can instead play off of it and integrate more Marian devotion. The Church has made December 31 and January 1 the Vigil and Solemnity of Mary, Mother of God, so let's take the secular customs of New Year's and make them Catholic. As faith-filled Catholics, we are called to elevate the New Year customs by making them, at least in part, focused on Mary and the great mystery of the Incarnation.

The Solemnity of Mary, Mother of God, is a holy day of obligation, which is a perfect way to begin the New Year. Gathering in church with our fellow parishioners, praying, listening to the Word, and celebrating the Eucharistic—there is no better way to equip oneself for all that the New Year will bring. This solemnity is also properly situated on the eighth day of Christmas, the last day of the octave, giving us a culminating feast to underscore the mystery of salvation and Mary's powerful role in that.

This date on which this solemnity is celebrated magnifies the intimate relationship between Mary and Jesus and between her and the rest of the Church. Mary is our queen, intercessor, and highly favored one. We begin the octave of Christmas with Jesus's birth and end it celebrating with the woman who ushered in his humanity. We begin a New Year under her motherly patronage and welcome her to walk with us and further direct us to her son, Jesus Christ.

I encourage you to continue all the aforementioned New Year's Eve festivities, but consider beginning the evening by attending the Vigil Mass with loved ones. When you extend an invitation for others to gather at your house, call it a New Year's and Solemnity of Mary, Mother of God, celebration. Suggestions follow for creating a festive celebration in your home. However you choose to commemorate the divine mystery of Mary, Mother of God, in your corner of the world, let it be done for her sake and for the good of the family and community. The Church has done her part to establish this calendar day as a solemnity; now it is time for us to do our part and make it a lived and vibrant expression of our Catholic faith and culture.

CARRYING ON THE TRADITION

AT HOME

In order to steer away from just the typical secular celebration that we are used to and focus more on the solemnity, think about hosting a gathering yourself or with other Catholic friends and family members who can assist you in leading the way to bring Mary's motherhood into focus on this day.

Consider This

- Make this celebration more Catholic by calling it a Solemnity of Mary, Mother of God, celebration.
- Incorporate a Marian prayer into your meal blessing, and specifically ask for her intercession.
- Place a statue of Our Lady in a prominent place for guests to see; what we see we can more easily call to mind.
- Decorate with blue, or make a Marian-inspired food or drink.
- Sing or say the Te Deum together to give thanks for the year that is coming to a close.

IN THE PARISH

Now is your time to shine! This date is in desperate need of a cultural shift, and the Church has already claimed it for Our Blessed Mother. In the same manner that Wren Day was transformed to St. Stephen's Day, we can lead the way in directing the celebrations to Our Lady by hosting a New Year's and Mary, Mother of God, celebration after the Vigil Mass on the evening of December 31. It's the perfect time as parishioners are already being called to Mass, so keep them there for a festive and faith-filled evening.

Consider This

- Regarding fireworks, I know what you're thinking—yikes, a liability! You may want to go a simple route with sparklers at midnight, or perhaps have your community meet somewhere after Mass where you can celebrate and watch a public fireworks display together.
- In some places, making noise at midnight ushers in the New Year, so if fireworks are off limits, consider noise makers and poppers instead. Perhaps try a mini-parade with festive music to move the party from the gathering hall to an outdoor area.

- Inspire families within your parish to host small-group gatherings at their homes, and give them the list of ideas that can be found in the "At Home" section above.
- Have the Knights of Columbus or another ministry grill or cook meals for the evening. Another group might be able to provide the drinks, and another the desserts.
- Move your parish's Mary statue to a more prominent place for everyone to see.
- Decorate the community hall in blue.
- Incorporate the Te Deum into your liturgical music selection.

Resource
At your gathering say the Prayer for the New Year found in the *Festive Faith Advent and Christmas Companion* at www.HisGirlSunday.com/FestiveFaith.

MAKING AND EATING KING CAKE FOR EPIPHANY

IN THE UNIVERSAL CALENDAR: JANUARY 6
IN THE UNITED STATES: SUNDAY BETWEEN JANUARY 2 AND JANUARY 8

THE STORY

The peculiar experience of discovering a plastic baby Jesus wrapped in a deliciously baked piece of braided cake has a fascinating origin story. It has its primordial roots in a French custom, which combined with Spanish cultural customs in the Americas to become its own unique tradition. The meeting ground for this fusion of cultures and customs was New Orleans. The French and Spanish cultures, each in their own way, had long celebrated the Solemnity of the Epiphany of the Lord with great festivity and celebration. Both populations were seeking to honor the visit of the Magi who followed the star and found the Christ child in a humble manger. From the French, New Orleans was inspired to carry on the Little Christmas—or *Le Petit Noel*, as the French call the Epiphany—as a day of family and community gathering, eating, drinking, and exchanging small gifts in imitation of the Magi. From the Spanish, New

Orleans received the communal experience of grand balls where a king and queen were selected and crowned.

Between the eighteenth century and the start of the nineteenth, in simplified terms, Spain and France had alternating control over New Orleans. This was fertile soil for two cultures that were very distinct, and often at odds with one another, to intermingle by observing the transcending feast of the Magi. As the French and Spanish lived in such close proximity, it was inevitable that each group would adopt common forms of festivity and ways of living from the other. That is especially observable in the Spanish celebration of King's Day, which eventually became an elaborate social event that starts on January 6, the twelfth day after Christmas. The French, too, have their own version of this called *Le Jour des Rois* (The Day of Kings), and the latter phrase has been the lasting Creole term used on the Solemnity of the Epiphany of the Lord.

Over time, the period between Epiphany and Ash Wednesday became known as Carnival season. The word *carnival* comes from the Latin *carnelevarium*, which means "the removal of meat." During these weeks of celebration Catholics would need to consume all remaining meat and animal products, such as eggs, cream, and butter, before the six-week Lenten fast. There are a couple of reasons for this. First, the laws of fasting and abstinence were significantly different from and much more demanding than what we practice now, and Catholics were obliged to abstain from all the items listed above and then some. Second, before in-home refrigeration, these perishable items would not have lasted through the weeks of Lent when they were not being eaten and therefore would have spoiled. The best thing to do was to use these ingredients to make delicious food. Carnival celebrations such as balls, masquerades, parades, and parties were held during the weeks before Lent began. However, many of the saints rightfully did not approve of what the Carnival season became. Many Catholics saw these celebrations as an excuse to overindulge beyond any sense of virtue. The weeks between Epiphany and Shrove (meaning absolution after confessing sin) Tuesday, also known as Fat Tuesday or Mardi Gras (the day before Ash Wednesday), are meant for feasting, but also for intentional preparation for the fasting and prayer that Lent demands. The faithful, seeking holiness in all things, should follow the Church's guidance and not adopt the more decadent and vulgar experience of Carnival season in many places.

The Carnival season originated long before the emergence of the current King Cake tradition, but these two customs are now intermingled. It is believed that King Cake was shared with New Orleans around 1870 by the French and had more of a resemblance to the Galette des Rois, a traditional French-styled buttery puff pastry that is deliciously flaky and filled with almond cream. The Spanish had their own adaptation of this called the *Rosca de Reyes* (Wreath of Kings), and eventually the Spanish style King Cake was served there too. The vibrant Louisiana-style Epiphany dessert that we know today holds a closer resemblance to the Spanish Rosca de Reyes in its wreath-like shape, decorative patterns, and sugary designs but you will not be able to overlook those unique Mardi Gras colors of gold, purple, and green.

THE TRADITION

King Cake is traditionally made during the short period of Ordinary Time (meaning ordered or numbered time) between Epiphany and Ash Wednesday. Although some will eat it only for Epiphany, others have it only on or just before Fat Tuesday. The Epiphany of the Lord is a special day to serve this cake because it is the day that we celebrate the three kings, or Magi, finding the Christ child by following the star. The custom goes that the host who is providing or baking the cake will hide a small baby Jesus inside, or in some places a bean, and whoever gets the piece of cake with the baby or bean will be declared king or queen of the day and will have to host the Epiphany party next year, or the next Carnival or Mardi Gras party. In French culture, it is customary also to provide a paper crown with your King Cake, and whoever finds the small Christ child or the bean will more visibly be the king or queen of the Epiphany event. In some homes, the hosts will ensure that the cake slices are given at random by having a child get under the table and call out the name of the next person to receive their slice of cake. Note, if you skipped around and are unsure of why there would be a bean in the cake, go back to the section on Nativity Scene practices.

Because I grew up in a small town in East Texas that was an easy drive to Louisiana, a King Cake has been a very common thing for us to make or buy during this season. There's no such thing as a cheater version of this cake, because for us, this is the tradition to focus on in preparation for January 6, and we all gather around to make and eat it at those ever-beloved Epiphany parties. It's a part of Catholic and non-Catholic culture alike down here, and it is a custom that is taken rather seriously. In fact, many will get into heated debates over how they make it and the preferences that they have—whether or not it will be filled or more traditional, have cream-cheese filling versus pecan-praline or fruit-flavored filling, and use a glaze or icing on top. Even the colors sprinkled on top have meaning, and they were purposefully chosen because purple, emerald green, and gold are gifts fit for a king. The purple signifies justice, the green represents growth or faith, and the gold expresses prosperity and wealth. We all have our own way to make the King Cake, and everyone thinks theirs is the best. That is the kind of ownership and pride that I wish everyone would take in festive traditions. Whether you're adopting or adapting a tradition, it doesn't matter. What's most important is that the traditions are yours to live and to share.

Tradition has a way of widening itself to embrace others, from the vastness of various cultures to the closeness of next-door neighbors. Here is a list of King Cakes from around the world that perhaps you might be interested in trying or find cultural connection to. In Spain and other Hispanic countries, you will taste the Rosca de Reyes, Germany and Switzerland eat Dreikönigskuchen, England enjoys Twelfth Night Cake and Lamb's Wool, Portugal makes Bolo Rei, and France delights in the Galette des Rois. All of these meaningful cakes are baked and enjoyed out of common belief in Christ as God's revelation to the whole world.

CARRYING ON THE TRADITION

AT HOME

Try your hand at making your own King Cake this year using the recipe in the *Festive Faith Advent and Christmas Companion* at www.HisGirlSunday.com/FestiveFaith. This truly is a family affair. Everyone puts their aprons on and spends the day in the kitchen making this delicious treat, playing games at the kitchen table, and sharing in lots of laughs. Don't forget to hide baby Jesus!

Consider This
- If you can't make it, go buy one this year and serve it as an after-dinner dessert. It's very tasty with a warm cup of coffee.
- Host an Epiphany party and serve the King Cake slices in the traditional way, at random.
- Tell your guests that whoever gets the baby or the bean hosts the next party.
- Provide a crown to whoever gets the baby Jesus or the bean in their slice of cake.
- Have your Magi figurines arrive at your Nativity Scene.

IN THE PARISH

Share King Cake with your parishioners at your Epiphany party!

Consider This

- Have the children's choir sign up to put on a performance in the parish community center as the Magi and to sing "We Three Kings" and other Christmastide hymns.
- Serve King Cake with refreshments and other treats or food platters.
- Have multiple King Cakes with hidden baby Jesus figurines. Whoever gets the Christ child in their cake becomes part of the group to serve on your Mardi Gras party team.
- Have your Magi figurines arrive at your Nativity Scene.

A LIVING TRADITION

I think the King Cake tradition is so interesting because it starts on the Solemnity of the Epiphany of the Lord. There is so much excitement as bakeries all through New Orleans begin making the cakes that will only be sold until Mardi Gras Day. I remember as a child wanting to enjoy this tradition as much as possible during the Christmas season because it was only available for a short time. On Ash Wednesday, we knew even as children that King Cakes were no longer sold, and it was time to start our Lenten penance. When I moved to Houston as an adult, I didn't want to lose this tradition that is rooted in my New Orleans culture. I remember going to my favorite bakery as a child to buy King Cake and the excitement of finding the baby Jesus in my slice. To keep the tradition alive each year for my family, I order a King Cake to be sent to Houston from New Orleans. When I don't do that, I try my best to make one from scratch using the colors purple, green, and yellow, which are the famous sprinkle colors of a traditional King Cake. This tradition matters to us today because even though every bakery and family has their own recipe, there is one thing that remains the same, and that is the baby Jesus being represented in each one of them. So, in our secular society, the King Cake represents at a basic level an important part of our faith: the three wise men bringing gifts to the baby Jesus. And in New Orleans, all bakeries sell these cakes without hesitation, knowing that it represents a greater message.

Gina Bergeron

EPIPHANY DOOR BLESSING

IN THE UNIVERSAL CALENDAR: JANUARY 6
IN THE UNITED STATES: SUNDAY BETWEEN
JANUARY 2 AND JANUARY 8

THE STORY

Have you heard of the three epiphanies? Three distinct but theologically inter-woven events in the life of Christ used to be celebrated all within the period of time called Epiphanytide. The term *epiphany* means to manifest or reveal, and these moments are times when God the Father has intimately revealed himself to us through his Son, Jesus Christ. These epiphanies are meant to direct us to the greatest epiphany, which will be Jesus's Second Coming. The three epiphanies are the Epiphany, also known as the Magi coming from the East to find the Christ child, the baptism of Christ in the Jordan River, and the wedding feast at Cana where Jesus turns water into wine. Epiphanytide is a period of time that is still honored in the Eastern Catholic and Orthodox liturgical traditions, but in the Roman Rite calendar Epiphanytide has been replaced by Winter Ordinary Time, which runs from the end of the Christmas season to the beginning of Lent on Ash Wednesday. We celebrate the Solemnity of the Epiphany of the Lord traditionally on January 6, for one day, and in the United States the celebration of Epiphany is moved to the Sunday between January 2 and 8.

Dating back to the Middle Ages in central Europe, chalking the doors with particular letters and numbers while praying a blessing is a Christian ritual that has now spread all over the world. In countries such as Poland, Switzerland, Germany, England, and the United States, to name a few, Catholics are witness-ing to their communities through this blessing that their homes are dwelling places for God among his people. To the passerby, or your mail carrier, the chalk writing may look like a random string of letters, but as Catholics we can identify this as asking for the intercession of the three Magi. The prescribed ritual has been the same throughout time and is written in this particular way for a reason. The CMB written in chalk above the home's front door holds two meanings. First, these are the initials of the traditional names for the Magi: Caspar, Melchior, and Balthazar. Second, CMB is an abbreviation for the Latin phrase *Christus mansionem benedicat*, "May Christ bless this house." A "+"

represents the Sign of the Cross, and the two numerals at the beginning and two at the end tell us the year the blessing occurs.

THE TRADITION

Partake in this time-honored tradition by chalking your door or the place just above it with the formula 20+C+M+B+24. Make note that the "24" will change to denote the current year. It is usually done on the Solemnity of the Epiphany of the Lord, but if that day is missed, it can certainly be prayed anytime between January 6 and the start of Lent. In the liturgical tradition of the Church, a priest or the head of the household can bless the home and chalk the doors, although the blessing of a priest is more efficacious. Regardless of who prays the blessing of the house, one element that merits clarification is, Who can bless the chalk? If you want your chalk to be used as a sacramental rather than simply decoration, then it must have a constitutive blessing (an authoritative blessing setting an object apart for strengthening the faith of people involved) that can only come from a bishop, priest, or deacon. In many places, the chalk tied to this tradition is customarily blessed on January 6 by a priest using the *Roman Ritual*. In addition to the blessing of chalk, some parishes have a small procession as well as an extra opportunity for charitable giving in remembrance of the Magi's gifts to Christ.

The blessing of chalk, the home, and all who dwell in it throughout the year is profound because it uniquely identifies us as Catholics and thus creates a sense of culture and belonging, but it also speaks to the very core of the domestic church. This custom provides families the opportunity to stand together in unity and offer God our humble lives and dwellings as places where we will strive to grow toward heaven together. The home is the first and most prominent place where we are taught the ways of virtue and prayer. We learn at our peaceful bedsides how to kneel down and say the Our Father, or at our tables how to give thanks, or in our living rooms to pray the Rosary. The domestic church is also where we experience in humility how to love one another and to be at each other's service. Every day we leave lasting relational impressions on our spouses, children, parents, or grandparents, whomever we share a home with. It is in those exchanges and time well spent that we express to one another our human desire and fundamental need for closeness with one another and with Our Lord. After the Mass and sacraments, the Catholic home is nothing short of essential in developing the liturgical life of the faithful. Standing on the thresholds of our homes with the members of our households, while calling upon the gifts of the Magi, we implore that our homes may become dedicated spaces for something extraordinary in the year ahead. The blessing used by the head of the household can be found on the USCCB website or in the *Festive Faith Advent and Christmas Companion* at www.HisGirlSunday.com/FestiveFaith for simple printing and usage.

A particularly lively custom connected to this time is one that goes back to sixteenth-century Germany. It is called *sternsinger*, which means "star singers." In certain regions Catholic churches will arrange this event where children dress up as the three Magi, and the leader for that year will carry a large star on the end of a wooden stick, while they all sing from house to house. There are traditional carols that the star singers will perform as they stop at each home, and when they have finished, they will inscribe C+M+B on the lintel of the door. In more recent years this tradition has also involved the request for donations for children's charities in Germany and surrounding countries. This practice truly does embrace all elements that were suggested in the *Directory on Popular Piety and the Liturgy*: the door blessing, procession, and charitable giving. *Sternsinger* is a lovely communal tradition that can easily be worked toward and revived in our neighborhoods, parish community, and friend groups too.

CARRYING ON THE TRADITION

AT HOME
Obtain blessed chalk and the text of the Epiphany Door Blessing. Have the head of household chalk the lintel of your home today, and invite the entire family outside to watch and participate.

Consider This
- You may want to print the blessing for the individual leading and for those responding.
- You can also sprinkle your home with holy water. Plan to fill up your bottle at church.
- Explain to your spouse, children, or roommates what each marking stands for beforehand.
- Save your chalk for next year; remember that blessed items should not be thrown away or discarded in the usual manner that you would when handling trash.
- Place a holy water font by your front door so you can bless yourself as you come and go, reminding yourself of the dedication you gave to your home.

IN THE PARISH

Provide your community with blessed chalk, holy water, and the Epiphany Door Blessing to be said when they get home.

Consider This

- Every year I lead the packaging of over one thousand Epiphany Blessing Kits for our community with a group of volunteers. The kits are a Ziploc bag filled with blessed chalk, a holy water bottle, and a card with the Epiphany Door Blessing on it. The parish priest blesses everything in advance, and a team of volunteers helps me assemble them. Think about doing this for your parishioners.
- Alternatively, you could have parishioners bring their own chalk to be blessed, and the home blessing can be printed in the bulletin or posted on your website. Remind them to fill their own holy water bottles at the font.
- Teach parishioners about this tradition and what the inscription means. Explain why we do this so that they can more fully embrace the custom.
- Chalk the lintel of the rectory, parish school if you have one, or the top of the church's door frame.

Resource

Use the Epiphany Door Blessing found in the *Festive Faith Advent and Christmas Companion* at www.HisGirlSunday.com/FestiveFaith.

A LIVING TRADITION

As my wife and I have worked to build up our domestic church, we have found the Epiphany blessing to be one of the most powerful annual traditions. The words of the blessing serve as an important reminder to us about the role that Christ should play in our home as well as the role our family should play in the building up of the kingdom. For our children, inscribing the letters on the door with chalk is a tangible experience that excites their imagination and prompts questions about the meaning behind the letters and numbers. Coming, as it does, at the beginning of the year, the Epiphany blessing is a way that we as Catholics remind ourselves that all time belongs to God. One of the great aspects of the inscription for me is that it continues to remain with us throughout the year, serving as a reminder of Christ's blessing on our home and family. It can also be a great evangelization tool when people ask you why you have "that code" written on your door. In the world today, the Epiphany blessing is a powerful reminder to our family and to all who visit our house that Jesus Christ is the Lord of all time and all places.

Chris Labadie

FOUR

WINTER ORDINARY TIME

The liturgy is the summit toward which
the activity of the Church is directed;
at the same time, it is the font from
which all her power flows.
—*Sacrosanctum Concilium*, 10

Begins: Day after the Feast of the Baptism of the Lord
Ends: Tuesday before Ash Wednesday
Natural Season: Winter
Ordinary Time Disciplines: Hope for the Second Coming,
Discipleship, and Growth
Recommended Prayer: Daily Examen
This prayer can be found in the Festive Faith Winter Ordinary
Time, Lent, and Triduum Companion *at www.HisGirlSunday.
com/FestiveFaith.*
Liturgical Color: Green

It occurs to me every time I journey through Ordinary Time that we, as Catholic people, make such a commendable effort in talking about and living out other seasons, especially Lent, Easter, Advent, and Christmas. We know exactly what the themes of these seasons are, resources and prayer books are plentiful, Catholics are discussing those seasons up and down our newsfeed, and liturgical life is bursting with seasonal activities. Yet, when Ordinary Time cycles back around, there seems to be little to say and do. It is apparent that the same understanding and efforts we have for other seasons do not always translate to Ordinary Time. Naturally, I have contemplated this and have arrived at the conclusion that perhaps this lack of active participation is a result of our very human response to the name. We associate the word *ordinary* with the way it is commonly defined, as being mundane or indistinct. With that reaction, we go about doing the normal things that we are called to do to live in the world such as school, work, family life, commuting, grocery shopping, and so on, without giving ourselves much permission to engage or pay attention to the Church calendar. Ordinary Time gets relegated as the season where nothing special is happening, and other seasons are where we long to be centered with ancient traditions and whimsy. This might be the perception, but there is certainly more to be discovered when looking further into the liturgical year.

Ordinary Time gets its name from the Latin term *ordinalis*, which stems from the term *ordo*, or in English, "order." *Ordinalis* refers to a specified order or sequence, and in reference to the liturgical calendar it is the way in which we number the weeks of Ordinary Time—the Second Sunday in Ordinary Time, the Third Sunday in Ordinary Time, and so on. In this way the Church is communicating to us that there is to be order within our lives during this season. The shape and structure that order provides to us is a way in which we can be more like God himself. God is order, and he creates with order. For example, mathematics, cosmological discovery, and the sciences have often been used as examples of ways in which God reveals himself to us in the order of creation. The liturgy also has order and ritual routine, imitating God's own nature and design. And so, Ordinary Time is establishing a pattern, a counted ordering of weeks, for us to direct our energy and attention toward living with Christ.

When we read in the Bible about the descent of the Holy Spirit and the days following that, we can see that the disciples were actively waiting for the Second Coming of Christ. They spent their days contemplating Christ's teaching, ministering to one another, spreading the Word of God, receiving the Eucharist, and cultivating their gifts. They supported one another as a community, and they sought to live in imitation of Christ in hopeful anticipation of his return. Their focus was to establish the kingdom of God on earth. We are called to carry on that same mission of the Church that was entrusted to the apostles with the coming of the Holy Spirit at Pentecost. That Christocentric, mission-oriented living that takes shape in the day-to-day is the essence and practicality of the season called Ordinary Time.

The term *Ordinary Time* does not always call to mind the events of Pentecost, the establishment of the Church, and our anticipation of Christ's Second Coming, but that is what it's meant to do. This season is unique in that the themes and the intentionality that Ordinary Time invites us to live rooted in are not meant only for this one season, but for all seasons while we wait for Jesus to return in glory. In fact, all other seasons have theological connections that draw us back to the Second Coming, reminding us that we ought to love God in word and deed so that when he returns, we are as ready as we can be. If we seek to comprehend this season in light of the Acts of the Apostles and later books in the Bible, we will see that Ordinary Time is a call to us to live liturgically, in hope, and with steady watchfulness.

Yet, Ordinary Time shouldn't be *that* ordinary. In reality it's meant to be a season of hope, growth, and discipleship. When considering how to integrate these dispositions into your liturgical living, I recommend that you give yourself time to pray, reflect, serve, learn, and rest. Usually after Christmas the world teaches that it's time to get back to work. It subtly and not so subtly reminds us that we have had our break and celebrated our "holidays," and now it's time to get back to business. There is indeed a time to work, but bear in mind that Ordinary Time is meant to elevate and sanctify the mundane, the everyday. We do not live to work; we work so that we may live. As Catholics, we live for glorifying God and we work so that we can achieve that as our highest good. This is the true sacramentality of the liturgical year: consecrating our ordinary life rhythms.

As we transition out of Christmas, prioritize cultivating hope and time for growth. The USCCB states, "Ordinary Time is a time for growth and maturation, a time in which the mystery of Christ is called to penetrate ever more deeply into history until all things are finally caught up in Christ."[1] Ordinary Time may hold our ordinary lives within its span, but we are still called to extraordinary faith. Let this season invite you into hopeful anticipation of the Second Coming through ancient and new liturgical customs that will certainly bring meaning and purpose to your home and parish.

THE BAPTISM OF THE LORD ICE CROSS SCULPTURE

FIRST SUNDAY FOLLOWING THE EPIPHANY OF THE LORD

THE STORY

The second epiphany that we honor is the Baptism of the Lord, which occurs every year on the first Sunday following the Solemnity of the Epiphany of the Lord in the United States, and it is considered a moveable feast. In the modern Roman calendar, this feast day brings a close to the Christmas season and transitions us into Ordinary Time. On this day we remember Jesus's own baptism, which was administered to him by St. John the Baptist in the Jordan River.

> Then Jesus came from Galilee to John at the Jordan to be baptized by him. John tried to prevent him, saying, "I need to be baptized by you, and yet you are coming to me?" Jesus said to him in reply, "Allow it now, for thus it is fitting for us to fulfill all righteousness." Then he allowed him. After Jesus was baptized, he came up from the water and behold, the heavens were opened [for him], and he saw the Spirit of God descending like a dove [and] coming upon him. And a voice came from the heavens, saying, "This is my beloved Son, with whom I am well pleased." (Mt 3:13–17)

This remarkable event in the life of Christ signifies an array of prominent realities not only for Jesus's life, but for our lives as well.

Christ's baptism is a watershed moment that begins his public ministry. From this point forward in the liturgical year we will hear about his stories, miracles, teachings, and healings through the readings at Mass. The mission of Jesus's life is now in full view, and we begin to see him reveal who he is and why he was ordained to live among us. His baptism expands our perspective, allowing us to partake in what Eastern Catholics still refer to as the Feast of Theophany. The term *theophany* comes from a combination of Greek words, *theos* meaning "God," and *phainein* meaning "to show or to appear." Catholics define this word to mean that God has manifested or directly communicated himself to humanity, and the baptism of Jesus is a primary example of this. Early Church Fathers, specifically St. John Chrysostom, really emphasized that this term be directly associated with the Baptism of the Lord since in this occasion we see the Trinitarian nature of God expressed in one instant. Jesus is in the water, we hear the voice of the Father, and the Holy Spirit descends upon them in the form of a dove.

Every year that I taught this topic to high school students I was asked, "If God is sinless, why did he need to be baptized?" Simply put, through this humble action, Jesus—who had no sin—entered fully into the human reality. In imitation of him we too are baptized so that we can live our own human reality striving for sinlessness, virtue, and closeness with God. By being baptized, Christ affirms the necessity of this action, which is further emphasized when we read that the heavens opened up and God the Father declared Jesus as his Son.

THE TRADITION

A couple of intriguing customs come to us from Ukraine. Remember that the exact date for this feast day may vary according to the calendar that is being followed. For some, it will be on January 6 when all three epiphanies are celebrated at once, and for others it will be on the first Sunday following the Solemnity of the Epiphany of the Lord. A more recent practice is to reenact Jesus's baptism by taking a deep plunge into a local lake or pond, regardless of the icy cold water in early January. In some places, people cut out the shape of a cross in the top layer of ice before jumping into the icy water. This frigid dip has been likened to the biblical themes of dying and rising, which we associate with baptism. The connection stems from the nervous-system stimulation that we receive when our bodies are plunged into icy waters. As we know from scripture, through the waters of baptism we die to our old selves, and we rise anew with Christ. This custom certainly gives new meaning to that!

An older tradition on this feast revolves around the consecration of water. Those in the Ukraine don't just bless the water within their churches but also bless lakes, rivers, and ponds within the area. Their prominent ice crosses, made out of large blocks of ice cut from local lakes or rivers, are certainly a source of fascination on this feast day. Faithful Ukrainian Catholics will stand an ice cross in front of their churches. The ice cross is then blessed, and as it begins to melt the parishioners will bottle the holy water to take home. They keep this on hand so that they can bless their home and family for protection and grace. This symbol reminds their community and all who encounter it of the commemoration of Jesus's baptism and the promises we make through our own baptisms.

In more recent years I have witnessed a much greater effort by Catholic individuals and families to remember their own baptismal anniversaries and those of their children. Just as we celebrate our physical birthdays, celebrating your baptism day is an opportunity to call to mind your spiritual birthday, the day you were reborn into a life with Christ. This is an occasion to reflect on the day you officially entered into the Church, received the indelible mark of Christian character, and were adopted as God's child. Some individuals will renew their baptismal promises on their baptism day, refill the holy water fonts in their home, and light their baptismal candle for dinner that evening. You might also choose to do these on the Baptism of the Lord. These simple gestures remind us of our Christian vocation and the life we entered into with Christ.

CARRYING ON THE TRADITION

AT HOME
Remember your own baptismal anniversary and that of your children by seeking to make today special in your own way and lighting all the baptismal candles in your household.

Consider This
- Make stuffed pasta shells for dinner tonight. The scallop shell is a symbol of Baptism and often used during the conferral of the sacrament to pour the blessed water of the font over the head of the one being baptized. A festive meal of pasta shells makes for a deliciously festive connection!
- Go out for a baptismal anniversary treat like ice cream or cake.
- If you can't find your baptismal candle, buy another one in preparation for this special day.
- Renew your baptismal promises at home.
- Read the scripture passage about Jesus's baptism.

IN THE PARISH
Purposefully place baptisms on this day and encourage all parishioners to take some holy water from the font back to their homes.

Consider This
- While presiding over the baptisms, make the families aware of Jesus's own baptism, which we are seeking to unite ourselves with today.
- Inform your congregation of the importance of having holy water available, and encourage them to get a bottle or font for their home.

- Lead the parishioners in renewing their baptismal promises today.
- Use the sprinkling rite as the penitential act that can be found in the appendix of the *Roman Missal*.

Resource
Renew your baptismal promises with the text found in *Festive Faith Winter Ordinary Time, Lent, and Triduum Companion* at www.HisGirlSunday.com/FestiveFaith.

THE TRIDUUM OF FIRE: ST. BRIGID, CANDLEMAS, AND ST. BLAISE
FEBRUARY 1–3

We enter into the "Triduum of Fire," beginning February 1 with the Feast of St. Brigid. Following that, on February 2, we celebrate Candlemas, also known as the Feast of the Presentation of the Lord, and then on February 3 is the Feast of St. Blaise. These three days (a triduum) mark the midway point between winter and spring, when we still have short daylight and long darkness in the northern hemisphere. Each feast is appropriately highlighted by fire! In the story of St. Brigid, we will learn about the eternal fire, on Candlemas we will bless and light liturgical candles, and on the Feast of St. Blaise we will have our throats blessed with candles blessed the previous day—the Feast of the Presentation. More specifically, they each characterize the prophetic words of Simeon from Luke 2:32, that Jesus would be "a light for revelation to the Gentiles," which we can see closely related to each feast. There is theological and liturgical depth to these three days that makes each one rather remarkable.

ST. BRIGID CROSSES

FEBRUARY 1

THE STORY

While few details of the life of St. Brigid of Kildare are known to us, it is believed that she was born around AD 450 in what is now Ireland. She was said to be a very giving and thoughtful girl who became consecrated to Christ in a religious order and later became an abbess. The most popular story is about her cloak, which she was carrying as she approached the king to give her land to build a monastery. As was to be expected he denied her, but in her pleading, she countered him by asking for as much land as her cloak would cover. When she and the others there helped her stretch out the cloak, it covered several acres, which she was permitted to use for a monastery.

Tradition tells us that at the monastery she founded, the nuns kept an eternal fire burning for her. In fact, this fire is said to have lasted from St. Brigid's death in 525 to 1220! It was also said to have been lit again later and burned for four hundred years until the Protestant Reformation—hence the association of St. Brigid with the perpetual flame. Embodying the words of Simeon, this fire is said to have Christianized the Irish pagan rituals.

Some traditions tell us a tale of two Brigids. There was a Celtic goddess also named Brigid who was worshipped by many and who embodied the element of fire. Before Christianity a fire was kept lit in Kildare, the place St. Brigid is from, for the Celtic goddess Brigid, and women would tend to this ritual fire while praying for good harvests. However, as Christianity began to spread, this ritual flame that was once used as a pagan symbol was Christianized as many followers of the Celtic goddess saw the fire as a familiar sign and became believers in Christ through saints like Brigid. Light and fire became material symbols that kept the people of ancient Ireland searching for the divine.

THE TRADITION

One popular custom to take up on the vigil of her feast day is making St. Brigid Crosses. From Irish folklore we receive a story that directs our celebration. It tells us that the evening before her feast day St. Brigid walks the land to bestow her blessing over all the farms and homes that have her unique cross hung over their doors. You will find that this cross is made with different materials from region to region; some make them with straw, and others use rushes. This customary Irish cross is then hung in the home and viewed as a welcome to guests and neighbors while also standing as a sign of blessing for those who live there. Engage in this sacred story by making your own St. Brigid Crosses. Afterward you can bless them and hang them outside or within your home.

CARRYING ON THE TRADITION

AT HOME
Continue the generations-old custom of making St. Brigid Crosses, and hang one over your front door.

Consider This
- Think about the materials or resources that are available for you to make a St. Brigid Cross.
- Watch a video on YouTube or find a tutorial that will guide you.
- Bless your newly made cross with holy water.
- Explain the tradition to those participating while making them.
- Kick your feast-day celebration up a notch by making a St. Brigid fire. If you don't have a fireplace or you can't build a bonfire, simply light a candle in remembrance of her.
- Try an Irish-inspired recipe or drink.

IN THE PARISH
Share the folktale of St. Brigid's cloak in today's homily or in last week's communications to prepare your parishioners. Develop a celebration guide with the following options.

Consider This
- Encourage parishioners to make St. Brigid Crosses; provide them with a list of materials needed and a link to a helpful tutorial.
- Encourage parishioners to light their fireplace, a candle, or a bonfire in honor of St. Brigid.
- Try Irish-inspired recipes or drinks at a parish social gathering.

Resource
Bless your St. Brigid Crosses with the prayer found in the *Festive Faith Winter Ordinary Time, Lent, and Triduum Companion* at www.HisGirlSunday.com/FestiveFaith.

CANDLEMAS
BLESSING OF CANDLES

FEBRUARY 2

THE STORY

The Feast of the Presentation of Our Lord, also known as Candlemas, is celebrated forty days after Christmas. On this day Joseph and Mary took baby Jesus to the Temple to make an offering and dedicate their child to God. In the 1962 Missal this feast was also referred to as the Purification of Mary, which commemorates Mary's ritual purification according to Old Testament Law after childbirth. Even though this feast day isn't a part of the Christmas season, it has been considered in much of Catholic tradition as a Christmas feast because it is the last feast day pertaining to Christ's infancy.

The term *Candlemas* comes from the Canticle of Simeon's mention of light and the liturgical practices that developed in relation to it:

> Now, Master, you may let your servant go
> > in peace, according to your word,
> for my eyes have seen your salvation,
> > which you prepared in sight of all the peoples,
> a light for revelation to the Gentiles,
> > and glory for your people Israel. (Lk 2:29–32)

Beeswax candles especially have held ongoing importance in the liturgy and are brimming with substance. You can even find bees, an ancient symbol of the Church and producers of wax, on the columns of the towering bronze canopy or *baldacchino* in St. Peter's Basilica in Rome. The virginal nature of the worker bee symbolizes the way the Church brings forth her spiritual gifts and fruits. The Church purely provides us with grace through the sacraments, just as the worker bees give us honey and wax through their diligent efforts and pure bodies. Their wax is meaningful to the Church because it is considered to be the fruit of virgin labor and is thus worthy to burn as candles on the altar where the Body of Christ will rest. Every part of the candle holds symbolic meaning: the wax represents the flesh of Our Lord; the wick, which is within, represents Jesus's soul; and the flame, which burns on top, represents Christ's divinity.

THE TRADITION

As a way of sharing Christ's light with the world, the Church has used this feast day to bless all the liturgical candles that were to be used in the year ahead. In the past, candles were to be 100 percent beeswax, but the current standard is that they are to be 51 percent, to emphasize the importance of having only articles of faith that are worthy to rest upon the altar where the Lord will dwell. At the beginning of Mass on this Feast of the Presentation, or Candlemas, the congregants each receive a candle to hold in their hands, and the flame of Christ is passed around for all to receive. Another essential element of today's liturgy is to have a procession. Although in many parishes this has fallen out of practice, some will simply process around the inside of the parish, while others process outside on the parish grounds or nearby neighborhood. The symbolism of this liturgical action is to visibly express bringing Christ, "a light to the nations," out into the world. When entering back into the Church together with lit candles, we should remember the entry of Christ into the Temple of Jerusalem.

By extension we are also invited by the Church to bring our own beeswax candles to church to be blessed for use throughout the year in our domestic church. There is no requirement for beeswax candles in the home, but they do express holy meaning, smell lovely, and smoke less. Then on special occasions, such as family feast days, sacramental anniversaries, solemnities, birthdays, times of loss, prayer time, and Sundays, we can light our candles as a way of making the light of Christ present. These opportunities are there for the taking so that we can call to mind how Jesus is truly in our midst and present to us in our daily offerings.

Enjoy your blessed candles while also honoring National Crêpe Day. In France this day is called *La Chandeleur*, also known as Candlemas, and crêpes are on the menu. This tradition goes back to around 490 with Pope Gelasius, who was said to have distributed them to pilgrims arriving in Rome. The golden, round, and sun-like crêpe is supposed to draw our attention to the shifting of seasons from winter to early springtime. As Catholics we can draw a further connection to the Son of God, whose warmth and light guides us closer to his Church and to heaven. Try to get crêpes on the family table today, and if you can't, switch them out for something simpler like pancakes.

CARRYING ON THE TRADITION

AT HOME

Place the candles that you had blessed today in a prominent place such as your home altar, mantle, prayer corner, or dining-room table. Make crêpes or pancakes, and light your newly blessed candles for the observance of the Presentation of the Lord. Read the story of the presentation of Jesus in the Temple in the second chapter of Luke's gospel. Keep in mind that you can light these candles for upcoming solemnities, sacramental anniversaries, and special feast days that you like to honor.

Consider This
- Purchase beeswax candles before the feast day.
- Find a parish, if not your own, that is blessing candles today.
- Learn the significance of beeswax, and share that with those in your household.
- Make or order in crêpes or pancakes for one of your meals today.
- Plan your feast-day celebrations ahead of time so that you can remember to light your candles throughout the upcoming year.

IN THE PARISH

Offer the blessing of candles with the solemn entrance or procession as found in the *Roman Missal* for this date.

Consider This
- Plan your indoor or outdoor procession in advance.
- Make small taper candles available to those in attendance so that everyone can have a lit candle and participate in the liturgical procession.
- Invite parishioners to bring their candles from home to be blessed.
- Make sure to bless the candles to be used tomorrow for St. Blaise and the blessing of throats.
- If you can't do a procession, follow the Second Form found in the Missal for the Solemn Entrance.
- Explain this candle-blessing custom for those who may not be familiar with the liturgical meaning of this feast day.

Resource
After your candles have been blessed at Mass, receive the blessed candles into your home with the simple ritual celebration found in the *Festive Faith Winter Ordinary Time and Companion* at www.HisGirlSunday.com/FestiveFaith.

Between the various beautifully powerful prayers of blessings over the candles that the faithful bring to church to be blessed, the candlelight procession, and of course Holy Mass, this feast is one the world needs to experience, and as Catholics we ought to observe and keep it. Our Church brings into focus and commemorates these events as part of our salvation history, and so should we.

I've come to appreciate how Holy Mother Church holds a special place for all of God's amazing creation, even the bees! These busy little creatures provide beeswax, which is used in the liturgy via candles. During the year our family acquires local beeswax to eventually melt down and pour into different styles of candles our family would most use at home during the year. After the aroma of melting sweet beeswax fills our home and stirs the senses, we begin making candles and anticipating this feast. We pour and make lots of tealight candles to use in our family oratory for special prayer intentions, as well as votives that I may burn at our dining-room table when we are having a rough day or when a storm approaches. We've also simply purchased already made beeswax taper candles and pillars for use on our family altar during devotions or when praying the Rosary. It has become part of our family's tradition to work on building a little stash of candles right after Christmas to bring to church for blessing on Candlemas and then to use at home throughout the year.

God in his loving mercy has given us the Church, who provides her children with sacramentals such as holy water, crucifixes, medals, scapulars, and candles to use during our earthly pilgrimage toward heaven. Everyone at some time experiences illness, spiritual battles, earthly troubles, weather storms, and so on. We ought to use the tools (i.e., sacramentals) Our Lord has allowed for us to help us along our way. As a mom, if I'm striving to live in a state of grace, which also includes utilizing the sacramentals offered to me, not only do I benefit spiritually, but my children are benefiting also. I pray they also will form traditional Catholic habits for themselves as they grow and leave my care. I try to really encourage them to make regular use of sacramentals in their daily life. I encourage everyone to rely on them for use as we march onward and upward. Sacramentals, such as Candlemas blessed candles, are loving tools from Our Lord to the faithful.

Michelle and Joe McClane

ST. BLAISE
BLESSING OF THROATS

FEBRUARY 3

THE STORY

The Triduum of Fire concludes with the Feast of St. Blaise, who was a third-century bishop and physician known for his pastoral care of the faithful and miraculous healing abilities. One of the earliest mentions of his name comes to us from the medical journal of a court physician named Aetius Amidenus that was written in the sixth century. It speaks of how St. Blaise was often summoned to treat people who had objects stuck in their throats. Many of us know the enduring story of the miracle that St. Blaise performed on a young boy who was said to be choking on a fish bone. He blessed the child, and the boy was healed of his ailment. The liturgical custom of blessing throats on his feast day is derived from this story along with his legacy as a physician, bishop, and martyr. In fact, his popularity grew so much within the Middle Ages that he is revered as one of the "Fourteen Holy Helpers," a team of saints whose intercession is believed to be highly effective against diseases.

In the oral tradition of Blaise's life, we are also told that during the persecution of Licinius, Blaise fled to the wilderness to live in a cave. While there he was caught healing wounded animals and was subsequently captured and thrown into prison. It was there that a woman he had met earlier in his ministry brought him candles to light his dark and dreary cell. St. Blaise is kept in the darkness of prison under the pagan leadership of the Roman Empire. Yet, even here there is light, through St. Blaise's love for Christ, through the woman's care for St. Blaise, and ultimately through Christ, who by his light is able to convert Rome, now the home of Catholicism.

The blessing of throats is done with two candlesticks crossed over one another, which may be in remembrance of the woman who helped St. Blaise light his prison cell. The red ribbon that ties the two candles together is symbolic of the martyrdom that he endured. And the manner in which they are held across the throat recalls his miraculous work as a physician. On a special day like this, be assured by the flicker of the candles that Christ is the light that will dispel all darkness.

THE TRADITION

We rise in the morning on the Feast of St. Blaise with great anticipation for a blessing that is like no other. The Church extends a blessing of throats to each of the faithful with two of the candles that were blessed yesterday on Candlemas. In some parishes the candles that are crossed and placed near either side of our throats are even aflame, and I would imagine in this case the anticipation of a unique blessing might be coupled with a sense of holy concern! I have especially marveled at the thought of this as a woman from the south whose hair is held together by a good layer of hairspray; I myself could become a third candle in all of that. While it is preferable to go to Mass and have a priest or deacon bless your throat, the *Book of Blessings* does mention that the lay faithful can do this blessing if they are not able to go to Mass. In this circumstance the laity would need to follow the rites and prayers designated for lay individuals.

My family also makes a fish dinner this evening in remembrance of St. Blaise healing the boy who was choking on a fish bone. This feast-day meal brings back fond memories from my childhood. I grew up in a small town near the water, and from a very young age my dad taught my brother and me how to fish. While I don't go out and catch my own dinner, the fish recipes from my family are truly delicious, and making them brings me back to the feeling of home.

CARRYING ON THE TRADITION

AT HOME
Go to church to have your throat blessed, and whip up a special fish recipe for dinner.

Consider This
- If you're not able to make it to church, use the instructions for the laity to bless the throats of those within your household.
- Integrate a St. Blaise prayer into your mealtime.
- Plan your fish recipe in advance so you are prepared to make a feast-day dinner this evening.
- Light the candles that you had blessed yesterday again today.

IN THE PARISH

Offer the blessing of throats, found in the *Book of Blessings*, to your parishioners and explain to them why we invoke St. Blaise and hand on this Catholic practice.

Consider This

- Many within the pews likely do not know why we celebrate the blessing of throats. Explain it to them in the homily, bulletin, or another highly viewed form of communication.
- Bless each individual person or, if this feast day falls on a Sunday, the *Book of Blessings* allows for the entire congregation to receive the blessing at the same time.
- Explain to your parishioners the connections between today's feast day and yesterday's by sharing how you will be using candles that you blessed on Candlemas to bless their throats.
- Use this opportunity to foster a proper understanding of blessings and their place in the faith.

Resource

If you cannot go to Mass today, use the Blessing of Throats prayer proper to a lay minister found in the *Festive Faith Winter Ordinary Time, Lent, and Triduum Companion* at www.HisGirlSunday.com/FestiveFaith.

FESTA DI SANT'AGATA IN CATANIA

FEBRUARY 5

THE STORY

St. Agatha is one of the early Church's "virgins and martyrs" whose names we hear during Mass when Eucharistic Prayer I (The Roman Canon) is prayed. Her feast day is February 5, and she is the patron saint of breast-cancer patients, sexual-abuse victims, and Catania, Sicily. Her intercession is also invoked against natural disasters, fire, and lightning. Like many of the early Church martyrs, not much is known about her life, but she remains a highly revered saint because of her story and the devotional life that she inspired in the faithful.

It is estimated that she was born around 231 in Sicily to a noble family. Tradition tells us that when she was about fifteen years old, she made a personal vow of virginity so that she could dedicate herself entirely to Christ as her spouse. Yet her beauty and wealth caught the attention of a local Roman prefect named Quintianus, who wanted St. Agatha to be his wife. As the story goes, she refused his offer because of her wholehearted commitment to Christ. In an effort to manipulate Agatha into being with him, Quintianus devised a plan to have her arrested. During that time Emperor Decius issued a decree that mandated all citizens make sacrificial offerings to the Roman gods. Quintianus was convinced that under these circumstances he would be able to persuade her into denying her faith under the threat of torment and death. But St. Agatha grasped tightly to her love of Christ and refused his advances once again.

Enraged at having been denied again, Quintianus sought to change her mind by forcing her to stay in a brothel, where he was sure she would lose her purity. She was left there for at least a month to deal with assaults against her vow of virginity, but Agatha remained strong and confident in her virtue. When Quintianus caught word of her fervor and strength, he demanded that she be brought before him once more, but when she approached him joyfully proclaiming that she would endure anything for Christ her spouse, he ordered that she endure physical torture. After days of being beaten, whipped, having her breasts cut off, and being forced to roll over hot coals, she commended her soul to God. St. Agatha was martyred around the year 251 in Catania, Sicily.

This account of her life and martyrdom can be found in the *Roman Martyrology*, which was assembled from previously existing sources near the end of the ninth century. Her memorial can be found in some of the earliest Church calendars, but the details of her life are not well documented. We receive varying parts of it from sources such as *The Golden Legend* by Jacobus de Voragine and *Acts of the Martyrs* from the early centuries of Christianity. While there may be elements of historical truth or credibility in these accounts, there have been too many variations in detail to give clear factual evidence to Agatha's entire story. However, we faithfully continue to relay her martyrdom as oral tradition.

We can say confidently that Agatha has been venerated from the early days of the Church, which gives evidence to the merits of her intercession. Agatha is honored and depicted by a great number of treasured poems, artwork, hymns, mosaics, and stories that date back to the fifth century. You may also notice that when the priest prays Eucharistic Prayer I, her name is listed among other saints. Not many saints are invoked in the Roman Canon, and even fewer women. St. Agatha is one of only seven women detailed in this most ancient prayer of the Church. In the towns of Palermo and Catania you will find some of the most deeply rooted and established traditions related to her because both claim that she was born in their region of Sicily. While there might be a discrepancy in that regard, we do know that her death took place in Catania, and for that the people hold her devotion most dear. They show their veneration on two special occasions of the year.

THE TRADITION

If you were to attend the Festival of St. Agatha in Catania, Sicily, you would be absolutely beside yourself just by the sheer amount of people in attendance. This is said to be one of the largest Catholic processions in the world. Some years upwards of a million devotees, tourists, and townspeople have been present at the festival. From February 3 to February 5 and again on August 17, the people of the region give life to their cherished saint. They view St. Agatha as their town's patron saint and strive to keep her brave and bold faith close to their way of living. To see a saint-related tradition spark so much attention on two occasions throughout the liturgical year is quite distinctive. The first set of dates commemorates the anniversary of her martyrdom and her feast day, and the second date is when Catania celebrates the return of her relics after they were stolen and taken to Constantinople for more than nine years. The people of Catania were elated when her remains were brought back in 1126, and they have been at rest in their cathedral ever since. It has been more than seventeen hundred years since she was alive, and yet this entire town stops everything to participate in the life of a young girl's exceptional love for God.

In February, this three-part experience begins its first day with the procession of the ancient *cannalori*, also known as *candelore*. *Cannalori* are massive wooden candelabras that have been hand carved and gilded in the traditional Baroque style. They are intricately designed with artistic depictions of scenes from her martyrdom along with angel and saint adornments. Each single candle tower requires a crew of men to carry it. As they process down the streets, thousands of people trail behind them dancing, singing, and enjoying their patron saint. The day concludes with an elaborate firework show and the anticipation of the following day.

The Aurora Mass begins bright and early as a pre-dawn Mass, and after that the St. Agatha reliquary bust is brought out to be placed on a *fercolo*, a silver carriage, for another procession. The bust is something to behold, made of silver, gold, bronze, elaborate jewel work, and a beautiful blushing face. The townspeople adore her, applauding gleefully upon seeing the reliquary. Then the singing of hymns cues the start of their procession. Everyone follows behind with lit candles of all shapes and sizes while singing and chanting, "*Tutti devoti tutti, cittadini, viva Sant'Agata!*" ("We all devoted citizens, long live St. Agatha!"). Their pilgrimage through various parts of the city ends back at the cathedral, and from there everyone is off to indulge in festive food and drink. Some of the food is made to look like story elements from her miracles and martyrdom, such as the *olivette di Sant'Agata* (St. Agatha's Olives) and the *minne di Sant'Agata* (St. Agatha's Breasts).

On the final day there is Mass followed by another procession, which ends with one of the most distinctive elements of the weekend. St. Agatha's devotees enter into a feat of endurance and courage by pulling the heavy silver carriage up the long, steep Via Sangiuliano with crowds cheering them along. If it is done successfully, then they believe that the rest of the year will be filled with many blessings and a good harvest. It all concludes where the road intersects with a convent where cloistered Benedictine nuns sweetly sing their respect to St. Agatha.

While it might not be the norm to find an entire town that has embraced the patronage of a saint the way Catania has, we can find emulations of that within the smaller villages we call parishes. Shrines, cathedrals, and parishes across America are dedicated to various saints, names of Jesus and Our Lady, or prominent events in the life of Christ. Honoring a parish community's namesake is one of the most essential opportunities for festivity that we have as Catholics. Many have sought to do this in a plethora of ways, from extravagant festivals to humble potluck dinners. Alternatively, I have discovered while consulting with parishes across the United States that there is no shortage of spring and fall parish festivals without any recognition of their church's name. As Catholic communities, we know better than anyone that true praise is always something to be directed back to God, and our patronal feasts can be a gateway into that experience. These namesake celebrations can create a sense of belonging within the parish. Just as a family's last name speaks the story of their origin, heritage, and reputation, so do our parish names.

In another sense, because marriage and the family are the nucleus of society, we should also be encouraged to have a family patron. Having a family patron saint, or saints, can give us purpose in our daily family mission, provide someone to intercede for us, and keep our focus on heaven. As families we can celebrate our chosen patron saint on their feast day together with special dinners, by going to Mass, or by doing things that we each organically enjoy doing as families to make the day special such as having a picnic, enjoying a bowl of ice cream, or playing a game.

In these efforts, may we be motivated by the story of Catania, Sicily, so that we do not fall into a sense of laziness or lackluster. Let us be like Christ on the Cross, who gives everything to us, so that we can give all our loving and joy-filled efforts back in return.

CARRYING ON THE TRADITION

AT HOME
Following the example of Catania's devotion to their patron, St. Agatha, use this day as an opportunity to discern and choose a patron saint for your family or household, one who can intercede and model holiness for you at all times. Each year learn something new about your patron, and create festive foods and celebrations that you might then continue annually. Make your patron, and the celebration of God acting in and through him or her, part of your household.

Consider This
- Dig into Sicilian tradition by making St. Agatha bread or buns. Invite your spouse and children into the kitchen with you. Baking is an optimal way to bring your family together over meaningful conversation, quality time, and good food.
- If making bread or buns today is not within reach, consider making or picking up an Italian dinner.
- Let this feast day prompt you to consider your own family patron just as the entire city of Catania has embraced St. Agatha.
- When picking a family patron, consider the charisms and mission of your family; then discern saints who would be helpful, heavenly friends in guiding you.

IN THE PARISH
Use the example of Catania to develop a Catholic festival in honor of your parish namesake, or transform your current festival to be more clearly connected to your patronage.

Consider This
- Ask for St. Agatha's intercession today at Mass so that your congregation knows it's her feast day.
- Provide your congregation with the story of St. Agatha, and give them examples of how they can creatively model her virtue in today's world.
- Develop a monthly or quarterly plan to aid your parishioners in knowing your parish's namesake with more depth and outward fervor.
- In a world that does not value purity or outward devotedness to Christ, it's important to share this ancient story of heroic virtue.

Resource
Use the "Discerning and Learning Our Patron Guide" for families and parishes in the *Festive Faith Winter Ordinary Time, Lent, and Triduum Companion* at www.HisGirlSunday.com/FestiveFaith.

INSPIRING AUTHENTIC LOVE ON ST. VALENTINE'S DAY
FEBRUARY 14

THE STORY

If you were to look at the *Roman Martyrology* under the date of February 14, you would actually find a couple of men named St. Valentine. While the stories of these men are sparse and unquestionably inconsistent, there are a few things we can be certain of: St. Valentine was martyred, was buried on the Flaminian Way north of Rome, and was a devoted follower of Jesus Christ. Some legends say that both Valentines listed may have actually been the same person, while other accounts maintain their individuality. Either way, the tales have developed so much over time that it is impossible to know the original story. The commonly told biography comes from *Butler's Lives of the Saints*, which tells us, "Valentine was a holy priest in Rome, who, with Saint Marius and his family, assisted the martyrs in the persecution under Claudius II. He was apprehended, and sent by the emperor to the prefect of Rome; who, on finding all his promises to make him renounce his faith ineffectual, commanded him to be beaten with clubs, and afterward to be beheaded, which sentence was carried out on the 14 of February, about the year 270."[2]

The extended version of this story indicates that Valentine was befriended by Emperor Claudius II, who was drawn to Valentine's popularity for curing townspeople and his reputation of profound holiness. The emperor tried to convince Valentine to abandon his Christianity and worship the gods, but he proudly refused. In an attempt to change Valentine's mind, Claudius put him in custody in the house of Asterius, a Roman judge. It was there that he healed the judge's blind daughter named Julia and converted the entire household in response to this miracle. When Claudius II summoned Valentine to appear before him in hopes that he had converted to paganism, Claudius realized that Valentine was still firm in his Christian faith and had him beheaded. Valentine's martyrdom took place on the Flaminian Way, and sometime later Pope Julius I preserved his tomb by having a basilica built on that site.

The second St. Valentine is said to have lived approximately seventy years later. He was the bishop of Terni, Italy, from the third century who was also known for curing the sick and pushing the pagan boundaries. The breadth of lore associated with Bishop Valentine reaches from curing the disabled son of a philosopher named Crato and converting his household, to presiding over Christian marriages in secret.

Some theologians believe this is where Catholic oral tradition has made the association with love, romance, and courtship on February 14. Others claim that the association with love on this feast day actually has nothing to do with St. Valentine but is because this date marks the beginning of mating season for birds. In Geoffrey Chaucer's "Parliament of Fowles" he writes, "For this was on Saint Valentine's day, when every fowl comes there his mate to take."[3] Speculation has also driven some to believe that perhaps the connection between St. Valentine and the topic of love stems from a Christianization of the ancient Roman fertility festival Lupercalia, which fell on February 15. There is one thing we definitely know, which is that we don't know.

In any case, the news of the Christian work of Bishop Valentine made its way back to the authorities, and he too was put to death. His martyrdom is said to have happened at another location along the Flaminian Way. The parallels in the stories of the two Valentines are stark: they both were able to heal others, both had courageous faith, both were martyred, and both died on the Flaminian Way. It's not unrealistic to think that they could have been the same person whose story developed and changed over time. Regardless, the enduring testimony of St. Valentine's life is that of immense love for Christ in spite of great struggle and suffering. You can see the relic of St. Valentine's skull preserved in Rome at the minor basilica of Santa Maria in Cosmedin.

THE TRADITION

Since the 1969 revisions of the General Roman Calendar, St. Valentine is technically not recognized on February 14 anymore. The calendar adjustment is mostly due to the fact that we don't have enough concrete information about his life. He is undoubtedly still recognized as a saint, and his name is currently maintained in the *Roman Martyrology*, but Sts. Cyril and Methodius are liturgically commemorated on this day. Although, I think it would take some meticulous searching to find a Valentine's Day card with Sts. Cyril and Methodius on it. Therein lies the strength of culturally adopted feast days within the liturgical year. You see, the Church has declared two other men the more prominent saints to be celebrated on this day, but given the dominance of Valentine's Day within Catholic and secular culture, there's no changing the path of our romantically inspired customs. While the secularly celebrated "Valentine's Day" has certainly lost the awareness of the saint, it's a rather curious thing to see that everyone is still carrying out his reputation in blissful oblivion. Looking at the glass half full, we can recognize that despite it being a highly commercialized holiday, this is a day to express love to those around us. As Catholics we are afforded the true gift of this feast day, which is to experience that love twofold: we not only extend our affection to those that we care for, but also to Our Lord, who is the fount of true love.

Out of all the sentimental gestures associated with February 14, the "Valentines" letter to a loved one stands out. It is said to have derived from the Middle Ages. As one can imagine, the custom of two people in love desiring to share their emotions for the other is certainly not a groundbreaking practice. Yet, often these affectionate writings were inspired because of the everlasting tale of the patron saint of lovers and written on or around his feast day. Within these writings are references to "my Valentine," a term of endearment that is directly related to the man of God who refused to abandon his love for Christ, and who is said to have helped couples marry under God's authority. It wasn't until the mid-nineteenth century within the aristocratic class that we see a distinct change in gift- and card-giving that has become more profit-oriented.

Now, well-intended Catholics have sought to reorient this holiday back to its original meaning as the feast day of a saint. The intentional use of the word *saint* when referring to St. Valentine's Day is just the first step in recovering the origin and truths that underlie it. Present-day Catholic customs also include attending Mass or Eucharistic Adoration with loved ones to draw the focus of authentic love back to Christ. Many couples are now more desiring of Catholic-inspired date nights that include fewer gifts, less romantic pressure, and more quality time together. Husbands and wives with children have purposefully chosen to celebrate this saint as a family all together, as opposed to hiring a babysitter, so that all can share in their love for one another as a family. And many have gone back to the old custom of writing heartfelt St. Valentine's letters, to show their loved ones how they truly feel.

CARRYING ON THE TRADITION

AT HOME
Honor the patron saint of lovers in an explicitly Catholic way by using this holiday to focus more on quality time, enjoying your beloved, and inviting Christ into the date-night plans.

Consider This
- Instead of buying Valentines, write one another letters.
- Consider involving the entire family in your St. Valentine's date-night festivities.
- Integrate prayer, Mass, or Eucharistic Adoration into the feast-day plans.
- Contemplate the depth and nature of St. Valentine's love for Christ and the sacrifices he endured for it. How can this inspire us to greater love for God and one another?
- Share Catholic-themed St. Valentine's Day cards. You can find printable options online.

IN THE PARISH
The weekend before or after the Feast of St. Valentine, offer a parish-wide date night, including a daycare option for those who have children. Couple the date-night events with Mass or Eucharistic Adoration.

Consider This
- Create an RSVP so you know how many couples to provide for.
- Incorporate fun couple activities such as a rendition of the newlywed game or a DJ with time for dancing.
- Oftentimes marriage prep is the last time couples receive direct encouragement and support from their parish. Give husbands and wives the

opportunity to be encouraged in their vocation by offering an evening of enrichment with a speaker who can talk on the topics of marriage, love, or the domestic church. I would encourage you to keep these particular evenings focused on marriage and relationship as opposed to discussions on parenting, motherhood, and fatherhood so that more couples without children or whose children are out of the house can be included.

- In addition to a fun date night, you could also separately plan a marriage retreat for more focused and serious enrichment.

SHROVE TUESDAY PANCAKES AND PARTIES

IMMEDIATELY PRECEDING ASH WEDNESDAY AND TYPICALLY FALLS BETWEEN FEBRUARY 2 AND MARCH 9

THE STORY

Fat Tuesday, also known as *Mardi Gras* in French, or Shrove Tuesday, holds within it a liturgical dualism that simultaneously shows the human urge to festivity and the need to prepare for the somber road ahead. Many in secular culture will associate this day only with the former: the rabble-rousing and partying that takes place often to the point of outright debauchery. Don't let the fun and enjoyment of Mardi Gras distract you from the purifying trial that is to come—that is, Ash Wednesday, the solemn and sacrificial start to the season of Lent. In what seems like a desire for more Catholic awareness, the faithful in more recent years have gone back to referring to this liturgical date as Shrove Tuesday. For some, calling it by this name more clearly articulates that we are bringing Ordinary Time to a close and entering into Lent with our sins forgiven and hearts readied. *Shrove* is the past tense of the word *shrive*, which means to offer our Confession to a priest, to be absolved of our sins, and to fulfill our penance. This means that on the very day in which we are indulging, we are also balancing that with making sure we are in a state of grace and composing ourselves for Ash Wednesday.

In the history of the liturgical year, the balance between celebrating and preparatory discipline was to be done over a span of weeks commonly referred to as the 'gesimas. This is a season also known as pre-Lent, which hasn't been a part of the liturgical calendar since before Vatican II. The three Sundays that precede Lent are called Septuagesima (seventieth), Sexagesima (sixtieth), and Quinquagesima (fiftieth).

As we know, the Lenten season is a period of forty days that are meant to imitate Jesus's forty days of fasting and prayer in the desert. Hence, the three Sundays before Quadragesima Sunday were named after the round numbers fifty, sixty, seventy. In the current version of the General Roman Calendar, some of the principles of pre-Lent are found in the readings that are still proclaimed on the days leading up to Ash Wednesday. Unfortunately, we now have a much shorter and more abrupt transition into Lent that takes place all in one day on Shrove Tuesday.

Culturally the weeks before Lent were referred to as the Carnival season, as we explored in the section on King Cake in the Christmas chapter. In many places the season, not just the day, is referred to as Mardi Gras, meaning Fat Tuesday, the day before Ash Wednesday.

THE TRADITION

In Fr. Francis X. Weiser's 1958 book, *The Handbook of Christian Feasts and Customs*, he wrote, "it is a trait of human nature to anticipate approaching privations," and that "the intensity of this urge, however, should not be judged from the mild Lenten laws of today, but from the strict and harsh observance of ancient times. Another reason for the feasting, and a very practical one, was the necessity for finishing those foods which could not be eaten during Lent, and which, in fact, could not even be kept in homes during the fast—meat, butter, cheese, milk, eggs, fats, and bacon."[4] These intense fasting rules governed the faithful for many years and thus gave rise to the creative way of emptying the refrigerator by making pancakes for Shrove Tuesday. In fact, places like Australia, the United Kingdom, and some parts of Canada will still refer to this day as Pancake Day. A particularly intriguing custom from the United Kingdom is the Pancake Bell, which is still alive and well in many churches today. The initial intention of ringing the church bells in the early afternoon on Shrove Tuesday was to signal the townspeople to come to Confession. Over time, and with this much beloved table tradition, the bell was also rung to signal the woman of the home to begin making pancakes. This blending of our need for Confession and good food has produced the attention-grabbing Pancake Bell. Some love the chiming and others are overwhelmed by it, but either way it's a cherished sound of Catholic culture ringing throughout the town.

There is also a liturgical tradition that has been revitalized in many parishes and homes in the United States that is directly tied to the change of seasons. This tradition, "Burying the Alleluia" before Lent, is another example of the power of visible signs and actions in human activity. It can be found as early as the 1200s throughout Christian parts of the world, and it has taken on many forms and variations over time. Basically, the faithful would gather on the evening of the last day that the Alleluia is sung in the liturgy, and they would lay the Alleluia to rest. Laying this word of praise to rest would include a burying ceremony, which is likened to a "little funeral." Inside a small wooden coffin or box would be prepared a banner with "Alleluia" written on it. Following Vespers (Evening Prayer), all would process with candles and the cross to a place outside the church building where the Alleluia banner would be sprinkled, incensed, and then buried until Easter.

This custom should be done with reverence and a somber tone. Historically, the Alleluia would be buried on the Saturday before Septuagesima Sunday, since that is the last day that Alleluia was sung in the liturgy. So, if you attend a parish that offers the Latin Mass according to the 1962 Missal, then you would carry on this tradition on that day. In the current Roman calendar, however, the last Alleluia is sung during Evening Prayer on Shrove Tuesday, the day before Ash Wednesday. So, for most, the custom would be appropriate on Shrove Tuesday. It has also become increasingly common that parishes will offer a blessing and burning of ashes to end their Fat Tuesday events, and they include the burying of the Alleluia here. Others will arrange opportunities to pray Evening Prayer together before burying the Alleluia. These days we are blessed with an abundance of Catholic artisans who provide beautiful or special Alleluia banners to be buried by parishes and families.

CARRYING ON THE TRADITION

AT HOME
Go to Confession today in preparation for Ash Wednesday, and make pancakes for dinner. If you have a bell, you could also institute your own version of the Pancake Bell.

Consider This
- You could serve Louisiana-style Mardi Gras food such as gumbo or jambalaya.
- This is the last time for King Cake before next season, so don't forget to have a piece.

- Pencil in time to go to Confession sometime this week, if not today.
- Ask a friend to join you in hosting a Mardi Gras celebration.
- Decorate and/or dress in traditional green, purple, and gold colors.

IN THE PARISH

Offer more opportunities for Confession today, and facilitate a Shrove Tuesday celebration in the parish hall.

Consider This

- Bring your parishioners together on this evening of festivity by throwing a Mardi Gras gathering.
- Ask the Knights of Columbus if they will make pancakes and bacon for the community.
- Perhaps the parents who have children in faith formation can lead a children's parade around the property.
- Play music and give everyone the chance to get to know one another, dance, and partake in fun games.
- This is a great opportunity to have parishioners bring their palms from the previous year to be burned. These ashes can be used tomorrow or buried.
- Offer the chance to pray Evening Prayer followed by burying the Alleluia.

Resource

With a bell in one hand and a whisk in the other, you can bring Shrove Tuesday to life with my delicious pancake recipe. You can find this recipe in the *Festive Faith Winter Ordinary Time, Lent, and Triduum Companion* at www. HisGirlSunday.com/FestiveFaith.

=========== *A LIVING TRADITION* ===========

As a native New Orleanian, and now a Texan of thirty-seven years, one of the most vibrant and memorable traditions in my past and present is our family celebration of Mardi Gras. To me it is Mardi Gras Day, while to many it's Fat Tuesday or Carnival. This is a season of revelry and enjoying excess before the fasting and "giving up" things during Lent. Mardi Gras is a time of pageantry, excitement, and fun, including elegant balls, lavish dinners, and themed parades with costumed riders, beautifully decorated floats, and lots of throws. The joy is celebrating good times with family and friends! You could attend an opulent ball, spend the day and evening watching extravagantly designed floats, or enjoy the rhythmic marching bands while taking breaks to delight in delicious, rich food and drink. The days of krewes throwing beads, riders regaled in their costumes, and crowds of spectators often dressed in the Mardi Gras colors of purple (justice), green (faith), and gold (power) is such an exciting time preceding the Lenten observances.

Enjoying delicious King Cakes throughout this three- or four-week season was a natural part of growing up and a tradition we passed on to our children and grandchildren. They all love Mardi Gras, the Catholic culture of New Orleans, and attending the parades when possible. They have also developed their own Texas traditions of enjoying many sweet King Cakes during this season. It's a reminder to all of us that Mardi Gras is the last day of richness before the leaner days of Lent.

Charlotte Noto

FIVE

LENT

Therefore, brothers, stand firm and hold fast
to the traditions that you were taught, either
by an oral statement or by a letter of ours.
—2 Thessalonians 2:15

Begins: Ash Wednesday
Ends: Sundown on Holy Thursday
Natural Seasons: Winter and Early Spring
Lenten Disciplines: Prayer, Fasting, and Almsgiving
Recommended Prayer: Stations of the Cross
This prayer can be found in the Festive Faith Winter Ordinary
Time, Lent, and Triduum Companion *at www.HisGirlSunday.
com/FestiveFaith.*
Liturgical Colors: Violet and Rose

The season of Lent is a widely known and relatively short season in which we commit ourselves to intensified prayer, fasting, and almsgiving in order that we will be ready to celebrate the Paschal Triduum—the three holiest days of our year, counted from the evening of Holy Thursday through evening on Easter Sunday. Lent is rich with highly recognizable practices such as receiving ashes, making personal sacrifices, not eating meat on Fridays, and the ever-so-popular parish fish fry.

The term *Lent* is brought to us from the Old English word *lencten*, which means to lengthen, a term that correlates to the lengthening of daylight as we approach springtime. Everything God has created grows in steady silence during Lent here in the northern hemisphere, so that even the smallest flowers are ready for the grandeur of Easter. We, too, are called to cooperate in this period of spiritual growth so that our praises might be properly ordered to God's salvific action. Lent reminds me of the many years I spent as a ballerina, sacrificing, training, and disciplining myself so that I might be able to express a true sense of beauty and art. Similarly, Lent trains and purifies us; these days of increased prayer, fasting, and the discipline of giving to others in need are a time of dedication to the practice of self-discipline for our spiritual growth. It's not the easiest season to enter into because of that reality, but it's one that we inevitably need so that we can enter into the celebration of the Triduum and be utterly transformed by the Death and Resurrection of Christ, which we call the Paschal Mystery. As with all good things, God grants us the respective time we need to engage with our hearts, minds, and actions so that we not only cognitively learn the disciplines of Lent, but are fully impacted by them through all our senses. Every day of this season becomes a new opportunity to contemplate and practice the countercultural skills of silence, meekness, prayer, charity, fasting, and humility.

I have often found that, similar to Advent, Lent is a season that we enter with high hopes for slowing down. We tell ourselves that this year is going to be different. We are going to stick to our sacrifices, pray more, and not do so many extra things that distract us from the true spirit of it all. Then Lent begins, and in the midst of our spiritual training, our imperfections are highlighted and we quickly learn our frailty. With slightly dashed hopes for our Lenten efforts, we come to see the real lesson of the season, which is that we desperately need and are utterly dependent upon God. It's no coincidence that we start this season with ashes placed on our foreheads in the shape of cross to remind us and the world that we are imperfect beings in need of a Savior.

As you enter the Lenten desert with Christ, lean on the necessary tools by fortifying yourself with prayer, fasting, and almsgiving. Remove extra busyness that might distract you from the focus you need to receive the fruits of this season. Seek courage to walk closely enough to Christ to feel the suffering he bore on our behalf. Remember that Jesus fell with his Cross, and so will we. But in the same spirit of sacrificing with love, you must get back up and move forward. The customs brought to life in this chapter will all speak of this great tension that we hold in our faith between sin and salvation, feasting and fasting, dying and rising to new life.

SACKCLOTH AND ASHES FOR ASH WEDNESDAY

ASH WEDNESDAY, FORTY-SIX DAYS BEFORE EASTER

THE STORY

The ancient liturgical practice of sackcloth and ashes is an easily identifiable custom of the Lenten season. There is evidence of this practice that goes as far back as the book of Job in the Old Testament. "I have sewn sackcloth on my skin, laid my horn low in the dust" (Jb 16:15). We can read examples of this penitential practice peppered all throughout the Old Testament and into the New Testament. Jesus himself references these things when speaking to towns who are refusing to repent of their sins and turn away from their wrongdoings. These external signs of sackcloth and ashes were carried on by early Christians to remind penitents and the community of their mortality and need for repentance.

Sackcloth is a type of garment that was woven with coarse fabric mostly made out of goat's hair and worn either as a shirt or girdled around the loin. It was worn as a discipline in self-mortification because of how uncomfortable it was to wear. The sackcloth was supposed to act as a physical reminder to resist sinful temptations and as a help in repenting of one's sinfulness in sincere sorrow.

The use of ashes by early Christians had a similar meaning but was different from what we witness in today's Ash Wednesday liturgy. At times, ashes were sprinkled on top of a person's head, and in other scenarios a person might have been told to sit in the dust and ashes. Wearing sackcloth and ashes wasn't an indicator of the beginning of Lent, but was done throughout the Lenten season for those who had committed grave public sins. It was a very public custom aimed not only at the one who had sinned, but the whole community, calling to mind the communal effects of sin and of eventually being reconciled to God and to one's community.

THE TRADITION

By the eighth century, ashes were customarily used to indicate that Lent had begun and that Christians were starting a forty-day fast and a season of increased prayer and repentance. We can find the earliest copies of the ceremony for the "Day of Ashes" in the *Gregorian Sacramentary*. This particular text shows a start to the Ash Wednesday liturgy that looks similar to what we are accustomed to celebrating today. This same sign, ashes, that publicly expressed a need for repentance before the life of Christ and throughout the years of the early Church is the same public expression that we present to the world at the start of Lent in our contemporary practice. The enduring message remains that we are sorrowful sinners asking for forgiveness and seeking to do penance for our misdeeds. This is what we humbly communicate to anyone who sees us after we receive ashes on our foreheads. While it's certainly no public confession, it makes clear that as Christians we are unified in our humanity, brokenness, and need for salvation. A seldom-discussed principle that is integral to our Catholic belief is that we are intricately connected to all the other members of the Body of Christ, here on earth and in heaven. Consequently, the repercussions of our sins are never in complete isolation but impact the entire Body of Christ, in ways large and small. Ash Wednesday invites us into a custom that proclaims this principle when we receive ashes as a community.

As a practical and symbolic practice, the ashes that we receive are created from the palms of the previous year's Palm Sunday liturgy. This is why many parishes will invite parishioners to bring their blessed palm branches back to the church so that they can be burned and used for the distribution of ashes. The parish priest will then bless the ashes and traces a cross on the forehead of each person present with those very ashes. There are two phrases offered by the *Roman Missal*, either one of which can be said when the ashes are being given, "Remember that you are dust, and to dust you shall return" and "Repent and believe in the gospel." While it's not a holy day of obligation, for many the start of Lent is just not the same without receiving ashes.

Ash Wednesday is, however, an obligatory day of fasting and abstinence. "For members of the Latin Catholic Church, the norms for fasting are obligatory from age 18 until age 59. When fasting, a person is permitted to eat one full meal, as well as two smaller meals that together are not equal to a full meal. The norms concerning abstinence from meat are binding upon members of the Latin Catholic Church from age 14 onwards."[1] Many Catholics, in preparation for the start of this season, will have planned their personal sacrifice and a few meatless meals in advance to get them started on the right foot. These practices and symbols are to remind us that this is an extraordinary time of simplicity, not just on this one day, but throughout all of Lent.

CARRYING ON THE TRADITION

AT HOME

Be prepared to begin your personal sacrifice, and if you meet the requirements for fasting and abstinence, be sure to participate. Try to attend Mass or a Liturgy of the Word to receive your ashes.

Consider This

- Plan your meatless meal ahead of time so you feel prepared.
- If you forgot to think about your personal sacrifice, try to choose something today.
- Keep your ashes on all day; don't be afraid to wear them.
- Share with your children, spouse, or friends why this day is important.
- Invite the solemn nature of this day into your home with prayer or a period of quiet time that is appropriate for the ages of those in your household.

IN THE PARISH

Offer ashes to the community, and review the prescribed rules for fasting and abstinence.

Consider This

- You might consider offering preparatory materials to encourage everyone at the start of Lent such as a schedule of your Lenten prayer opportunities, how to fast and abstain, and the meaning of Ash Wednesday.
- Provide a small meatless meal for those stopping in on their lunch break on Ash Wednesday.
- Offer an additional Confession time today.
- Encourage meaningful sacrifices by offering an inspiring list of ideas.

Resource

Struggling to come up with Lenten sacrifice ideas? You can find ideas in the *Festive Faith Winter Ordinary Time, Lent, and Triduum Companion* at www. HisGirlSunday.com/FestiveFaith.

ST. PATRICK'S DAY HUMBLE AND GRAND TRADITIONS

MARCH 17

THE STORY

St. Patrick was a fifth-century bishop who became the patron saint of Ireland and is largely credited with converting Ireland to Christianity. Before receiving such great titles, he endured many trials in his life. When he was around the age of sixteen, he was captured and made a slave. We can explore some stories of his enslavement and the depth of prayer that he found solace in by reading his autobiographical writing called St. Patrick's *Confessio*. The most important thing to grasp from this writing is the deep conversion he underwent through perpetual prayer and his recognition of God's greatness. He recounts his escape from Irish pirates, who held him captive for roughly six years. He tells about following a voice that told him his escape was near, and that a ship would be ready for him. Not long after his escape, he had a vision in which he saw his mission: St. Patrick was being asked to share the message of Christ with pagan Ireland. He described his vision like this: "I saw a man coming, as it were, from Ireland. His name was Victoricus, and he carried many letters, and he gave me one of them. I read the heading: 'The Voice of the Irish.' As I began the letter, I imagined in that moment that I heard the voice of those very people who were near the wood of Foclut, which is beside the western sea—and they cried out, as with one voice: 'We appeal to you, holy servant boy, to come and walk among us!'"[2]

Patrick's devotion drew him to France, where he studied to become a priest, and as his missionary work developed, he was later ordained a bishop. Convincing the Irish to set aside the pagan lifestyle they were accustomed to presented many challenges, especially among the Druids, who were the priestly and ruling class of ancient Celtic cultures. But he didn't let that deter him from proclaiming the Christian message. St. Patrick's humble ministry converted thousands of Irish people and led to establishing churches and monasteries and ordaining priests from among the native peoples. St. Patrick was a tireless communicator of the faith because he knew the Lord's grace so profoundly and he wanted others to receive that too.

The legends that surround St. Patrick are brimming with Irish symbolism and history blended with authentic Christian meaning. A popular one that many have heard explains that while St. Patrick was doing his missionary work, he was attacked by a swarm of snakes, and in reaction to this he cast all the snakes out of Ireland. From Genesis we understand that serpents are symbolic of evil and deception. The snake was also a common symbol of the pagan Druids, who openly fought to undermine St. Patrick's missionary efforts. The story of St. Patrick and the snakes is not meant to be a historical account, but a narrative that effectively teaches us about how he used his authority and power to drive out evil and establish Christianity. St. Patrick's unfailing work and determination allowed him to convert the people of Ireland and place them under Christ's protection.

Throughout Ireland, St. Patrick's feast day is celebrated by telling the stories of his life and heroic deeds, feasting on traditional Irish food and drink, and singing local folk songs. The Irish have declared St. Patrick as their country's patron, and they celebrate with strong elements of their ancient culture to keep his legacy alive. Previous customs were far humbler—one might pick a few shamrocks to pin to their dress or lapel and go to Mass. At the end of Mass, the priest would impart the Blessing of the Shamrocks. The shamrock represents Irish heritage while also reminding the Irish of a story about St. Patrick using shamrocks to teach about the Trinity. While there isn't actual proof of that, and many argue that he didn't do that at all, the three-leafed Irish symbol has become a representation of our Trinitarian belief.

Because this feast day is also situated in Lent, up until the 1970s pubs in Ireland were closed on the Feast of St. Patrick. March 17 was viewed as a religious day, and there was worry that if the bars were open, people would be too tempted to go in and drink excessively on such a holy day within a solemn season. Until recent decades, St. Patrick's Day was predominantly enjoyed by embracing both Irish and Catholic culture. Not unlike Carnival season, however, this patronal day has given rise to excess, and for some it is just another excuse to drink and carouse. But the intemperance of some should not deter you from celebrating this saint's day with moderation and fitting festivity.

THE TRADITION

The growth of St. Patrick's Day has been exponential, not only in Ireland, but also in the United States. This is in part due to the fact that he is one of the most popular Catholic saints around the world and also because of the large Irish immigrant community that dwells here. While his feast day may have had small beginnings more closely rooted in our faith, it's more commonly associated with well-known parades, dressing up in Ireland's colors, and drinking beer. Places like Boston and New York have long boasted of hosting the first St. Patrick's Day parades, but it turns out that the first was actually held in St. Augustine, Florida, in 1601. Since this tradition didn't prominently endure in St. Augustine as it has in other cities, we can see why Boston and New York would claim ownership. Interestingly enough, Ireland didn't see its first major and more formalized parade until around 1903 in Waterford.

All that considered, perhaps the most iconic Irish-American celebration of St. Patrick's Day comes from Chicago. The city hosts its largest annual parade in celebration of the day, and the Chicago River is dyed green. You can drink a green beer, which is a uniquely American thing to do (frowned upon by most residents of Ireland), enjoy live entertainment, and eat traditional Irish foods. Irish Catholics may venture to find a balance between having a good time at community celebrations and going to Mass and seeking St. Patrick's intercession. Some parishes might also bless beer on this day, while others maintain an older tradition by blessing shamrocks. In places where festivities aren't offered, individuals or families will do their own liturgical living by playing Irish music, sharing a loaf of Irish soda bread, wearing green, and reciting the St. Patrick's Breastplate Prayer.

Celebrating a saint within the season of Lent can be a source of confusion. Some are unsure of what celebrations to partake of when approaching St. Patrick's Day within the greater context of Lent. Begin by prayerfully evaluating what may seem to be at face value a conflicting combination of festivity and the penitential nature of the Lenten season. Take time to consider that this tension is a manifestation of the complex mystery at the core of our human nature—the harmony of celebration and humble simplicity. Although we are in the midst of our Lenten observances, we still live in a time that is post-Resurrection. As faithful Christians we hold in each hand our joy and suffering, the sacrifice and celebration of the Mass, and the death and the resurrection of Christ and of ourselves. While this feast day does not supersede Lent, you can still embrace St. Patrick's Day with praise while also observing your Lenten sacrifices and meatless Fridays.

CARRYING ON THE TRADITION

AT HOME

Let's start with humble beginnings! If St. Patrick's Day should fall on a Friday of Lent, try recipes for Irish fish stew or fish pie. Many authentic recipes are available online. While continuing your Lenten disciplines, you can honor this great saint by playing Irish music, baking a loaf of soda bread, wearing green, and reciting or listening to St. Patrick's Breastplate Prayer first thing in the morning or maybe at the dinner table. Many beautiful musical versions are available online.

Consider This
- During dinner, read or share the legend of how St. Patrick banished the snakes from Ireland.
- Pin fresh shamrocks to your jacket, dress, or shirt today, or decorate with them, and then discuss the basics of the Trinity. We believe in one God, three persons.
- Honor St. Patrick by going to Mass today.
- If there are local celebrations near you, try to attend one of them and soak in your neighborhood customs.

IN THE PARISH

Draw parishioners' main focus away from the purely secular aspects that have overcome this feast day, and direct their attention back to the saint. Whatever liturgies, meetings, or social events are scheduled in the parish on March 17, find simple ways to draw attention to the legend of St. Patrick and to pray for the people of Ireland.

Consider This
- Sometimes the congregation doesn't know whose feast day it is until you tell them. Especially for popular saints, state their name at the beginning or end of Mass, or integrate them into your ministry meetings or programming.
- If this feast falls on a Sunday, use this golden opportunity to bring everyone together in the parish hall for coffee and Irish treats. Use simple and inexpensive decorations to indicate that it is a special feast day, have Irish

music playing lightly in the background, and give your hospitality volunteers shamrocks to pin on their shirts or jackets. When most of your Mass attendees have strolled over, pray the St. Patrick Breastplate Prayer with them before serving.

- If you have a significant Irish population, I encourage you to take that opportunity to invite them to lead the community in learning about their culture and patron saint.
- Share the story of this saint through your usual communication methods.

Resource
Pray the St. Patrick's Breastplate Prayer found in the *Festive Faith Winter Ordinary Time, Lent, and Triduum Companion* at www.HisGirlSunday.com/FestiveFaith.

A LIVING TRADITION

From a very young age, in an Irish family of ten children, we knew who St. Patrick was and the meaning of his being the patron saint of Ireland. It is a national holiday there; everyone is off for the day, and towns and villages around the country display their pride with parades and festivals. For us, the day always started with Mass, and we had to be wearing something green and always had a St. Patrick's Day badge or pin on our coats or a bunch of shamrocks.

Members of older generations in my family were committed to picking fresh shamrocks from the mossy ditches in the morning before Mass. As children it was our job to find a nice bunch of them for our mother's coat. We came to understand the meaning of the shamrock and the tale of how St. Patrick picked it up and explained to the pagans that the three leaves represented the Father, Son, and Holy Spirit of the Trinity. I believe these traditions are important for us to carry on today because they unite our faith to the sense of pride we have in being Irish. But most important is an understanding of the life of St. Patrick, who was brought to Ireland as a slave, but came back as an ordained priest to teach and preach the faith and convert the pagans to Catholicism by using symbols of our land and country.

Josephine Dolan

ST. JOSEPH'S ALTAR

MARCH 19

THE STORY

St. Joseph was the spouse of the Blessed Virgin Mary and the earthly father of Jesus. Known as a just man, his character of righteousness gave him the ability to accept God's plan with obedient devotion unlike any other. Although he is known as a "silent man" because no words were recorded from him in the gospels, he of course played a vital role in the Holy Family and in God's will for our salvation. Joseph is a descendent of the house of David, which makes him a part of God's Chosen People and plan. This is an important element in his fatherhood because prophecies from the Old Testament foretold the Messiah would come from the line of King David. In the anticipation of marriage to Mary, he was met with great difficulty and suffering when she was found to be with child. He knew this could lead to her potential death if it was made known to the public, so he chose to leave her quietly. Before doing so he was met by an angel in a dream who revealed the truth to him, and Joseph chose to trust that this was a message from God and stayed with Mary. Joseph provided Mary with loving support and stood as a model of fidelity, strength, and holiness.

The Solemnity of St. Joseph is not just a typical feast day but is elevated in importance because of his virtue and commitment to God's will, his wife Mary, and the child Jesus. In Italy this day is called *La Festa Di San Giuseppe,* or the Feast of St. Joseph, and is celebrated all over the country, but it has a special tradition of festivity in the region of Sicily.

The Sicilians consider St. Joseph to be their patron saint because of a story dating back to the Middle Ages. He was credited with saving them from a drought after they prayed for his intercession. The people had promised that if he would bring rain, they would be devoted in honoring him. St. Joseph heard their cry and responded to them favorably by ending the drought, thus giving them the ability to grow their crops again. The harvest came, and the Sicilian people kept their vow and prepared a great offering for him by using the bounty to make a great feast for their families and villages. Everyone gathered to share in the blessing of food and offer thanksgiving to God and the saint who helped them. This feast became known as a St. Joseph's Altar and became an annual tradition on St. Joseph's feast day. The blessing of St. Joseph was carried to America by many Sicilian immigrants, who continued the tradition of a St. Joseph's Altar in their new country.

THE TRADITION

This tradition continues in Sicily today with liveliness and pride. If you ever have the chance to visit there around the Solemnity of St. Joseph, you will most likely see altars or tables displayed in homes, churches, and even some Italian cafes. The understanding is that no one is to be turned away from a St. Joseph's Altar. Typically, these will be three tiered, symbolic of the Holy Trinity and the Holy Family, and placed in an area for all to see and partake in. The table will be nicely displayed with colorful tablecloths and filled with gifts of food and religious items. Bread is the predominant food displayed on the table, and it comes in many shapes and sizes. Some of them are molded in the shape of popular symbols of St. Joseph, such as a staff, carpentry tools, and crosses. Community members and families will also add traditional Italian pastries like *zeppole* and a variety of fish since the feast is celebrated within the Lenten season.

While many dishes will grace this table, it is also beautifully decorated. In the center of the highest table there is typically a statue of St. Joseph, lest we forget the source of our gratitude and joy on this day. A crown of thorns might be displayed to remember the Crucifixion of Jesus, and palm branches are laid under dishes and placed in vases to represent his victory. Vases hold the flower of St. Joseph—white lilies in full bloom. Many people add wine bottles that represent the miracle of the wedding at Cana, holy cards, icons, and other Catholic symbols. Sicilians add items that speak to their homeland such as grapes, figs, olives, and lemons.

The most meaningful food that you will find on the table brings connection to the story of the drought, and that is the fava bean. It is said that during the drought the fava bean was the only thing that would grow, and while this was usually grown to feed livestock, the people were forced to sustain themselves with fava beans during this drought. They referred to this as the lucky bean, and many Sicilians continue to see it as a reminder to pray for the intercession of St. Joseph for their needs and the needs of others.

This yearly act of gratitude to St. Joseph is one that has spread to homes and parishes across the United States, even for those who are not of Sicilian descent. With the same intention in mind, you and your community can show St. Joseph reverence and devotion by creating your own St. Joseph Altar.

CARRYING ON THE TRADITION

AT HOME
Arrange a small one-, two-, or three-tiered altar in your home, and adorn it with a St. Joseph statue, flowers, and baked goods.

Consider This
- Bake a loaf of bread, and shape it as a staff or carpenter's tool.
- If you prefer sweets, you could make an Italian dessert instead of bread.
- Sometimes we don't have time to bake, so it's okay to buy something from the store and share it as an after-dinner solemnity dessert.
- Ask for St. Joseph's intercession during personal and group prayer time today.
- Solemnities are a feast day of the highest rank; try to go to Mass today or spend time in Eucharistic Adoration.

IN THE PARISH
Develop a team that can coordinate and lead the creation and celebration of a St. Joseph Altar. Create a tiered altar, and encourage parishioners to bring baked or store-bought goods to share. This is best done on the closest Sunday to the Solemnity of St. Joseph when the parishioners can partake of this beautiful tradition.

Consider This
- Plan this a few months in advance so there is ease in arranging the tables and coordinating the food.
- Start educating your parish community about this tradition and encourage participation well in advance.
- Recruit volunteers who can help serve the food from the table.
- Recruit a small group to organize cleanup.
- Ask your pastor to bless your St. Joseph Altar at the first Mass of the morning.
- Lead everyone in a St. Joseph prayer and explain the importance of his feast day before participants enjoy the festive foods.

Resource
Once you've assembled your St. Joseph Altar, pray a blessing over it in honor of this beloved saint. You can find a blessing in the *Festive Faith Winter Ordinary Time, Lent, and Triduum Companion* at www.HisGirlSunday.com/FestiveFaith.

My family is from the Mississippi Gulf Coast, which was a huge port for immigrants through much of the eighteenth, nineteenth, and twentieth centuries. Many immigrants from coastal countries in the Mediterranean, such as Italy and Croatia, settled in the Gulf Coast region of the United States in order to continue the trades they were already skilled in. Both sides of my family, primarily Italian, Croatian, and German, are Catholics who immigrated here in just that way. My ancestors came to the Gulf Coast to continue the fishing, shrimping, crabbing, and oyster harvesting that they did in their home countries. The practice of Catholicism has been strong on the coast as long as anyone can remember, and the St. Joseph Altar is no exception. The St. Joseph Altar is an annual tradition that the whole community supports.

As a child, I watched my grandmother's church put out the most amazing St. Joseph Altar with copious amounts of bread, pictures, and baked goods. Big-haired ladies would spend days and days perfecting it. I marveled at it, or at the pictures when I couldn't go see it. Such a sight would capture the attention of any child! Without me knowing at the time, a regard and devotion to St. Joseph was cultivated in me through this honoring of him and watching others honor him. It was not until college that I realized I had a special devotion to St. Joseph that others did not have. After an incredibly moving experience with St. Joseph on a mission trip in Honduras that overlapped his March 19 feast day, I began practicing the St. Joseph Altar too. He is so humble and so much in the background in scripture; I find that pulling him forward and really recognizing the incredible role he had in the Holy Family truly highlights the force of his intercession and care for us on earth. Now, I get to share the St. Joseph Altar tradition with my kids, and they love it too.

This tradition is important to carry on so that Catholics across the world can fully experience the love, protection, and devotion that St. Joseph can offer us! Mother Mary has a multitude of feast days honoring her and her role in our salvation, whereas St. Joseph has just a couple. The act of putting together a St. Joseph Altar is a natural exposure to him, as well as a way to ponder his role and how he protected and guided the Holy Family. This tradition particularly matters today. Our contemporary culture makes it difficult for many men to find their place in families, as husbands and fathers, and even within their faith communities. By making a point of honoring the earthly father of Jesus and spouse of our Mother Mary, honoring the distinct, invaluable role he had in Jesus's life counteracts the confusion many men feel today about what it means to be a virtuous and faithful man. Celebrating St. Joseph in this way upholds the Church's value of male and female complementarity and the powerful role of a father. Making a point to celebrate St. Joseph in a grand way will carry on his legacy by encouraging people to ponder the powerful role he had in Jesus's time, as well as the powerful role he can have in our lives today.

Taylor Alsobrooks

THE VEILING OF SACRED IMAGES DURING PASSIONTIDE

FIFTH SUNDAY OF LENT

THE STORY

Before First Vespers on the Saturday evening before the Fifth Sunday of Lent, crosses, statues, and other sacred images in many Catholic churches are covered. The Fifth Sunday of Lent was historically celebrated as the first day of Passiontide—a term used to describe the last two weeks of Lent—and was known as Passion Sunday. There is little record of the history behind this first Sunday of Passiontide, but we know it had been called this for centuries. As Dom Prosper Gueranger writes in *The Liturgical Year: Passiontide and Holy Week*, "The most ancient sacramentaries and antiphonaries of the several Churches attest, by the prayers, the lessons, and the whole liturgy of these two weeks, that the Passion of our Lord is now the one sole thought of the Christian world."[3]

In the current edition of the *Roman Missal*, the Fifth Sunday of Lent, while not referred to as Passion Sunday, does mark a notable change in the liturgical themes of the season. Our attention turns to Christ's sufferings in the prayers and readings that we hear in the liturgy. The Fifth Sunday remains the day on which crosses and other sacred images are veiled, if parishes choose to take up this custom. After several weeks of traveling through the Lenten desert, Passiontide calls us out of the wastelands to realize the fulfillment of what we have prepared for. The practice of veiling statues on this Sunday creates a distinct shift that helps us intensify our gaze on Christ's salvific action.

It is believed that the veiling of statues evolved from a practice in Germanic churches called the Hunger Cloth. The Hunger Cloth was a large white cloth hung in a way to hide the entire altar from the view of the faithful. This was connected to the older practice of expelling public sinners from the Church for the duration of Lent. Fr. Edward McNamara explains it in this way: "After the ritual of public penance fell into disuse—but the entire congregation symbolically entered the order of penitents by receiving ashes on Ash Wednesday—it was no longer possible to expel them from the church. Rather, the altar or 'Holy of Holies' was shielded from view until they were reconciled to God at Easter."[4] At one time public sinners were expelled from the churches and denied the sacraments during Lent to foster a longing for communion with Christ and his Church by deprivation. When this became less common, the entire congregation began coming together on Ash Wednesday within the church to receive ashes and collectively admit the need for repentance. In this case, churches would lay a large purple, and in some countries white, cloth entirely over the altar to keep the congregation from seeing it. Not only was it meant to guard the Holy of Holies, but it gave the people a visual image of the separation that results from sin. Through the years, veiling the altar expanded to covering statues and images as a way of hiding their divine message, a representation of the way that Jesus hid himself from those who did not accept his divinity.

This custom can be further attributed to the pre-conciliar gospel reading for Passion Sunday which says, "They therefore took up stones to cast at him; but Jesus hid himself, and went out from the temple" (Jn 8:59). As it relates to the tradition at hand, we see that Christ veils, or hides, his presence to flee those who persecute him as an expression of submission to the Father's will. The Church echoes this by covering statues and images as a veil of sorrow for the suffering and death that is to come.

THE TRADITION

Covering sacred images and statues is an ongoing tradition that continuously prompts us not to run from but to stay with the suffering of Good Friday, which we are quickly approaching, so that we can ardently receive the glory of Easter. The *Roman Missal* gives clear instruction for this optional practice: "In the Dioceses of the United States, the practice of covering crosses and images throughout the church from [the fifth] Sunday [of Lent] may be observed. Crosses remain covered until the end of the Celebration of the Lord's Passion on Good Friday, but images remain covered until the beginning of the Easter

Vigil."[5] The Missal further instructs that the only things not to be covered are the Stations of the Cross. You may also not hear the term *Passion Sunday* or *Passiontide* used because in the liturgical reforms of the Second Vatican Council, the Church combined Passion Sunday with Palm Sunday, giving it the liturgical name of Palm Sunday of the Lord's Passion, which is celebrated on the Sixth Sunday of Lent and marks the beginning of Holy Week.

The practice of entirely veiling the altar has fallen out of practice in many places, but especially within the United States. However, many parishes continue to veil the images and statues that adorn their church with plain and simple purple cloth. Removing the covering takes place without any special ceremony. In the order dictated by the *Roman Missal*, crucifixes are unveiled on Good Friday, and the rest are unveiled before the Easter Vigil.

Many Catholics are reclaiming the traditional practices of Passiontide. Those who have decorated their homes with saint statues, crucifixes, and other sacred art can heighten their awareness of the shift in tone by veiling these images for the final two weeks of Lent. There is certainly no requirement that this be done, or that you need to have expensive fabric veils tailor-made in a manner that your parish church might. Above all, this involves a humble acceptance of an invitation to immerse oneself in the rhythms of the Church during the Lenten cycle. Our domestic churches are encouraged to do as the Church does within our homes so that we further sanctify, or make holy, our day-to-day lives. Those seeking to participate in veiling will need to obtain purple fabric that can easily be cut and laid upon the sacred images in their home. Following the cues of the *Roman Missal*, these go up on the Fifth Sunday in Lent and come down in two parts: cross coverings on Good Friday and other image coverings on Holy Saturday, just before the Easter Vigil begins.

CARRYING ON THE TRADITION

AT HOME

As the Fifth Sunday of Lent approaches, identify within your home the images and statues that you would like to cover, and purchase enough inexpensive purple fabric to cover them.

Consider This
- You may have to take some measurements before purchasing the purple fabric.
- Don't worry about having things sewn or tailored; you can simply cut and lay the fabric over your statues and images.

- Perhaps you cover some but not all images. Start with just the crucifixes.

IN THE PARISH

Some parishes partake in veiling and others don't, but I encourage every parish to do this because it speaks volumes to Catholics in the pews. The coverings act as a stark indication that something is happening or changing in our Lenten journey. It pulls our senses away from what we are used to and signals to us that we are deeper in the desert. It is another impactful reminder of our Catholic culture. The uniqueness of these liturgical experiences brings Catholics closer together and unites us in a depth of shared custom.

Consider This

- You might need to explain this custom to your congregation in advance so that the action can be deepened with understanding and not primarily a distraction.
- If you have a sewing group in your parish, you could provide them with the materials and dimensions for each statue and image and ask them to make the coverings for you.
- Perhaps you have others in the parish who would happily donate the materials needed to make the veils. Maybe you can also find volunteers to do the covering in a prayerful manner.
- Follow the instruction of the Missal and uncover the crucifixes on Good Friday and the rest of the statues before the Easter Vigil.

=============== *A LIVING TRADITION* ===============

We cover statues and crucifixes when we begin Passiontide during the final days of Lent. To me it means the celebration of the great Paschal Mystery is near. It's also a time for me to finalize my preparation for the Sacred Triduum and Easter. Because I also help with initiation ministry in our parish, the final preparations of those adults and children getting ready to receive the Sacraments of Initiation at the Easter Vigil are ever present when Passiontide is upon us. To see the faces of those being baptized helps me see the beauty of what my parents gave me when I was an infant. Like the statues being uncovered at the Easter Vigil, their eyes and hearts are uncovered and opened to sanctifying grace. Their witness is what our faith is about, a conversion of heart to be a disciple of Christ.

The importance of carrying on this tradition is that we, in our fallen nature, need a continual reminder of what God did for us and our salvation. Covering statues allows us to focus on Christ's sacrifice for us and the Church he gave us. Our nature makes it easy for us to be distracted and attached to things that are unholy. This liturgical tradition is relevant today, as it was from the beginning, to remind us to focus on Christ and not material and temporal things. Similar to receiving any wrapped gift, the joy we have when the cover is removed and we see the beauty of the gift is the same yet even greater as we are surrounded by the saints, angels, and the Holy Spirit.

Deacon Stuart Neck

FLOWERS, FIGS, AND PALMS FOR PALM SUNDAY
PALM SUNDAY OF THE PASSION OF THE LORD

THE STORY

On Palm Sunday we commemorate Jesus's triumphant entry into Jerusalem, an entry that will directly lead to the Passion, Death, and Resurrection of Jesus. It is important for us to understand the meaning behind this day so that we can understand the Old and New Testaments in their fullness. Through the readings we see that Jesus claims his kingship and authority over us when he enters Jerusalem. His actions reveal fulfillment of Old Testament promises, and he shows that his power does not come from man but from God. The people recognize him as their Messiah, their king, and we can see this in the way that they lay out their garments on the street while waving their palm branches and proclaiming, "Hosanna! Blessed is he who comes in the name of the Lord! Blessed is the kingdom of our father David that is to come! Hosanna in the highest!" (Mk 11:9b–10).

The tradition of processing with palms began in Jerusalem and spread throughout most of the Christian world in a short time. As early as the fourth century, the Church in Jerusalem marked the occasion of Palm Sunday by processing to different sites around the city. Everyone gathered to walk with the clergy as they carried and waved their palm branches while chanting, "Hosanna!" Choirs set the tone as they sang sacred hymns, while the clergy and altar servers took the lead in bringing Jesus's messianic entry into Jerusalem back to life. While we know this day to be the start of Holy Week, and many of us feel the knot in our stomachs beginning to form ahead of Good Friday, this procession is marked with a celebratory character.

While the procession with palms was present from the beginning of the Palm Sunday observance, the Blessing of Palms that many of us are accustomed to didn't arise until around the seventh or eighth century. We find mention of this Blessing of Palms in the Sacramentary of the Abbey of Bobbio in Piacenza, Emilia-Romagna, Italy. Because they are blessed, the palms hold great religious meaning and should be carried, held, and displayed or otherwise kept in our homes with true reverence. As the *Directory on Popular Piety and the Liturgy* states, "Palm and olive branches are kept in the home as a witness to faith in Jesus Christ, the messianic king, and his paschal victory."[6]

From the fourth century to the twenty-first century, the traditions around Palm Sunday have remained consistent while also being regularly adapted to specific cultures. Recognition of local celebration in the midst of the universal liturgical calendar brings our attention to two current Palm Sunday activities that might enrich your experience of this festive day.

THE TRADITION

Palms have not always been easily accessible in every place, and it can still be hard for parishes in parts of the world far from the tropics to acquire them. As an alternative, people have used what was available to them, such as olive branches, willows, or yews, and adapted the name of this Sunday to fit their offering. Poland, for example, will call Palm Sunday "Willow Sunday" because of the branches that are grown there. In many areas, native flowers in bloom are also blessed on this day so that they can be woven into the branches that are being used. Especially in England, Germany, Croatia, Serbia, and Armenia, this day is beautifully referred to as "Flower Sunday," "Flowering Sunday," or "Blossom Sunday." It is no longer common in the United States to include flowers in the procession, partly due to the rubrics limiting flowers in the season of Lent. However, it is not inappropriate to include local flowers or other types of branches that are more accessible to your community. Any variation on these liturgical practices should be done with careful discernment, reverence for the liturgy, and a sense of authenticity to the local community. Flowers in the liturgical environment are not simply pretty décor. They highlight and enhance the space and observances to show in a visible way that something special or extraordinary is occurring. In the same manner that Laetare Sunday (the Third Sunday of Lent) calls for rejoicing in the middle of our Lenten penitence, so does the Palm Sunday procession. You might consider weaving or braiding local flowers into your palm branches.

In the past, Palm Sunday has also been referred to as "Fig Sunday," more commonly in England, but also in some parts of the United States where individuals and families have sought to incorporate varied Holy Week customs. Fig Sunday is derived from the scriptural story of Jesus cursing the fig tree after his entry into Jerusalem. "The next day as they were leaving Bethany, he was hungry. Seeing from a distance a fig tree in leaf, he went over to see if he could find anything on it. When he reached it he found nothing but leaves; it was not the time for figs. And he said to it in reply, 'May no one ever eat of your fruit again!' And his disciples heard it" (Mk 11:12–14). In keeping with the custom, it would be fitting for you to add figs to the dinner table today. Recipes are abundant, but some of my favorites include fig cookies, a charcuterie board with figs and honey drizzle, and fig and prosciutto crostini. You can find a fig recipe in the *Festive Faith Winter Ordinary Time, Lent, and Triduum Companion* at www.HisGirlSunday.com/FestiveFaith.

CARRYING ON THE TRADITION

AT HOME
When the palms are blessed, handle them with reverence. If you are following the tradition of Flower Sunday, braid or weave small flowers into your palm branches. Continue the custom of making palm crosses for your home, or simply slide the palm frond behind your hanging crucifixes. Let these be a reminder to your home of the paschal victory of Christ.

Consider This
- Use the palms as an arrangement for your dining-room table. Having them displayed in a central location can remind us of the themes of Holy Week.
- Attach palms to a wreath, and hang it on your front door. I do this every year, and it has been a symbol of our family's faith to our neighbors.
- Serve a fig dish: fig cookies, a charcuterie board with figs, or fig and prosciutto crostini.

IN THE PARISH
It is traditional on this day to do the Blessing of Palms with a Palm Sunday procession, recalling Jesus's entry into Jerusalem.

Consider This
- Plan your procession carefully with the help of volunteers or a liturgy committee. Think about whether you would like to start inside or outside.
- Involve your ushers and/or hospitality ministers.
- Purchase palms ahead of time, and decide how you would like them to be distributed. This might be a great opportunity to invite children and youth of the parish to serve.
- Arrange enough clergy for the Blessing of Palms.
- Be sure to give notice to your parishioners so that they can plan to attend.

=========== **A LIVING TRADITION** ===========

I find it difficult at times to hold together the paradoxes presented by Christ, victorious in defeat, made glorious in his shame, and bringing life through death. Palm Sunday helps to push it all together. With a palm in my hand, I cheer on Christ's entrance into Jerusalem, while only moments later I ponder him hanging upon the Cross. I'm so used to the opposite: a struggle through difficulty to attain glory. Palm Sunday helps me see beyond that. It's not just an end of pain that he has promised us, an end of suffering, but the peace that surpasses all understanding. Palm Sunday drives me to that. It's a kind of precursor to the Triduum and even an invitation to see beyond it. "Remember," it whispers in my ears, "the victory of Easter is but a foreshadowing." I am made, as the promise holds, for even greater glories. We all are. Christ is greater even than his Resurrection. The palm of true victory is so much more than the palm we now hold.

Tomas Diaz

EXTRAVAGANT MONDAY
MONDAY OF HOLY WEEK

THE STORY

"One of the peculiarities of the Roman liturgy is its fondness for counting the days intervening until a feast," Pius Parsch writes.[7] This is remarkably true for Holy Week, when there is a yearning to mark each and every day leading to Easter with intentional participation. However, the Monday of Holy Week often gets left in the shadow of Palm Sunday and the quickly approaching celebrations of the Triduum. Especially with regard to liturgical living, it may appear at first glance that there isn't any tradition to be done on this day. Instead, some homes will enter into the vigorous Holy Week house cleaning ritual that goes from Monday to Wednesday, but I encourage you to wait to pick up your duster until tomorrow.

There is a lesson to be learned here about not forgetting the daily scripture readings. Often this intersection between God's Word, the liturgy, and our at-home liturgical lives gets overlooked in the rush of trying to just make something happen. When that urge to "just get it done" rises up, I encourage you to slow down and intentionally look at where we are in commemorating the story of Jesus's life. Remember, that is what using the liturgical year is for: weaving our life into the life of Christ and allowing that to influence our actions.

Extravagant Monday gets its name and meaning from the gospel reading for today, which tells the story about Mary of Bethany anointing Jesus's feet with perfumed oil. In the gospel story, Mary takes a costly jar of perfumed oil made from pure nard and pours it over the feet of Jesus. The entire house is said to have been consumed by this lovely aroma, but in the midst of her grand gesture, Judas speaks out. He rudely complains that this expensive ointment should have been sold for money, which could have been given to the poor. It's not that he truly cared for the poor, but he would often steal for himself out of the money bag. Jesus reprimands Judas, telling him to let her continue this extravagant act of love, because we will always have the task of caring for the poor, but Jesus will only be with us for a short time. From this reading we get the foretelling of Jesus's burial, and we also witness the completely selfless action of Mary that is meant to be an imitation of the extravagant offering that Christ makes of his own body.

THE TRADITION

As we've seen, some historic traditions extend themselves strongly over time, steadfast and never changing. Other traditions arise and remain in the local community: the home, parish, or culture that nourishes it. Extravagant Monday is one of the latter. Some communities and families will make this a day of service to the community by giving generously of their time toward the needs of others. Others seek to combat any reluctance that might be within themselves to hold on to what they own, as we saw in the story with Judas, by giving more charitably of their belongings. Collecting unused clothes, goods, and items that others might be in need of is another way that people spend their Monday of Holy Week.

When my husband and I got married, we created an annual custom on Holy Monday of hospitality and service centered around the dinner table. We invite a group of friends and family over to our home, and we make an extravagant dinner with foods and recipes that we would certainly not enjoy on any other Monday. In the name of being more extravagant, we make menu cards, set the table, prepare bread from scratch, and serve a multicourse dinner with a specialty drink. Mirroring Mary, we serve each course to our friends in gratitude for the love and support that they offer to us. In the midst of what is often a busy Holy Week, this multicourse meal slows us down and affords us the time to pray with and belong to our community. What we are seeking to do is share in the fullness of this earthly life, as we await the time of fulfillment for our eternal life. If you are intrigued by the idea of imitating this, you can find more adaptations in the next section.

CARRYING ON THE TRADITION

AT HOME
If there is any one particular thing that should be done today, it is displaying an extravagant gesture of love. With so much variation, see the ideas below.

Consider This
- Arrange and prepare a fancy dinner for family and/or friends tonight.
- Bake a more elaborate dessert tonight to add to dinner.
- Give an extra charitable donation to the Church or your local nonprofit.
- Don't put off that service project you've been wanting to do, but extend your efforts to those in need.
- Bring special foods to a local shelter for unhoused members of your town or city.
- Take balloons or flowers to a local care facility or assisted living residence.

IN THE PARISH
As with the Seven Fishes appreciation dinner mentioned in the Advent chapter, during this busy season when our volunteers put in many extra hours to help make Holy Week happen, you could arrange for another extravagant gratitude dinner for those members of your community.

Consider This
- Host a dinner in the parish hall for one of your special committees that puts in a lot of work around this season.
- Extend the gift of a Catholic book to your parishioners or groups. My parish has done this at times, and it has been helpful to receive free and enriching materials, especially to read during the Easter season.
- For those who are not at work during the day, you could lead a parish service project at a local shelter or even on your campus by making care packages.
- Give your congregation the opportunity to do something extraordinary this day, and highlight the story of Mary of Bethany.

Resource
You can find an Extravagant Monday dinner party guide and menu in the *Festive Faith Winter Ordinary Time, Lent, and Triduum Companion* at www. HisGirlSunday.com/FestiveFaith.

HOLY WEEK HOUSE CLEANING
MONDAY, TUESDAY, AND WEDNESDAY OF HOLY WEEK

THE STORY

Regularly referred to as spring cleaning, this ancient cleaning tradition is one that I look forward to every year, and it is typically done on the Monday, Tuesday, and Wednesday of Holy Week. Many homes can probably relate to the manner in which things begin to pile up over the months of the year, and busy schedules keep us from doing more detailed housework like dusting cracks and corners. From the customary Passover cleaning, we have received and adapted this practice from Jewish culture. With roots in the Old Testament the Jewish people would sweep, clean, and sanitize their homes of any food that can leaven or rise in preparation for Passover. As prescribed in Exodus 12:15, "For seven days you must eat unleavened bread. From the very first day you will have your houses clear of all leaven. For whoever eats leavened bread from the first day to the seventh will be cut off from Israel." Immediately following this was the direction to further ready their homes by slaughtering the Passover lamb and brushing its blood on the lintel and doorposts. In a similar way we, too, prepare our homes for the greatest feast of the year, Easter. Motivated by the upcoming celebration of Christ's Resurrection, as well as the passage from the cold and dark of winter into spring warmth, in various countries around the world Catholics will present some of the tidiest homes during Holy Week.

THE TRADITION

"All hands on deck" is a phrase that we use when cleaning a home that has been well lived in. Everyone has enjoyed the home and made the mess, so everyone must pitch in with readying the home for Easter and preparing a place for Christ. In the Czech Republic, each of these three days has its own unique name to reflect the duties assigned for the entire family to help with Easter preparations. On Blue Monday people typically didn't have to go to work, and spring break usually began at this time so children didn't have to go to school. Some believe that this name is from the Czech title of this day, *Modré pondělí*, which would translate to mean that everyone is called to rest from work. From a more Catholic perspective, Blue Monday is believed to have come from the local church's custom of hanging blue fabric in honor of Our Lady. In some smaller towns, parishes still do this. Either way, Monday of Holy Week is said to have been a day for rest in preparation for the upcoming days of cleaning. Gray Tuesday gets its name from the dust, dirt, and cobwebs that would get swept out and wiped down. Ugly Wednesday, or Black Wednesday, is when the chimneys would be swept after their frequent winter use.

It's not uncommon in the Czech Republic and in other places still to find some variation of this cleaning custom. Not everyone uses all three days, and of course because many homes no longer use chimneys to keep warm, the order of tasks has evolved a bit too. You can create your own chore chart for the Monday, Tuesday, and Wednesday of Holy Week that fits your own routine, local weather, and Catholic culture. If you're like me, Monday is for fine dining, and Tuesday and Wednesday are for cleaning to-dos, but be inspired to make this your own.

CARRYING ON THE TRADITION

AT HOME

Prepare your home for the Resurrection of Christ by developing a chore chart for these three days.

Consider This
- Create a routine and displayable cleaning chart that works for your family.
- An example might be that Monday is for clearing out and donating gently used clothes, toys, and home goods. Tuesday is for cleaning bedrooms, living spaces, and doing laundry. Wednesday is for cleaning bathrooms, the kitchen, and floors.
- You might also try assigning certain rooms in the house to specific days as opposed to tasks. Make this your own!
- Since we are only at the beginning of Holy Week, I recommend saving Easter decorating for Holy Saturday.

IN THE PARISH

The parish is the house of the Lord, and in the same manner that we clean our homes, the parish can also be cleaned and tidied before celebrating Easter. You might find it beneficial to encourage volunteers to sign up for this.

Consider This
- Tasks that volunteers can help with might include dusting, tidying, organizing, vacuuming, watering outdoor and indoor plants, and wiping down pews or walls.
- Arrange this as a day of service with Mass at the beginning, followed by an hour or two of cleaning, and then provide lunch or coordinate meeting somewhere to eat.
- You might consider adding other Holy Week tasks that the parish needs help with and presenting this as a parish work day where as a parish family we give back to our community and to God.

Resource
Don't be overwhelmed by the prospect of cleaning your home or parish; use the handy cleaning schedule that is in the *Festive Faith Winter Ordinary Time, Lent, and Triduum Companion* at www.HisGirlSunday.com/FestiveFaith.

SPY WEDNESDAY
THEMES LIVED OUT
WEDNESDAY OF HOLY WEEK

THE STORY

Holy Wednesday, or Spy Wednesday, gets its name from the sly and devious actions of Judas, who betrayed Jesus for thirty pieces of silver in the Gospel of Matthew. From the fifth century until recently, it was tradition to proclaim the Passion narrative of St. Luke at Mass on the Wednesday of Holy Week, which features prominently the betrayal of Judas. St. Luke's Passion tells how, before the Last Supper, Judas goes before the chief priests and makes a bargain to hand over Jesus in exchange for money. The agreement was for the chief priests to wait for the crowds around Jesus to dissipate, and Judas would "spy" for the right opportunity for them to arrest him. With a simple kiss, he compromises his friendship with Jesus and sets into motion the events that will lead to the death of Our Lord. The term "Spy Wednesday" was first recorded in Ireland in the early nineteenth century and has become popular again in recent years. It is a time of intense preparation, both externally and internally. For example, in Ireland Spy Wednesday's disciplines also included abstaining from milk and butter.

THE TRADITION

From spy movies to spy games, the creativity of modern Catholics has not disappointed. Every effort is an eager attempt to remember the betrayal of Christ in the garden, especially as it relates to us. The harsh reality is that we all want to be Mary from Extravagant Monday, while often forgetting how our own sinfulness also makes us Judas from time to time. Pius Parsch writes, "In everyone's heart, in my own too, there dwell two souls: a Judas-soul and a Mary-soul."[8] The gestures made on Wednesday of Holy Week pour forth from the hearts of those of us seeking greater recognition of our own frailty. Some Catholics seek to go to Confession today, if it is available to them, so that they can reflect on their own motives and actions. Being purified from the sins that keep us from Christ and his Church before Easter is one of the most important things we can do during this week. Faith-filled mothers and fathers also share the story of Judas in an age-appropriate way so that their children become more aware of the events leading to Jesus's Death and Resurrection. Conversations on honesty, true friendship, and right action are themes that unfold at the dining-room table. Coupled with sincere dialogue are activities such as hunting thirty coins throughout the house or enjoying a spy movie together. Most of these customs, which have developed within our American culture, are concrete ways for us to push away distraction and orient our homes toward Jesus.

CARRYING ON THE TRADITION

AT HOME

Given the newness of some of these traditions, it's important to let customs grow naturally and from a place of authentic desire to pass them on to others, particularly to members of a younger generation. Seek to embody the themes of Spy Wednesday by enriching your home with one of the following ideas that speaks to you most.

Consider This
- Go to Confession at a local parish.
- If you have children, let them hunt for thirty coins throughout the house. Once they have found those coins, they can save them in their piggy bank, or put them in the collection basket next time you go to Mass.
- Play a spy-inspired game like "I Spy."
- Watch a spy movie with a friend or your spouse.
- Give an extra thirty dollars to the Church on this day.

IN THE PARISH

Although the parish is readying itself for the Triduum, which begins tomorrow evening, it might still be beneficial to offer the opportunity for parishioners to come to Confession on this day. Tie this into the story of Judas's betrayal, reminding everyone that God always waits for us with love, renewal, and forgiveness.

Consider This
- Invite your local community to attend the Chrism Mass, the liturgy during which the sacramental oils and chrism are blessed and distributed to all the local parishes. This is typically held on Holy Thursday, at the diocesan cathedral, but in some dioceses it is celebrated earlier during Holy Week.

- Plan a time this evening for a Holy Thursday rehearsal.
- Before the Triduum begins, take a deep breath and create a last-minute checklist of remaining to-dos.

Resource
You can find a list of classic spy movies in the *Festive Faith Winter Ordinary Time, Lent, and Triduum Companion* at www.HisGirlSunday.com/FestiveFaith.

SIX

THE PASCHAL TRIDUUM

Let them mark the seasons, the days and the years.
—Genesis 1:14b

Begins: Mass of the Lord's Supper on Holy Thursday Evening
Ends: First Vespers of Easter on Easter Sunday
Natural Season: Early Spring
Triduum Disciplines: Accompaniment, Watchfulness, and
Rejoicing
Recommended Prayer: Prayer before the Crucifix
This prayer can be found in the Festive Faith Winter Ordinary
Time, Lent, and Triduum Companion *at www.HisGirlSunday.
com/FestiveFaith.*
Liturgical Colors: White and Red
*For planning purposes, some liturgical-living traditions from
the chapter on the Easter season can also be done within the
Paschal Triduum.*

The Easter Triduum, or the Paschal Triduum, is the summit of our liturgical year. *Triduum*, taken from the Latin, means "three days," and in the Catholic context they usually precede a feast of great importance. Regarding the Easter Triduum, the term is used to express the solemn three days of prayer that commemorate the Paschal Mystery—the mystery of Christ's Passion, Death, and Resurrection. The Easter Triduum begins at sundown on Holy Thursday with the Mass of the Lord's Supper and ends with Vespers on Easter Sunday near sundown. While our liturgical prayer spans three calendar days, it is in fact a single liturgical celebration. You may notice that we begin the Mass of the Lord's Supper as we do all Masses, but there is not a dismissal as with all other Masses. The Good Friday Celebration of the Lord's Passion begins with the Liturgy of the Word, and there is again no dismissal. The Easter Vigil, which is not to begin until the sun has well set, also doesn't begin with the usual introductory rites. Rather, it begins with the Service of Light, also known as the Lucernarium, which is usually outdoors where we all gather around for the lighting of the new fire, the Easter Candle, and then candles held by everyone attending. We all process into our churches, carrying our lit candles, representing Christ, our Light, and singing. Once in our places, the great Easter Proclamation is sung as we stand in the glow of candlelight. This is the mother of all vigils and appropriately lasts late into the night. This Mass concludes in the usual fashion, and then the Easter Sunday Masses are celebrated in much the same manner as other Sunday Masses.

Out of all the feasts and seasons that we celebrate each year, this is the most significant, because within the Paschal Triduum we can see and behold fulfillment of the prophets, the scriptures, and the covenants between God and his people. God kept his promise, and those promises were made so that original holiness, which was lost after the Fall, could be restored through the gift of eternal life in heaven. Christ is the Paschal Lamb and the spotless victim who is offered for our sins. In these three days we come to deeply know and feel the dying and the rising of Jesus and the reverberation of that throughout our own lives. In our broken state, all creation enters the darkness of death and the hope of resurrection. This unavoidable cycle can be witnessed through the seasons, the liturgical year, and our human existence. Even going to sleep has been considered a little death, a prefiguring of what is inevitable, coupled with our rising each morning. All things that die and rise are held within the sovereign power of God. This tells us that every fiber of our being is connected to the Paschal Mystery and the breadth of all of creation. The Passion, Death, and Resurrection of Jesus is not just an acclaimed series of events from a story in the Bible, nor simply historical events that occurred in the ancient Middle East. Rather, these events and our commemoration of them each and every year hold the fundamental and inescapable reality that marks us as God's people, holy and beloved, and as disciples of the Lord Jesus Christ.

God further reveals our participation in the Paschal Mystery by unfolding the Easter Triduum every Sunday, if not every day, through the Mass. In one solemn hour we enter into the Last Supper of Holy Thursday, the Sacrifice of Good Friday, and the Resurrection of Easter Sunday. The Eucharist, like the Easter Triduum, is called the summit of the Christian life, not coincidentally. Together the precious Body and Blood of Christ and the Triduum weave together a hallowed tapestry that depicts the redemptive work of God. Our liturgical living, while unquestionably heightened throughout these three days, can and should extend these liturgical truths throughout our every waking moment. When you can embrace that God created you for himself, that any separation from that must be reconciled, and that he loves *you,* then you can authentically and endlessly embody the Paschal Mystery, which is the heart of these three holy days, in your home and community.

ST. PHILIP NERI'S SEVEN CHURCHES TRADITION

THURSDAY OF HOLY WEEK

THE STORY

Holy Thursday, also known as Maundy Thursday, is the day on which we celebrate the institution of the Eucharist and of the ordained priesthood. At the Chrism Mass, held on Holy Thursday, or in some places earlier in Holy Week, priests will renew their vows. Some priests also renew their vows in their parish churches on Holy Thursday evening.

Holy Thursday commemorates the Last Supper, where Jesus gave his mandate—or *mandatum*, from which we get *Maundy*—to love one another as he has loved us and to "go, therefore, and make disciples of all nations, baptizing them in the name of the Father, and of the Son, and of the holy Spirit" (Mt 28:19). We commemorate this mandate by participating in the washing of feet, listening to the biblical account of the Last Supper, and recalling the institution of the Eucharist. After the Communion Rite of Mass, the altar is completely stripped and the tabernacle is emptied. All leave in silence and join in a procession to a special altar of repose for adoration. In some places a simple Eucharistic chant or hymn is sung during the procession to the place of reposition. The altar of repose is an altar other than the main altar where the consecrated host is kept for adoration and reserved for use on Good Friday. This altar should be unadorned and in a place that is removed from any trafficked areas of the parish campus. Adoration should take place continuously until the beginning of the Good Friday Celebration of the Lord's Passion.

St. Philip Neri, a sixteenth-century Italian priest, and his friends are said to have begun the tradition of visiting seven churches on the night of Holy Thursday. Together they would go on a pilgrimage to seven churches in one night. This grew out of a desire to increase prayer and keep with Christ's request to "remain here and keep watch" (Mk 14:34). This is also why this tradition is given the name *Night Watch*. By keeping with this custom, we, too, can become pilgrims staying with Christ in the garden and consoling him in his agony.

THE TRADITION

Countries around the globe, such as Mexico, Italy, the Philippines, Poland, and the United States, model St. Philip Neri's Holy Thursday ritual by gathering their friends and family to visit seven churches after the Mass of the Lord's Supper. The custom was meant to be done at night in honor of staying awake with Christ in the garden of Gethsemane, where he endured his agony before being arrested. As this tradition spread, it was adapted and began to take place during the day on Holy Thursday. This allowed for more participation, particularly by families with young children. Keep in mind that you might not find seven churches within your area with scheduled adoration, but you can still draw close to the tabernacle for a few minutes of quiet prayer time.

This particular tradition has long been a part of our family life and is a highlight of the Triduum for us. Going from church to church is like being welcomed into another parish family. You get the opportunity to breathe in the beauty of that church while sitting with Jesus in pensive prayer and contemplation.

We have attempted to do this tradition in various parts of our sprawling city, and one year we weren't even able to make it to all seven churches after the Holy Thursday liturgy because it took so much time to get from point A to point B. We knew in advance where we were going, but didn't detail each drive time, nor did we know the various hours that each church would be open for adoration. I realized then that I could help support Catholics in my city by coordinating with seven churches that were close to one another. The majority of parishes that I have worked with had never even heard of this, so it became a prime opportunity to revitalize a saintly tradition. From there I was able to arrange for seven churches to publicize a map that I developed for them with addresses, adoration times, an explanation of the tradition, and recommended prayers. If you are a part of a ministry group or a leader in a parish, you can do this too. This is a good opportunity to use your traditional adoration prayers such as the Anima Christi, Tantum Ergo, and Pange Lingua.

CARRYING ON THE TRADITION

AT HOME
Coordinate with friends and family to make the seven churches pilgrimage with you. Visit seven parishes in your area that are having Eucharistic Adoration, and spend a few minutes at each one in prayer either during the day on Holy Thursday, or after the Mass of the Lord's Supper in the evening hours.

Consider This
- If you can't go at night, adapt this by visiting each church during the day on Holy Thursday.
- Plan ahead of time by seeing what parishes are closest to you, and call in advance to make sure each church will be open.
- Prepare a couple of adoration prayers to bring with you in advance.

IN THE PARISH
Create a seven churches guide and map for those in your community looking to participate. Call six other parishes nearest to you and see what time they will offer Eucharistic Adoration. In the weeks leading up to Holy Week, offer this guide to your parishioners.

Consider This
- Your guide could have any variation of the following things: Six parishes in addition to your own to visit, their adoration times, a map with drive time, the explanation of the tradition, and prayer suggestions for adoration.
- Since starting this in my city, the parishes that I have coordinated get an influx of visitors. To welcome new people, I placed a hospitality table at the entrance of our parish with upcoming event flyers and small treats for people to take on their way out. You might try something similar in your parish.

Fill in and share the Seven Churches Guide found in the *Festive Faith Winter Ordinary Time, Lent, and Triduum Companion* at www.HisGirlSunday.com/FestiveFaith. You can also use the list of suggested prayers for adoration.

HOT CROSS BUNS FOR GOOD FRIDAY

FRIDAY OF HOLY WEEK

THE STORY

Hot cross buns! Hot cross buns!
One a' penny, two a' penny,
Hot cross buns!
If you have no daughters,
Give them to your sons
One a' penny, Two a' penny,
Hot Cross Buns!

Hot cross buns are a delicious spiced bun traditionally made on Good Friday. They are believed to have been made in the fourteenth century by the monks at St. Alban's Abbey in Hertfordshire, England, who were seeking to feed the poor. The Alban bun, or the hot cross bun, was not piped with a cross as it is today, but scored in accordance with the widely accepted practice of blessing the bread in thanksgiving to God. The cross also stands to symbolize and remind us of the Crucifixion of Christ. Many current recipes call for the cross to be made with icing, which seems counterintuitive to the Good Friday penance of fasting and abstinence, so instead you could use a flour-based paste to pipe the cross. Hot cross buns are also packed with spices to signify the burial ritual that Jesus underwent. Some even use citrus fruits to remind us of the bitterness that comes with the Cross. You may find further variation from country to country, but the ideal of this tradition remains the same: to develop an internal hunger on Good Friday that only Christ himself can satiate.

THE TRADITION

Hot cross buns pair nicely with a simple soup that can be served after attending the Celebration of the Lord's Passion, once commonly known as the Liturgy of the Presanctified Gifts. Today is the only day in the liturgical year in which the Blessed Sacrament is not consecrated, instead we consume the Eucharist which was consecrated yesterday. You might even try baking the hot cross buns while keeping silence, praying, and reflecting on the sacrifice of Christ crucified. The healing that baking can bring to a home and heart is exactly what we need on a day when we recall and enter into anew the Passion and Death of Our Lord. And how much more might we feel consoled as we add each meaningful ingredient to create these buns with their rich tradition and theological symbolism.

In addition to making hot cross buns, some households attempt to observe an hour of silence on Good Friday. Others keep near silence, only speaking what is necessary from nine in the morning until three in the afternoon, the hours traditionally held as the time during which Jesus was crucified and died on the Cross. You might try doing this, too, with practical adaptations to fit the age ranges and needs of your household or your workplace. My husband and I usually pray one of these three prayers on Good Friday with unassuming desire to be joined with Christ in his death: Prayer before the Crucifix, Stations of the Cross, or the Sorrowful Mysteries of the Rosary.

The liturgy of Good Friday is one of somberness. It is stark and tightly focused. As mentioned earlier, the Celebration of the Passion of the Lord is not Mass, although the faithful receive the Body of Christ in hosts that were consecrated at the Holy Thursday Mass of the Lord's Supper. Rather, the focus of this liturgy is the proclamation of the Passion according to the Gospel of John, extended intercessions marked by kneeling in silent prayer between petitions, and the Veneration of the Cross. The rubrics of the *Roman Missal* call for the liturgy to begin at 3:00 p.m., the hour that the gospels tell us Jesus took his last breath. We walk into our churches with altars completely bare, and the Eucharist is not in the tabernacle. The door is left open so that we can see its emptiness and feel unsettled because this day is like no other. Today is the only day in the liturgical year when Mass is not permitted. According to Dom Gaspar Lefebvre, "Such is the impression produced on the whole Christian world on Good Friday, when the throne of the Cross, from the height of which God made man reigns, stands out stained with His Blood before the world on Calvary, that the Church shrinks on this day from renewing that sacrifice on her altars. She is content therefore . . . to consume the Holy Species that have previously been consecrated. Hence the term Mass of the Presanctified . . ."[1]

The tradition of venerating the wood of the cross comes to us from St. Helen, who was said to have discovered the wood of the True Cross after her conversion to Christianity. As early as the fourth century, the faithful of Jerusalem would come to honor the Cross on Good Friday by kissing it. Now we imitate this practice by venerating a cross in our parish churches. In some places, the faithful bow and kiss the cross, while others kneel and kiss the cross, and still others bow and reverently touch the cross. Expressions vary, and sometimes the physical needs of individuals dictate how the act of veneration is carried out. The specific manner is not as important as each member of the faithful being encouraged and helped to venerate the Cross on Good Friday with reverence and simplicity.

While Good Friday brings about big emotions, it is not meant to bring about big schedules. Go slowly, mourn the loss of Jesus beside Mary, and pray for all who suffer the pains of death and illness. Seek peace and strength through traditions like baking hot cross buns, reverencing the cross, and making space for silence and prayer.

CARRYING ON THE TRADITION

AT HOME
Before or after the Good Friday liturgy, gather your family or other loved ones around your kitchen to make hot cross buns. As you add each symbolic ingredient, explain why it is being used. Serve them warm with a simple bowl of meatless soup.

Consider This
- If you don't have time to bake them from scratch, you might pick them up from a local store or bakery.
- You could also bake simple dinner rolls and pipe a cross over the top.
- Serve them as they are, or pair them with your favorite meat-free soup for a simple Lenten Good Friday meal.
- Bake enough to share with a neighbor, friends, or coworkers as a way to spread the tradition. Write out the story to go along with them so that others know why you're making hot cross buns on this day.

IN THE PARISH

The monks who are credited with this practice were seeking to serve the poor. Imitate this sense of service to your community by organizing opportunities for parishioners to be among underserved populations in your locale. Perhaps invite parishioners to bake and share hot cross buns with those who are unhoused, are staying in a shelter, or live in a nursing-care facility. Attend to spiritual needs within the parish, helping the community embrace the humility of the Cross by becoming poor in spirit.

Consider This
- Offer the Sacrament of Penance on Good Friday and Holy Saturday, or if your parish cannot accommodate this, provide parishioners a list of parishes that will be available for the sacrament.
- Provide a time for a communal praying of the Stations of the Cross, or make Stations booklets available for individuals in church.
- Offer the Tre Ore (Three Hours) devotion to your parishioners. This is a prayer opportunity that is traditionally held on Good Friday that lasts from noon to 3:00 p.m. to commemorate the three hours that Jesus hung on the cross. Within that time, a series of reflections or homilies are given on the last seven words of Christ in addition to suitable hymns and silent reflection.
- Extend the opportunity for parishioners to bring nonperishable food items for the poor.

Resource
You can find a Hot Cross Buns recipe in the *Festive Faith Winter Ordinary Time, Lent, and Triduum Companion* at www.HisGirlSunday.com/FestiveFaith.

A LIVING TRADITION

While fasting on Good Friday is not "merely" a tradition, but an obligation for most Catholics, it still holds a special place in my heart. As a teenager, our Good Friday fast always started strong, but by the time we got home from the Good Friday liturgy with the Veneration of the Cross, everyone was hungry, and we all had to work at not letting our tempers get the best of us. We'd come home and make a big pot of pasta, our one meal for the day, before winding down and calling it an early night. In college, I really tried to "buckle down" and embrace the ascetic aspect of the fast, choosing less filling or less "tasty" foods for my two small meals, and stretching myself longer and longer before taking that first food for the day. I had this idea that one day I wouldn't even need the two small snacks, that I could be some sort of next-level Catholic and fast like the earliest Christians did.

Now that I am in my adult years, married, and experiencing pregnancy, fasting in these circumstances is often imprudent. At least in the United States, pregnant and nursing mothers are exempted from the annual fast. This definitive exemption has been a blessing to me in my often-prideful ambition to "be the best Catholic." I find that I miss fasting, even as I recognize that it would not be good for me in my current season. I miss the choice to let hunger gnaw away at my insides, a constantly recurring call from the Lord to return to him. An all-day, intentional fast means that even if I give in to the temptation to complain or let my hunger drive me to snap at someone, I can constantly choose to return to the Lord and to offer once again that small physical suffering to be joined to him in his Passion. It is easy to act as if we, in the twenty-first century, have grown past the need for signs and symbols. But the reality is that because we are embodied souls, fasting from the physical necessity of food offers us a unique and important opportunity to bring our awareness back to our infinite dependence on God for everything we have and are.

Sara Dietz

THE PASCHAL CANDLE
EASTER VIGIL ON HOLY SATURDAY

THE STORY

It is not clear exactly when the paschal candle became a universal part of the Easter Vigil, but we know the inspiration for it goes back as far as the third century. The tradition grew out of the custom of blessing a fire and lighting a candle as part of Vespers or Evening Prayer from what we now know as the Liturgy of the Hours. This custom of lighting candles just before nightfall is also thought to be inspired by the Jewish tradition of lighting the Shabbat (Sabbath) candles at the conclusion of the Sabbath. Early Christians saw this practice as a way to physically represent that Christ was in their midst. This is no longer commonly done as a part of Evening Prayer, but the Lucernarium has lived on in the Easter Vigil on Holy Saturday night.

From Christian antiquity, around the fourth century, we have the earliest references to the development of the *Laus Cerei* (Praise of the Candle), which is a prayer of blessing and praise for the candle. As the rites and prayers grew over the centuries, so did the size of the candle. The beeswax candle expanded in width and height to fit the description of it as a "pillar of brilliant light" by Eusebius at the time of Emperor Constantine. The emperor "transformed the night of the sacred vigil into the brilliancy of day, by lighting throughout the whole city pillars of wax . . . so that this mystic vigil was rendered brighter than the brightest daylight."[2] The paschal candle, new each year and blessed at the beginning of the Easter Vigil, is positioned within our churches as a revered sacramental that stands brightly and strongly as a sign that Christ is with us.

THE TRADITION

Tonight, we will encounter the most gloriously dramatic liturgy of the entire year, the "mother of all vigils," to celebrate the triumphant Resurrection of the Lord. The *Roman Missal* says this is the "greatest and most noble of all solemnities and it is to be unique in every single Church."[3] Just as we kept watch on Holy Thursday in the garden and Good Friday by the Cross, we keep watch again as we wait to be made new in the glory of Christ's Resurrection.

In accordance with ancient custom, we begin this evening with everyone assembled outside in the stillness of night. The Easter fire is kindled, and we are to receive it as a sign of hope, a light in the darkness that unifies us through its beauty and warmth. From this we can also draw the same connections that we did from the changing of seasons from Advent to Christmas. The liturgical cycle is yet again proclaiming the redemptive work of Christ. We must be attentive and watchful, not only to specific seasons, but as a more holistic integration of preparing ourselves for the Second Coming.

During this most holy night, as Lenten disciplines give way to Easter joy, the Paschal Candle is given light from the new fire, full of symbolism and meaning. The candle dispels not only the darkness in which we stand but the darkness of our hearts and minds. The fact that the candle is made predominantly, if not fully, out of beeswax recalls the praise of the purity of the bees that was described in the section on Candlemas in Winter Ordinary Time. The cross that is etched into the candle represents Christ and his suffering for our salvation. Greek letters for Alpha and Omega are also on the candle to show that Christ is our beginning and our end. The four numerals of the current calendar year remind us that Jesus reigns over time and eternity. The year in which we mark and bless this holy candle is now sanctified by our actions. Five grains of incense are also molded into wax nails and inserted into the candle to represent the five wounds of Christ.

The Paschal Candle is then lifted high for all to see, and a deacon or priest chants, "Christ our light!" Those assembled chant in response, "Thanks be to God!" A procession to the church entrance begins. At the door of the church, the procession stops, the Paschal Candle is again raised up, and the two-line call-and-response chant is again sung. Then the light of the great candle is shared with all those gathered, who light their own smaller candles from it and one another. All process by candlelight into the dark church, pausing once more for the raising of the Paschal Candle and singing of the simple chant. The United States Conference of Catholic Bishops notes, "Just as the children of Israel were guided at night by the pillar of fire, so Christians follow the risen Christ."[4]

The liturgical celebration of the Easter Vigil is an impactful encounter with God and with our fellow Catholics around the world. There is so much depth and generational history to this evening that each year you attend you might learn or receive something entirely new. As a way to hold on to this specific custom, Catholics have even sought to bring their own version of the Paschal Candle into their home. Because home is where we spend most of our time, it has become a way for us to harness the hope and acclamation of Easter into our everyday life. Some Catholics purchase a beeswax pillar candle and etch the same symbols into it as a way of imitating the church's candle. Catholic Paschal Candle stickers and pin sets have been created to affix to a candle. During dinner or prayer time, the home version of the Paschal Candle is lit to represent Christ being in our midst and as a clear reminder that we are called to be made new in him.

On Holy Saturday we sit metaphorically at the tomb of Christ in imitation of Mary and mourn his death. It is a solemn day when we remember the scars of his powerful suffering and wait faithfully for the Resurrection. On this day, apart from the Easter Vigil, no Mass is offered and Communion is only given to those near death, who receive the Sacrament of Anointing of the Sick and *viaticum* (meaning "food for the journey"). We also commemorate the "harrowing of hell," wherein Jesus descends into hell to deliver the holy souls into heaven. You may have noticed that we say this in the creed, and perhaps it seems like a rather peculiar event. The *Catechism of the Catholic Church* explains to us that Christ went down to Sheol, the abode of the dead, to free the just who had gone before him that were awaiting the redeemer (*CCC*, 633). We are taught that this is the last phase of Jesus's messianic mission.

CARRYING ON THE TRADITION

AT HOME

Create your own Paschal Candle as a way of bringing the light of Christ into your domestic church throughout the year.

Consider This

- Buy a pillar candle, and if you can, get one made out of beeswax.
- Think about how you want to secure the symbols to your candle. You can carve them or you can purchase a kit for this purpose.
- Explain to those in your household what each symbol means, or read the section from this book to them as you are getting your candle set up.
- Light your at-home Paschal Candle throughout the Easter Season, maybe at dinner time each day or each Sunday. Also, consider lighting the candle for festive celebrations all year long, such as sacramental anniversaries, solemnities, birthdays, special feast days, or regular prayer time.

IN THE PARISH

Keep the Paschal Candle in a stand, and place it in the sanctuary or next to the ambo during the Easter Season. While there is usually not enough time within the context of the Easter Vigil to explain the profound symbolism of the candle, find a time in the upcoming weeks to communicate its importance as being far more than just another candle. Include this explanation in the parish bulletin for Easter Sunday, with reference to the Service of Light at the Easter Vigil.

Consider This

- Throughout the Easter season, be sure the Paschal Candle is lit for every Mass and solemn liturgical celebration.
- After the Easter season, place the candle near your baptismal font and light it each time a new member of the Church is baptized.
- During funerals, place the candle next to the coffin and light it as a way of showing that the Christian who is deceased was baptized in Christ Jesus, was baptized into his Death, and, we pray, is baptized into his Resurrection.
- When changing to the new candle, if much remains of the previous year's candle, it can be given to a family or member of the parish to be

burned in the home so that it is honored to the last light and not discarded irreverently.

SEVEN

EASTERTIDE

Christ yesterday and today, the beginning and the end,
Alpha and omega, all time belongs to him and all the ages;
to him be glory and power through every age for ever.

—Service of Light, Easter Vigil

Begins: Easter Sunday
Ends: Pentecost Sunday
Natural Season: Spring
Easter Disciplines: Praise and Joy
Recommended Prayer: Regina Caeli
Liturgical Colors: White

The fifty days of the Easter season or Eastertide are a time in which all of creation seems to sings God's praises. Springtime begins to showcase its charming colors, with new growth and warmer days. People seem to walk with a lighter disposition, and the aroma of fresh flavors pours out of our homes as we shake off the chill and darker days of winter and early spring. Again, we see the harmony between the rebirth of the natural cycles here in the northern hemisphere and the cycles of our liturgical life, as both are ringing out the same proclamation, Jesus Christ is risen. The Easter Season begins with the Easter Octave—the eight days that begin on Easter Sunday and continue through to Divine Mercy Sunday, which ushers in the second week of Easter. You can think of the Easter Octave extending the solemnity of Easter Sunday over each day: Easter Monday, Tuesday, Wednesday and so on.

One of the things that I enjoy most about being Catholic is that important celebrations don't last only one day. The covenants have been fulfilled, Jesus has shown that he is Lord, the just souls have received their reward, darkness and death have been defeated, and the gates of heaven are open to us. Alleluia! Alleluia! Alleluia! We cannot comprehend the magnitude of this, especially within one day, and the Church in her wisdom knows this. We need time to meditate and immerse ourselves in the great mysteries of our faith. As Pius Parsch explains, "Mother Church is a good psychologist; she understands human nature perfectly. When a feast comes, the soul is amazed and not quite prepared to think profoundly upon its mystery; but on the following days the mind finds it easy to consider the mystery from all sides, sympathetically and deeply; and an eighth day affords a wonderful opportunity to make a synthesis of all points covered."[1] It is indeed true that we need more time, not only for rejoicing, but to learn how to celebrate for the length of a season.

The fifty days of the Easter season provide an opportunity to adjust our thoughts and patterns of behavior, reflecting on all that has been given to us. Within this chapter you will find Easter-oriented experiences to help you stay focused on the gift of Christ's Resurrection. St. John Paul II wrote, "We are an Easter people, and Alleluia is our song." What comes next in his writing speaks to the responsibility we have to live joyfully for the sake of the kingdom of God. St. John Paul II goes on to say, "We are not looking for shallow joy but rather a joy that comes from faith, that grows through unselfish love, that respects the 'fundamental duty of love of neighbor, without which it would be unbecoming to speak of joy.' We realize that joy is demanding; it demands unselfishness; it demands a readiness to say with Mary: 'Be it done unto me according to thy word.'"[2] Nurturing joy takes effort, and the same holds true for liturgical living. So often we want to make things short, sweet, and easy; however, offering love and praise requires us to deepen our commitments to God, Mary, and the saints. Jesus gives everything to us, holding nothing back, and now we must diligently offer the same to him and others.

Extend your sense of wonder with me over this principal feast. Bask in the season of triumph in blessedness and gratitude. Be inspired to live in accordance with this new life that has been offered to us through the Resurrection of Christ Jesus, Our Lord.

RED EASTER EGGS

THE STORY

The story goes that after the Death and Resurrection of Jesus, Mary Magdalene went to Rome to have an audience with Emperor Tiberius Caesar to criticize the way that Jesus's trial was handled. Her desire was to try to have Pontius Pilate removed from his role as governor of Judea for having Jesus, an innocent man, sentenced to death. She told the emperor that Jesus had risen from the dead and that he was no longer in the tomb. To further prove her point, she picked up an egg from his table, which was a pre-Christian symbol of the earth's springtime regeneration, and extended it toward him, declaring what is now known as the universal Easter proclamation, "Christ is risen!" The emperor mocked her by saying that Jesus had no more risen from the dead and returned to life than the egg in her hand was red. As he sarcastically spoke these words, the egg that she held miraculously turned red.

A Polish version of this story says that Mary Magdalene brought a basket of white hard-boiled eggs with her to the tomb of Jesus, possibly as a meal for herself and the others that joined her that morning. When she arrived at the tomb and saw that the stone had been rolled away and the tomb was empty, the eggs in her basket changed from white to all the colors of a rainbow. These legends of the saints from our Catholic folk heritage may not be historically precise, but they serve as beautiful stories that convey deeper truths of the faith.

THE TRADITION

The egg is considered to be a symbol of the Resurrection because it signifies new life. The hardness of the shell has been likened to the tomb that Jesus was laid in after his Passion and Death. Customarily the eggs are dyed on Holy Thursday in various shades of red to represent the blood of Christ. Unlike our modern egg-dyeing technique, in the past natural onion skins were used as opposed to food coloring to achieve the bold colors. In both Eastern and Western Christianity, there has long been a practice of blessing the dyed eggs as a part of concluding the Lenten fast.

A traditional Greek Easter egg game that follows the Resurrection Service is a competitive egg-cracking game called *tsougrisma*, which means "clinking-together" or "clashing." In this game one person taps their egg against another person's, the one with the cracked egg is declared as the loser, and the winner gets to play again against the winner from another pair. This continues on until only one person and their uncracked red egg remains. While done in good fun, this game also symbolizes the shattering of hell and Christ's victory over the tomb. There are newspaper accounts from the 1930s and 1940s in New York City of the various games, rituals, and rules surrounding this popular tradition.

You can continue this tradition by dyeing your own red eggs during the Triduum or the Easter season. Try playing the egg-tapping game with your family or friends, or pass on a red egg as a way to proclaim to those in your community that Christ is risen. One year I bought small wooden eggs and painted them red with delicate designs as Easter gifts for loved ones. Now every year they can put their red egg out in their home and let it proclaim the Good News of the Resurrection to all their guests.

CARRYING ON THE TRADITION

AT HOME
During the Easter season, continue proclaiming and unveiling the joy of the Resurrection by painting or dyeing Easter eggs red.

Consider This
- You can integrate this tradition into your usual Easter egg dyeing routine, or you can turn this into another opportunity within the Easter season.
- Play the egg-cracking game with your family or friends, and give a small prize to the winner.
- Give a red egg to someone else—a neighbor, friend, coworker, or family member—as a festive way to share the joy of the Resurrection of Christ.
- Dyeing the eggs is one option, but you could also hand-paint the eggs.

IN THE PARISH
Organize an egg-coloring event for one of your ministry groups or the faith formation families. Encourage participants to paint or dye red eggs, and share the stories of St. Mary Magdalene and the eggs.

Consider This

- Plan ahead and provide the materials for your participants, or ask them to donate eggs, red dye, or red paint with brushes.
- Play the egg-cracking game, and give a small prize to the winner.
- Display the red eggs in the public spaces of your parish as a way to share with parishioners and visitors the story of the Resurrection.
- Share the origin stories and details of the tradition in your publications at some point throughout the Easter season. Encourage parishioners to adapt the custom in their homes with friends or family.

Resource
Color your Easter eggs red with my recipe for natural egg dye listed in the *Festive Faith Easter and Summer Ordinary Time Companion* at www.HisGirlSunday.com/FestiveFaith.

GERMANY'S CHARMING EASTER EGG TREES

HOLY SATURDAY, EASTER SUNDAY, OR WITHIN THE EASTER SEASON

THE STORY

This quaint Easter custom is a tradition with a mysterious beginning, but it finds its most prominent history in Germany. The Easter egg is a universally known Christian symbol that represents renewal, rebirth, and new life. In homes across the world, friends and family sit down to dye this Resurrection symbol. While some German families and their children do that, too, their longer-standing observance has been to paint the eggs. After they are creatively adorned, it's common in some places to have an Easter egg hunt. In neighborhoods across Germany, however, they hang their eggs on trees or bushes. This tree or bush is known as an *Ostereierbaum*, or Easter egg tree. It can also be found in Poland, Austria, and Hungary. Some individuals are known for their considerable effort in adorning their Easter egg trees, and as others walk or drive by their homes, they are captivated by the splendor of the season. The

Easter egg tree stands as a reminder of the gladness we share as we reflect and rejoice over the Resurrection of Jesus.

THE TRADITION

Decorating indoor and outdoor trees with eggs is an Eastertide ritual that is still leaving impressions on the hearts and minds of the faithful. As I was giving a talk to a group of military wives on how they can live liturgically in the midst of a transitory lifestyle, a woman raised her hand and shared her experience of these elegant egg trees from when her husband and family were stationed in Germany. She explained to me that during this season it is impossible to go outside and not see and feel the Easter season all around you. In fact, there is a popularly shared story of a local family who has decorated their trees with eggs for the last several decades, each year striving to add more. In 2012 they had more than ten thousand eggs bringing life and color to their property. It is nothing short of amazing to see what people will do out of honest love for their Catholic faith, culture of origin, their neighbors, and God.

I remember Easter egg trees from my childhood; somehow this enchanting tradition made its way to some of the Southern states, but the trees were mostly enjoyed indoors. Where I live now, many, if not most, Christians don't decorate the exteriors of their homes for the Easter season, yet I can identify many other religious and secular instances where doorsteps are embellished. If we acknowledge that we are in the holiest time of our year, it seems reasonable that we should proclaim that outwardly.

Easter egg trees are within our reach; all we need is a tree or bush in our front yard, or even a faux or real plant inside our home. There are various techniques that you can use for stringing eggs, including blowing out the yolk of a natural egg, placing a hook with string in a wooden egg, or more simply purchasing eggs ready to hang. Maybe you can turn the task of gathering branches into an exciting adventure. Arrange them in a vase, and then hang your dyed or painted eggs on the branches. You can also string festive ribbons on your branches to add more color and fullness. Keep the Easter egg tree up for the entire fifty days of Easter as a way to rekindle a tradition that makes us more aware of Jesus's sacrificial love for us and the new life we continually find in him.

CARRYING ON THE TRADITION

AT HOME
Imitate Germany's attention-grabbing Easter custom by adorning your outdoor or indoor trees with beautifully dyed or painted Easter eggs.

Consider This
- You can practice blowing out natural eggs to hang them, or you can use plastic or wooden eggs to embellish your trees and bushes.
- Invite your family, friends, or children to help you hang Easter eggs.
- Think about adorning your trees and bushes with colorful ribbon.

IN THE PARISH
Proclaim the Resurrection through the symbol of the Easter egg on your parish grounds. Create an opportunity for parishioners and guests to be inspired by the colorful expression of Easter joy as they drive onto your campus.

Consider This
- Gather a group of volunteers to string and hang Easter eggs on trees or bushes on your parish property.
- Allow the children in faith formation and the youth group, and other parish groups who might be interested, to decorate the eggs that will be displayed.
- Explain the meaning of the Easter egg and the reason why this outward expression of Easter is important to see in a secular world.

A LIVING TRADITION

In the summer of 1987, my parents moved our family from northern Louisiana to Northwest Houston, Texas. My father transitioned from truck stop owner to executive oil marketer. Our new lifestyle came with experiences we had never known before—for instance, shopping all day for the mere pleasure of shopping. The local favorite was a section of town named Old Town Spring. The streets of Old Town Spring were lined with old houses that now held cafes, antiques, and the delicacies of yesteryear. When my mother and I visited during the springtime, it seemed everyone displayed the same décor welcoming the Easter season, specifically Easter eggs that hung on strings in trees. Some homes had small trees or just branches inside that dangled the colored ovals from fishing line. Other shops had moved the levitating eggs to outside trees, like confetti thrown within the green of the leaves. It was not until I was a married woman, spending my days scrolling the empty promises of social media, that I saw these beautiful displays dispersed on various accounts, and my memory was reengaged. I found myself desperately wanting to re-create my own version of this Easter egg kaleidoscope inside my home. The desire felt nostalgic and familiar. I wanted to have Easter eggs hanging from anywhere I could "plant" a tree! When I discovered this tradition was established in Germany—way before 1987—it made perfect sense. The part of Texas where my family had landed, and where I decided to raise my own family, had been a German settlement. My French-Cajun heart had fallen in love with a German Easter tradition, and I was home.

Liv Harrison

FLYING EASTER BELLS AND EGG HUNTS

EASTER SUNDAY OR WITHIN THE EASTER SEASON

THE STORY

The church bells of France ring brilliantly throughout towns and villages multiple times a day. They chime out their call for the faithful to come to church and to be aware of a special holy hour. It is a regular sound of life, until we get to Maundy Thursday. On the first day of the Triduum the bells fall silent, and while you might think they have been turned off or not rung out of ceremonial respect, you are mistaken. According to tradition, the bells have sprouted wings, packed up their bags, and flown out to Rome. The silence is attributed to them being gone. Folklore has it that the church bells carry with them to the Vatican the grief of everyone who is mourning the death of Our Lord. Every year on this day they go to visit the pope so they can be blessed before proudly ringing out the Resurrection on Easter Sunday. On their way back from their papal blessing, the bells fill themselves with chocolates, treats, and Easter eggs for the children to enjoy on Easter Sunday. Before returning to their steeples, the bells toss chocolates in Easter baskets left out overnight and scatter eggs in the gardens. On the morning of Easter Sunday as the church bells jubilantly toll their song, the children wake up to find what the Easter bells have left for them.

THE TRADITION

From this tale comes a morning of Easter excitement and playfulness. This story somewhat coincides with what many American children have been told: that the Easter Bunny will come overnight to leave a special treat in their Easter baskets and to hide the decorated eggs in the yard (or around the house if the weather isn't suitable for outdoor egg hunting). Yet this fantastical story of flying bells also signals to those who hear it a sense of alignment with the liturgical season. The way in which the bells fall silent reflects the restraint we practice at the start of the Triduum as we approach the stark somberness of Good Friday. The bells are blessed by the pope so that they can ring more triumphantly for the greatest feast of the year. This sort of rich, resonant storytelling gives voice to our faith and preserves our cultural heritages, which can be delighted in from generation to generation.

This story and practice are especially worth considering in our American culture that tends to separate the tradition of hunting eggs from the meaning of Easter. While the religious association is not strictly in the egg hunt itself, there is meaning to the egg, which represents springtime and resurrection, and in the reason we dye them, as we discussed in the "Red Easter Eggs" section above. The stories we tell give language to the beliefs we hold dear to us. Perhaps this tradition can become an invitation to reflect on the current Easter egg hunt practices that are within your family. Waiting to participate in egg hunts until we have reached the appropriate time in the Church's calendar can help us to live in the present liturgical moment. While our traditions may therefore look a little different from what others around us are doing, our Catholic-centered customs can be an anchor of faith.

CARRYING ON THE TRADITION

AT HOME

On Holy Saturday, share the story of the French church bells flying off to Rome at Easter with children in your home, neighborhood, or extended family. Encourage the children (or everyone gathered) to leave their Easter baskets on the dining-room table or other special place that night. Tell them to come see on Easter morning what the Easter bells left them in their baskets. On Easter Sunday, enjoy an egg hunt together.

Consider This
- Think about waiting to partake in Easter egg hunts until the Easter season itself.
- Have you been looking for a more Catholic tale to share with your Easter basket and egg hunting traditions? Begin telling this one!
- Add a few religious Catholic items to Easter baskets this year to help all who receive them grow in the faith.

IN THE PARISH

Share the story of the Easter bells with the members of your community so they can carry that out into their homes. Offer an Easter egg hunt on Sunday morning or one day during the Easter Octave for the children of your parish to partake in.

Consider This
- Convene a team of volunteers to hide Easter eggs for the children of your parish. Maybe this needs to happen at some point on Saturday, since most have family obligations on Sunday. Or perhaps there is another day more suitable; if so, recruit egg hiders for that day.
- If there are a lot of children at your parish, create Easter egg hunt rotations: one in the morning and one in the evening. Adapt the times to fit your parish needs.
- For the Easter egg hunt, create a photo booth where families can gather and take an Easter picture.
- Invite your parish priests or deacons to make themselves available to be a part of these festivities.

BLESSED BASKETS OF FOOD: AN EASTER MEAL PREPARATION

BEFORE OR AFTER THE EASTER VIGIL,
ON HOLY SATURDAY, OR ON EASTER SUNDAY

THE STORY

Most commonly associated with the Polish community, the blessing of the Easter baskets is said to have started in the seventh century and spread to a multitude of ethnic groups across the globe. After a long and difficult Lenten fast of not eating meat, eggs, dairy, and fats, we can imagine Christians had a pronounced anticipation for the start of Eastertide. The morning of Holy Saturday, families would gather in the kitchen to collect the special foods that would be used for their Easter meal into a basket. Each item was given a symbolic meaning. Butter might be shaped like a paschal lamb; special Easter bread was made in honor of Christ who is the True Bread; eggs were elaborately painted and embellished with markings made from beeswax; ham or sausage showed that Jesus fulfilled the Old Law, which forbade these meats; salt reminded the faithful of how we are to flavor the earth or to be witnesses of the Resurrection. Poppy-seed rolls prompted people to consider the sweetness of loving Christ; candles served as a reminder that Jesus is the Light of the World; flowers or greenery acted as a sign of joyful springtime; horseradish symbolized the bitterness of Jesus's Passion and Death; and wine represented the blood of Christ. A linen cover that was often delicately embroidered and pulled back during the blessing symbolized the veil being torn when Jesus conquered death. These linens were regularly kept as family heirlooms and handed down to help keep this Holy Saturday practice alive and to share the faith with next generations. On Saturday afternoon there would be a small ceremony at local churches for the faithful to gather and receive priestly blessings for the contents of their Easter baskets, which they would then enjoy on Easter Sunday.

THE TRADITION

Blessing food is commonplace for us, especially as Catholics, as we do this every time we sit down to have a meal. We pray Grace before Meals: "Bless us, O Lord, and these thy gifts, which we are about to receive from thy bounty, through Christ our Lord. Amen." The extraordinary thing about the Easter food blessing is the way that it draws upon our human experience. We have a physical need and connectedness to the land that sustains us and gives us life. After several weeks of being without some key ingredients, especially in the early centuries of the Church, Christians experienced a physical deprivation. To be able to compile and offer this basket of rich foods to God and then share it with their families was an imitation of the way Jesus offers his body for us as eternal bread. While we today do not know the same strictness of the Lenten fast as our ancestors in faith, we have still been in a spiritual desert if we have faithfully kept our Lenten disciplines. Having our festive foods blessed by our parish priest affords us the opportunity to be claimed by Jesus and consecrated to him anew. We are spiritually nourished by the Paschal Mystery, and in this case the food that we bring is given a sacred purpose and benefit.

I have noticed that more parishes are starting to offer this blessing on Holy Saturday as people have grown more aware of it and truly desire to have their Easter food blessed. You can include the ingredients listed above, each with their own Catholic connection, or you can load your basket with the ingredients that you will be using to create Easter's feast—no matter how big or small, fancy or simple. Whatever you fill your basket with, seek out a parish that offers this blessing, if your own does not.

Maybe this year you can mold your butter into the shape of a lamb for your family (many grocery stores also sell lamb-shaped butter), helping to remind everyone at the table of the underlying meaning of your Easter lunch or dinner. This might also be the perfect occasion to begin the warm family practice of handing down an heirloom linen. Purchase or make one for covering your basket, or over several years, make one for each child you want to become a recipient. Hand down these Easter linens to your children or godchildren. Through enriching experiences such as these, we can show our families the gift of hospitality, memories, and meals together.

CARRYING ON THE TRADITION

AT HOME

Prepare a basket of meaningful foods or the items that you will use to make your Easter Sunday meal. Then take it to your parish or a neighboring parish to have it blessed.

Consider This

- Create a list of the foods you want to gather in your basket.
- If your own culture or family has meaningful ingredients or foods used on Easter, ensure that they make the list.
- Find a worthy and large-enough basket to hold your foods. You don't need to spend a lot of money! Often thrift shops have good offerings, or if you plan well in advance, you can check at yard sales throughout the summer. Crafting store sales can also be helpful here.
- Use an heirloom linen to cover your basket. If you don't have one, think about purchasing one or making one if you are able, and then eventually hand it down to the next generation. Explain the importance of the linen covering the Easter food, and encourage your children or godchildren to keep the linen and the tradition in the family for generations.
- Look ahead of time for parishes in your area that will be blessing Easter foods. Encourage your parish priest to offer this special opportunity to your community.

IN THE PARISH

Extend the gift of this festive Catholic custom to all the faithful by arranging a time to bless the Easter foods of your parishioners.

Consider This

- In the weeks leading up to Easter, explain the tradition and gift of this practice in an announcement at the end of Mass or in your parish communications. Be sure to include the details and suggestions for how to put together an Easter food basket.
- Arrange a time that works for you and your community to bless the baskets, and turn this into a tradition by offering it every year.
- Create Easter baskets of food for the poor by having parishioners donate goods and/or prepare baskets. Then bless these baskets along with those of your parishioners. Arrange for volunteers to deliver these immediately after the blessing, on Easter morning, or at another suitable time.

Fill your Easter baskets with meaningful food items. Use the suggested list found in the *Festive Faith Easter and Summer Ordinary Time Companion* at www.HisGirlSunday.com/FestiveFaith.

A LIVING TRADITION

My earliest memories of Easter actually were of Holy Saturday more so than Easter Sunday. Each year, my grandparents, who lived in a predominately Polish town in northeast Pennsylvania, took a basket filled with hard-boiled eggs, ham, sauerkraut, kiełbasa (Polish sausage), babka (a traditional Polish Easter bread), and makowiec (poppy-seed roll) to the church for Święconka, the blessing of the Easter baskets. While our basket typically didn't hold a beautiful lamb carved from butter, many of the other baskets there for the blessing that morning did. I loved knowing how the food we would be eating the next day had been blessed by Father in preparation for our delicious brunch.

This tradition continues in my family today, though we live on the opposite coast from where I grew up. We were fortunate to have a Polish priest at our parish who also took joy in celebrating Święconka, so each year on Holy Saturday we pack our basket full of the same foods my grandparents packed into theirs. My family now also makes a lamb out of butter for the Easter brunch table. This simple act of packing an Easter basket for blessing feels like an anchor to my soul; it grounds me in the traditions of my family and reminds me of who I am and where I came from. It refocuses my heart on the beauty of keeping these traditions alive, on the importance of the Easter celebration, and on Jesus's sacrifice for us amid the busy preparations we undertake each year. Today, this matters even more to me than it did as a child. As a Polish Catholic, this and other traditions ground me in both my faith and my cultural heritage. They enable me to hand on things my family has done for generations, giving younger members the same anchoring that I received so many years ago. This blessing of Easter foods provides me with a sense of continuity that grows each time we relive and recelebrate the tradition year after year. Joy blooms in my heart as I think of my relatives, many of whom I hope to one day meet in heaven, looking down as I bake the same bread that they themselves baked more than a hundred years ago.

Jen Frost

PYSANKY EASTER EGGS

WEEKS LEADING UP TO EASTER OR
DURING THE EASTER SEASON

THE STORY

Vibrantly painted Easter eggs grant us another window to see the delights of Eastertide. These eye-catching eggs are an artistic expression that tells the story of ancestral culture and the way our forebears relate to the world. *Pysanky* is a word derived from the Ukrainian term *pysaty*, which means to write, and in this ancient custom it refers to the delicate and intricate art of writing designs on Easter eggs. Specifically, it refers to the initial method of ornamentation, when the designs were written on the egg using a stylus and melted beeswax. Today the eggs can also be hand-painted with bright colors, folk motifs, small patterns, and symbolic designs.

These decorated eggs originated in primitive, agrarian societies when people worshipped the sun. The sun was a highly reverenced deity, and the only creature that could get close enough to it was the bird. Birds were challenging for people to catch, but they could grab hold of bird eggs. People would gather eggs and decorate them with symbols of springtime and nature as an offering to the sun. It was an honored ritual during rite-of-spring festivals.

As we have seen in our exploration of other festive customs, superstitions and folklore often were blended with Christian beliefs. While the painted eggs we see today may have had pagan roots, the egg became a symbol of the risen Christ and was incorporated into Easter festivities in many places, particularly Ukraine. Even St. Augustine is attributed with describing how the Resurrection of Jesus from the dead can be likened to the hope of new life that is brought forth from an egg. With the conversion of the peoples of what is now Ukraine came the conversion of the interpretation of these exquisite eggs. From this, a myth developed that says that when Jesus was being investigated by Pilate, Our Lady went to him wearing an apron filled with eggs. While pleading for them to be less cruel to her precious Jesus, her tears dropped on the eggs, and they created dots of dazzling colors—thus the creation of the pysanky egg.

THE TRADITION

Ornately decorating eggs not only is an occasion for offering artistic expression, but communicates a sense of pride. It shows pride in one's abilities, culture, family history, and Christian faith, which everyone could use a little more of. Pysanky eggs are painted over the course of days, weeks, and sometimes even months leading up to Easter and throughout the Easter season. The eggs are shared as gifts or displayed as decoration within the home. You can use a variety of eggs, not just chicken, but also goose, quail, duck, or ostrich. Some dye the eggs in a more natural and traditional way, by taking dried plants, roots, berries, flowers, or onion skins and combining these with water and vinegar. The creation of the dye, in some families, is said to be a mother's secret that she hands down to her daughter in confidence. This becomes a beholden family recipe that is kept with a sense of honor for the next generation.

While some individuals use the dye and wax method, and others stick with paint, every egg is meant to display Easter symbolism. Depictions to include on your eggs might be lines that extend around the circumference of the egg to express eternity. Designs that section the egg into four quarters represent the four gospel messages that were shared to convert the world. You could also paint a cross for the Death and Resurrection of Jesus, plants to show new life, small dots that represent the tears of Mary at Christ's Crucifixion, triangles for the Holy Trinity, ladders that signify rising prayers, or fish as an ancient symbol for Christianity. Painting intentionally with specific colors can also imbue your egg with more meaning: white stands for purity and rejoicing, red for the blood of Christ and the hope of Resurrection, yellow for wisdom, blue for Our Lady, and purple for fasting and loyal faith.

This unique tradition is a noteworthy experience and one that can give your Easter days excitement. Do this on your own, or gather friends, neighbors, your children, or grandchildren around every evening to paint a portion of the egg and pray together.

CARRYING ON THE TRADITION

AT HOME
Try dyeing or painting pysanky eggs at home, perhaps over various days with family or friends.

Consider This

- Try your hand at using the traditional melted wax and dye, or use paint with delicate brushes to make intricate designs.
- Let this be an ongoing project, something that takes time to make, and while you paint you can pray and reflect on the Resurrection.
- Invite friends over for brunch and a painting project.
- Adorn the egg with special symbols that speak to our Catholic faith.

IN THE PARISH
Host an Easter workshop with pysanky egg painting and treats.

Consider This

- Pick a Saturday within the Easter season when everyone can come spend an afternoon or evening painting eggs and enjoying drinks and treats, or even a potluck meal.
- Develop a symbol guide for those attending so they have ideas already laid out for them to paint on their eggs.
- Share the story of the pysanky egg so parishioners understand the custom.
- Encourage participants to decorate their homes with their newly painted eggs.

Resource

Design and decorate your pysanky eggs purposefully with the guide provided in the *Festive Faith Easter and Summer Ordinary Time Companion* at www. HisGirlSunday.com/FestiveFaith.

DYNGUS DAY
EASTER MONDAY

THE STORY

Easter Monday, sometimes called Dyngus Day, is given a lively expression in Poland with the age-old sprinkling custom. A tradition that still endures today in a more playful manner developed out of somewhat superstitious pre-Christian practices associated with fertility and cleansing. One pagan courtship practice is said to have gone like this. Early in the morning, everyone would wake to get dressed in traditional attire, and the women of the town would wait in front of their homes for the men to come to their doors with buckets of water. The men would recite a folk rhyme for the ladies and ask if they had permission to sprinkle or splash them with water from the buckets. In exchange for being sprinkled, the women would offer the men a pysanky egg.

In 966 when the Polish people met Catholicism through the baptism of Mieszko I, duke of Polans, the meaning behind the water ritual began to transform. He is believed to have been baptized on Easter Monday, and the experience of the Catholic rite of sprinkling gave new life to the preexisting water custom. No longer about fertility or purification, it became a joyous opportunity to have a bit of fun throwing water at one another during the Easter season and to give thanks for the spread of Christianity to Poland. Boys and girls couldn't wait to hurl water at one another, but to spare themselves from being drenched they could offer one another a ransom in the form of a pysanky egg. The word *dyngus* is believed to be a variation on the German word *dingeier*, which means "the eggs that are owed," or *dingnis*, which translates to "ransom." From the pre-Christian era to now, exchanging an egg has endured as an offering of newness, springtime, and life.

THE TRADITION

Today, Easter Monday water fights carry on with great enthusiasm in many places. Still intertwined is the theme of baptism, not only of the Polish people, but of all of us. New Christians join the Church through baptism at the Easter Vigil, and all who are already Christians renew our baptismal promises each year at Easter. Through the waters of Baptism, we die to our old selves and rise to new life in Christ. It is through this first Sacrament of Initiation that we receive entrance into Christ's Church and the kingdom of God. As the *Catechism* states, "This sacrament is also called 'the washing of regeneration and renewal by the Holy Spirit,' for it signifies and actually brings about the birth of water and the Spirit without which no one 'can enter the kingdom of God'" (*CCC*, 1215). This is the true water that cleanses us from sin and leads us to everlasting life, which is made possible through Jesus's Death and Resurrection. At Dyngus Day celebrations, the custom of sprinkling water, the sacramental matter of baptism, vividly reminds us of these baptismal truths.

Polish families have brought this same practice with them to the United States, where you can find parades, festivals, and water fights in places like Ohio, Indiana, and New York. Easter Sunday is only the beginning of the joyous celebration of the Resurrection, as Easter Monday follows up with entertainment, music, costumes, and delicious Polish foods. If this celebration is offered in your area, you might consider sharing in the festivities as a way to unite yourself to customs that may not be of your own heritage but that speak to the same shared desire for communal festivity and Catholic culture. On a small scale, families and friends who are longing to keep the spirit of Easter alive have adopted this practice by hosting a lunch followed by water bucket and balloon fights. Don't be afraid to dive into this one.

CARRYING ON THE TRADITION

AT HOME
Bring Easter Monday to life by starting a water bucket and balloon fight in your yard.

Consider This
- Explain where the custom comes from so that your family, friends, and neighbors know its origin.
- Articulate the importance of water as a symbol of faith, especially as it pertains to Baptism and Easter.
- Invite friends and family for an Easter Monday brunch followed by water games.

IN THE PARISH
Oftentimes the parish is closed on Easter Monday after what can feel like a long and self-giving Triduum and Easter Sunday. With the help of volunteers, host an hour of water games for the youth group or faith-formation children.

Consider This
- Pop up a simple snack table with water bottles.
- If you have a Polish community, invite them to share their culture with the larger community, perhaps by sharing special foods and music. This would take advanced planning, but it is a worthy endeavor for bringing Catholic tradition to life within our neighborhoods.
- Develop manageable water games for those attending to have fun while keeping the preparations simple.
- Explain where this custom comes from so those attending have a greater understanding.

ASCENSION CELEBRATIONS AND PICNICS

ON THURSDAY, THE FORTIETH DAY OF EASTER,
OR THE FOLLOWING SUNDAY

THE STORY

The Ascension may appear at face value to be a feast with seemingly less tradition and merriment than the first days of the Easter season—after all, it is a rather somber event to commemorate Jesus departing from the apostles—but celebrations actually date back to St. Gregory of Nyssa, who lived through the mid- to late fourth century, provides us with a brief homily regarding the Ascension that gives venerable witness to this feast day's observances. St. Augustine writes about the feast as well, expressing that this was celebrated well before his life. It is awe-inspiring that by continuing to celebrate this feast day and others, we are continuing the life of the Church that harkens all the way back to the earliest centuries of Christianity.

On the Solemnity of the Ascension of the Lord, we give glory to Jesus, who ascended into heaven and took his seat at the right hand of the Father. This feast is seen as the work of completion. "When he had said this, as they were looking on, he was lifted up, and a cloud took him from their sight" (Acts 1:9). The Ascension, celebrated on the fortieth day of Easter or the following Sunday, is the culmination of Jesus's earthly life in which he returns to the Father, body and soul. The liturgical celebration for Ascension Thursday is celebrated on that day because the Bible tells us that after the Resurrection Jesus spent time with the apostles and disciples to share with them how to establish the Church on earth; then on the fortieth day he took them up to the mountain, and he ascended into heaven.

The Solemnity of the Ascension of the Lord inspired an outpouring of celebrations and devotions in the early Church such as blessings of beans, first fruits, and beeswax candles. The first fruits are the initial produce harvest of the season which is to be offered to God in thanksgiving for blessing us and the land. People brought what was naturally a part of the life around them and offered it to God. This is a lesson in simplicity that everyone can learn from when starting to live liturgically—we do well to use what is already at hand. The faithful saw the springtime new growth in the natural world as a gift from

God. Following the example of Christ, they received the blessings of the earth with gratitude by offering them back to him in their Ascension celebrations. This is a fitting blessing on the Solemnity of the Ascension as we recall that Jesus is the first fruit of Messianic fulfillment.

Until the 1970 *Roman Missal*, the liturgy for the Solemnity of the Ascension of the Lord called for the Paschal Candle to be extinguished following the gospel reading recounting Jesus's ascent to heaven. This was a dramatic way to show that Jesus is no longer with us on earth as he had been, but with the Father in heaven. In the current edition of *Roman Missal*, the Paschal Candle is kept lit until Pentecost.

Processions were also once common on Ascension Day. Led by the clergy, the laity carried with them lit candles and banners with symbols that represented Christ's victory over evil. Some of these processions even developed into more elaborate plays where figures and images of Christ would be raised into the air, in some cases even through windows nearest the roof of the church.

The breadth of these traditions is a beautiful example of the simplicity and the splendor that Catholic life can bring forth. The uncomplicated offering of humble fruits for blessing, for instance, reminds us that the heart of liturgical living is to bring all that we have, no matter how humble, to the Lord. The splendor of liturgical processions and elaborate plays also reminds us to offer the highest of our accomplishments, creations, and abilities in praise of our Redeemer.

Tied to the Solemnity of the Ascension of the Lord are Rogation Days. These are days set aside for prayer and penance in reparation for sin, begging God's mercy, and asking for God's blessing on the spring planting season and a fruitful harvest. The major Rogation Day is on April 25, and the three minor Rogation Days take place on the three days (Monday, Tuesday, and Wednesday) preceding Ascension Thursday. The word *rogation* has its origins in the Latin word *rogare,* which means to supplicate or ask God for his mercy, to turn away his anger, and to request his blessing on the fruits of the earth while protecting us from natural disasters. Traditionally the minor Rogation Days associated with the Ascension were observed with abstinence but not fasting since they take place within the Easter season. Each Rogation Day can be observed with Mass and a procession. The Rogation Days were removed from the General Roman Calendar, but are still encouraged. Their administration is now given to regional conferences of bishops and individual bishops in their dioceses. I explain more about the history, meaning, and observances of the Rogation and

Ember Days in the *Festive Faith Rhythms of Fasting and Abstinence Companion* at www.HisGirlSunday.com/FestiveFaith.

THE TRADITION

Feasts such as the Ascension connect us to our Christian ancestry while also paving a way for us to move forward in unity and hope. Catholics around the world have made this solemnity their own, with each tradition giving importance to Jesus being lifted up into heaven. Looking up is an important thread in Ascension traditions; much as the way our prayers rise with burning incense, our minds and hearts are drawn upward to heaven. Germany might inspire your dinner preparations for the Solemnity of the Ascension of the Lord because in parts of the country it is customary to make and eat a roasted bird of some kind. Drawing upon the image of Christ "flying" to heaven, it would be appropriate to prepare quail, goose, pheasant, turkey, duck, or chicken. Yes, chicken can take flight, even if not for long distances. We'll count it because it makes for an attainable dinner recipe. If you do not eat meat, there are plenty of ways to use the symbol of birds in your festive meals for the day. In some German bakeries you will find pastries shaped like various birds; you might copy this tradition if you are a bread baker. Or perhaps today you might pull out a special cookie cutter that is shaped like a bird of some kind. Maybe cut sandwich bread with it and prepare a simple Ascension Day picnic. With similar intent to look upward, parts of central Europe have been known for their mountain hiking and hilltop picnics on this day.

Having your fruit blessed and packing it up for a picnic along with an oven-roasted chicken, bird-shaped meatless sandwiches, or loaves of home-made bread would make for a delightful day outside with family and friends. Bring along games or toys that draw your gaze to the sky, such as bubbles and kites. We have done this every year since getting married, and it's now treasured family time that keeps Jesus's Ascension at the forefront of our minds. Remember, this divine event is not to be simply interpreted as Christ leaving us, but it is an encouragement for us to wait and watch for his return. It is a feast that should inspire hope within us as well as anticipation for Christ's return and our eternal life with him in heaven.

CARRYING ON THE TRADITION

AT HOME

Prepare a meaningful festive meal with fruits, sandwiches, breads, and roast chicken or turkey if you eat meat, or beans, and enjoy it as a picnic this evening.

Consider This
- Encourage your extended family to attend, and make it a potluck.
- Integrate activities that make you look up such as blowing bubbles or flying kites.
- Have fruit to be used in baking blessed by your local parish priest if possible. If a priest is not available, find a suitable prayer of thanksgiving and blessing to pray before preparing celebratory foods and feasting.
- Light and extinguish your domestic church's Paschal Candle as a way of expressing that Christ has ascended to heaven.
- Partake in the Rogation Days leading up to the Ascension.

Resource
For more information on how to observe the Rogation Days, reference the *Festive Faith Rhythms of Fasting and Abstinence Companion* at www.HisGirlSunday.com/FestiveFaith.

IN THE PARISH

Offer the traditional blessing of beans and first fruits, found in the *Roman Ritual*, and create an opportunity for a parish picnic.

Consider This
- On Ascension Thursday or Sunday bless the fruit and beans of your congregation.
- Create time for a parish picnic, where everyone can bring their own food and you can provide music, kites, and outdoor games.
- Carry on the tradition of a celebratory Ascension procession around your parish grounds.
- Offer a penitential rogation procession on one of the appointed days, chant the Litany of Saints, and bless your parish grounds.

MAY CROWNING

WITHIN THE MONTH OF MAY

THE STORY

Crowning our Blessed Mother Mary stems from an ardent response of deep devotion and love for Mary's role in salvation history and the affection she has for all her children, the Church. This tradition is said to have originated from the dedication of the month of May to the Blessed Mother near the end of the eighteenth century by a Fr. Latomia from the Roman College of the Society of Jesus (the Jesuits). The tradition tells us that Fr. Latomia was trying to curb immorality by replacing it with greater devotion among his socially distracted students. This practice of devoting the month of May to the Blessed Mother gained popularity, and over the next hundred years it became customary throughout the Church. May is filled with special Marian observances, so it is only fitting that we spend the entire month reflecting on her role as mother and queen.

With the momentum of this monthly dedication came the pious tradition of May Crownings in the nineteenth century. In the Basilica of St. Mary Major hangs an image called the *Salus Populi Romani*, which according to tradition is believed to have been painted by St. Luke the Evangelist. Popes throughout the years have made many offerings of crowns and jewels to the icon as a way of entrusting the Church to her care during times of challenge. Pope Clement VIII (1592–1605) gave the Marian icon in the Basilica of St. Mary Major two crowns, one for Mary and one for Our Lord. Through the years those crowns were lost, but Pope Gregory XVI crowned this image again on August 15, 1837. With the attendance of cardinals and bishops, he blessed two crowns with a special prayer, incensed and sprinkled them with holy water, and adorned the icon with the crowns while singing the *Regina Caeli*. This marked the beginning of what became the widely known and highly anticipated practice of May Crowning.

THE TRADITION

This popular devotion is repeated annually during the month of May by placing a gold, silver, or floral crown on a venerated image of Our Lady. Often a space for Mary's statue or image is set apart by decorating the area with flower arrangements and candles. The Order of Crowning the Blessed Virgin Mary has many variations that can be used by bishops in cathedrals, individuals in homes and classrooms, and communities of the faithful. Wherever you are, this is a spiritually enriching practice that you should feel empowered to do.

In many parishes, May Crowing celebrations include a procession with one or more people carrying an image or statue of Our Lady and others carrying bouquets of flowers and candles. At some parishes you might find children who have recently received their First Communion dressed in blue or white attire and given a special place within the procession. Resounding through streets and churches is the unifying melody of beloved Marian hymns.

If you are doing a May Crowning within your home or classroom, you and other adults living in your home, your children, or students can learn to weave together flower crowns for Marian statues. Every part of this special tradition is an offering of gratitude to our Blessed Mother. It is Mary who is considered the "crown" of creation, and by celebrating her in this special way, we join with her in a perfect yes to God.

CARRYING ON THE TRADITION

AT HOME
Crown a statue or image of Mary within your domestic church and offer her a bouquet of flowers.

Consider This
- You can purchase a crown or make one out of flowers as a craft project.
- Make sure your statue or image of Mary is in a prominent place in your home, garden, or yard.
- Have your parish priest bless the image of Mary that you will be crowning.
- Arrange a bouquet of flowers for Our Lady.
- Say a Marian prayer or sing a Marian hymn before or after crowning her.

IN THE PARISH
Arrange a procession, and publicly crown a statue or other sacred image of Mary.

Consider This
- Sing Marian hymns as you process.
- Invite the children or First Communicants of your parish to wear blue or white and walk at the front of the procession with flowers.

- Place the image or statue that you are crowning in a prominent place.
- Encourage participants to bring flowers for Mary.
- Strengthen community ties by planning and inviting everyone who participates in the May Crowning to a reception of springtime treats after the crowning. If you crown a statue outside, perhaps gather near it to continue your celebration.

A LIVING TRADITION

Many people love the month of May because the weather is nice in many places, trees and lawns are green again, and many flowers are blooming. Spiritually, the month of May is also a magnificent month for Catholic tradition. It is the month of Mary, the most beautiful flower of God's creation. In Vietnam, one can see this clearly in Catholic churches during the annual May Crowning. Most, if not all, churches in Vietnam have beautiful May Crowning dances called *dâng hoa* in honor of the Blessed Mother. The people express their devotion to her by dancing alongside the tune of a Marian hymn and then placing flowers around her statue.

Personally, this experience moved and heightened my own devotion to the Blessed Virgin Mary through the words of the song, the movement of the traditional dancing, and the crowning of Mary with flowers. My relationship with her grew so much that I believe Mary spared me from being horribly injured after falling backward off of a seven-foot-tall Marian shrine I was helping to construct. Vietnamese Catholics are deeply rooted in their Marian devotion, and that was only made more powerful after the Blessed Mother appeared at La Vang to help the Catholics during an era of persecution. The tradition of crowning and honoring Mary during the month of May has persisted in the Vietnamese Catholic community because we believe it is important to express on the outside the love that we have for our Blessed Mother in our hearts.

Fr. Steven Tran

EIGHT

SUMMER ORDINARY TIME

On the feasts of the saints consider their virtues,
and beseech God to deign to adorn you with them.

St. Teresa of Ávila, OCD

Begins: Monday after Pentecost
Ends: Before First Vespers for the First Sunday of Advent
Natural Seasons: Spring, Summer, and Fall
Disciplines: Maturation, Discipleship, Hope for the Second Coming
Recommended Prayer: The Angelus
This prayer can be found in the Festive Faith Easter and Summer Ordinary Time Companion *at www.HisGirlSunday.com/ FestiveFaith.*
Liturgical Color: Green

During the first stretch of Ordinary Time, following the Christmas season, the liturgical readings show us who Jesus is. We learn anew to walk with him through the biblical stories, observing how he treated others, listening to his words, trying to absorb his miracles, and coming to know him again as the Son of God. By keeping the days of Ordinary Time, the Church desires that each of us grows in our relationship with Jesus. Throughout those weeks we follow Christ around as did those who lived with him and learn how to grow and mature in deeper devotion. We dwell in the peace of Christ's first coming and grow in faith. Now, in the second stretch of Ordinary Time, which takes us through mid-spring, summer, and fall, we live and grow with the apostles and the disciples in anticipation of his Second Coming.

The scripture stories we hear throughout these weeks pertain to the early Church receiving the gifts of the Holy Spirit and using those to share the Good News with all whom they encounter. Proclaiming the mission of Christ was their duty and responsibility because of what they had experienced. They didn't just hear the Gospel message as we do; they lived through its first proclamation. The earliest Christians allowed themselves to be totally transformed by the life and message of Jesus. Those who were Jewish began to see how everything they had heard from the prophets and their ancestors was coming to fulfillment in Jesus. Instead of being consumed by doubt or fear, they accepted it with courage. Even in the midst of persecution, it was up to them to keep these truths alive by proclaiming that the kingdom of God is at hand. This same experiential conversion is what we are called to seek in our lives today and in our homes, parishes, and wider communities. Our Christian obligation is never passive; it is an active command to live the life of Christ. Thankfully, Ordinary Time offers us the bounty of three natural seasons that can be used to graft ourselves onto the Paschal Mystery.

It is true that we might settle back into our mundane routines, but we are also meant to develop a sense of readiness and preparation for Jesus's return. The USCCB says, "Ordinary Time is a time for growth and maturation, a time in which the mystery of Christ is called to penetrate ever more deeply into history until all things are finally caught up in Christ."[1] God is substantially making his way through history, in visible time and space, by means of his Church. We—you and I—are making Christ present now, just as generations of Christians did before us and will do again after us. This influential and generational activity leaves behind a legacy of faith as we progress forward toward the eternal. Even in our finite lives, we penetrate through time by our union with Christ. This was the wisdom of the early Church and the many saints who consistently wrote about living with the goal of heaven. They understood that one day we will all be "finally caught up in Christ."

Enrich your journey through this stretch of Ordinary Time that runs from late spring through fall with the mentality of the saints by looking upon these weeks as a chance to know and love Christ, yourself, your family, and your community with a full and grateful heart. Root your days in prayer, the sacraments, and celebration. Do this while time is within reach. In this chapter the traditions are plentiful—bonfires, blessings, parties. Offer to God and his Church a proclamation of your faith as Mary, the apostles, and the disciples did.

In this lengthy season I often remind myself that God can never be outdone in generosity, and in the spirit of that lesson, I challenge myself to offer him all that I have in return, even if this means forgoing other things so that I have the time and energy for liturgical living. May we allow the gifts of the Holy Spirit to work within our homes and parishes so that our Catholic legacy is left as a blessing for those to come. Ordinary Time isn't so ordinary after all!

CORPUS CHRISTI PROCESSIONS AND FLOWER CARPETS

THURSDAY AFTER TRINITY SUNDAY, EIGHT WEEKS AFTER HOLY THURSDAY

THE STORY

Among the most widely revered feasts is the Solemnity of the Most Holy Body and Blood of Christ. Many Catholics know this feast by its Latin name, *Corpus Christi*, meaning "Body of Christ." With the significance of the Eucharist to our Catholic faith, it's no surprise that it was designated its own feast day in the thirteenth century. Corpus Christi is among the feast days whose dates are set in relation to Easter. In the General Roman Calendar, it is celebrated on the Thursday after Trinity Sunday, harkening back to Holy Thursday and emphasizing how the Eucharist sustains us through time after the Resurrection until Christ comes again in glory. In the United States and some other countries, the observance has been transferred to the Sunday after Trinity Sunday. Recognizing the parallels among Holy Thursday, the institution of the Eucharist, and the Solemnity of Corpus Christi should lead to a stronger appreciation for the sacrament and a deeper devotion. As Pope Benedict XVI taught, "Corpus Christi, is thus a renewal of the mystery of Holy Thursday, as it were, in obedience to Jesus's invitation to proclaim from 'the housetops' what he told us in secret."[2] During the Last Supper the apostles received the extraordinary gift of the Eucharist in private, but they proclaimed and shared it with all of us. Jesus's Body and Blood is our perpetual inheritance that we are to reencounter weekly, if not daily, through reception of the Blessed Sacrament and in Eucharistic Adoration.

Many Catholics are confused about or, sadly, reject the doctrines of transubstantiation and the Real Presence. We know that many during the time of Jesus also struggled to accept the radical action that he was telling them to take (John 6:64–66). "Jesus said to them, 'Amen, amen, I say to you, unless you eat the flesh of the Son of Man and drink his blood, you do not have life within you. Whoever eats my flesh and drinks my blood has eternal life, and I will raise him on the last day'" (Jn 6:53–54). With much of the world drifting further away from finding peace and hope in religious faith, we can't be surprised that there is an increased lack of acceptance, even among some Catholics, that we see and consume the Real Presence of Christ when we receive Holy Communion. Without getting too far into Aristotelian metaphysics, the Church uses the term *transubstantiation* to express this fundamental change of bread and wine to Christ's Body and Blood. The accidents of the bread and wine (taste, shape, texture, appearance) stay the same, but the substance (the bread-ness and wine-ness) changes. So, while it may taste like bread and wine, after the Prayer of Consecration is said by the priest, it is substantially, fully, and truly the Real Presence of Christ. If this is what we adhere to, then this truth must be wholeheartedly shared and proclaimed to others in the same manner in which we received it from the apostles. Eucharistic processions and celebrations have long been a way for Catholics to express belief that Christ is present in the Eucharist. By publicly sharing our devotion to his Body and Blood, Christ is made manifest in our neighborhoods, towns, and cities, giving others the opportunity to encounter him anew.

THE TRADITION

Eucharistic processions are traditionally done and given pride of place on Corpus Christi as a public proclamation of the Real Presence of Jesus in the Eucharist. Although the idea of carrying the Blessed Sacrament through town was established in the early fourteenth century, it was not until the Council of Trent (1545–1563) that it was officially proposed. Popes encouraged Catholics to participate in this procession by offering a special indulgence. In some locations it is a simple walk around the parish grounds with prayers and hymns of thanksgiving. Others prefer to celebrate with grandeur by progressing through city streets, tossing rose petals, ringing bells, and drawing the attention of thousands. The liturgical guides leave plenty of room for local expressions of the community so that everyone can offer their own particular gifts. Some processions grew with such popularity throughout Spain that Eucharistic pageants began to take shape. Performed on the streets following the procession, these dramatizations were meant to teach viewers about biblical stories, virtues and vices, and the story of the Eucharist.

Italy also has a jaw-dropping Corpus Christi custom called *infiorata*, which translates to "decorated with flowers." Italian artists, florists, and townspeople spend days and countless hours creating flower-carpet depictions. Entire towns gather together to collect materials and assemble buckets of petals for the upcoming artistry. Sprawling across the grounds of plazas are sacred depictions of the Catholic faith, which are assembled with thousands upon thousands of flower petals, wood cuttings, dirt, and rock. All these natural materials are used together to add further color and artistry. The elaborate design work can typically be found in areas leading up to monasteries and Catholic churches. Some towns in Italy go well beyond that by dedicating themselves to covering an entire street in floral artwork so that the Blessed Sacrament can be processed through these glorious displays.

There is no end to the number of ways in which faithful people come together to offer God all that they have on the Solemnity of Corpus Christi. Jesus gave us every part of himself, down to his physical Body and Blood, and in return this day is filled with processions, acting, singing, dancing, artistry, and flowers to aid this festive celebration of his ongoing presence among us. This should be inspiring to us! Finding a procession near you can be one of the more notable things to do on this day, but if that isn't a real option for you, then celebrate the Eucharist in other ways. Sitting next to the tabernacle after Mass or finding a parish with Eucharistic Adoration are a couple of doable options. Cling to the Body and Blood of Christ as your source of strength on this feast and through the days that follow. Collecting flowers, dirt, mulch, and rocks to create an outdoor sidewalk, driveway, or yard icon is another creative way to live liturgically today. Chalk a simple outline of a Catholic symbol, and fill it in with the goods you gathered from nature.

My family has always appreciated the expression of faith in the Eucharistic presence of Christ as the Bread of Life. After Church on Corpus Christi, we come home and make a homemade loaf of bread. Handed down from my mother-in-law is an easy table loaf recipe that we make in our Dutch oven. Our festivities are full of flour fingerprints and happy hearts.

CARRYING ON THE TRADITION

AT HOME
Attend a Corpus Christi procession at your parish or within your town, or spend time in front of the Blessed Sacrament today.

Consider This
- Locate and plan to join in a local Corpus Christi procession. Invite your extended family, friends, and perhaps your neighbors to join you.
- Spend time in Eucharistic Adoration, or sit in front of the tabernacle. Prepare printed prayers, Catholic books, prayer manipulatives, or an "adoration bag" if you are going with children.
- Sing a Eucharistic hymn with your family before dinner or during your prayer time.
- Bake a fresh loaf of bread together, and explain the importance of bread in connection to the Eucharist.
- Create and display your own *infiorata* flower carpet. On your driveway or patio sketch out an easy Catholic symbol in chalk, and fill it with flowers, rocks, and dirt.

IN THE PARISH
Prepare a Corpus Christi procession for your parishioners, and allow time for adoration in front of the Blessed Sacrament.

Consider This
- Work with your liturgical ministers and fellow clergy members to arrange the procession in advance.
- Share this opportunity with parishioners in advance, and ask nearby parishes to join you. Maybe they can publicize this in their bulletin too.
- Invite the First Communicants from the last year to wear their white suits and dresses and walk at the front of the procession.
- In the weeks leading up to Corpus Christi, encourage faith formation and other parish ministries to explore the doctrine of the Real Presence. Encourage leaders to invite faith-sharing about what the Eucharistic means in the lives of participants.
- Adopt the Italian tradition of *infiorata* flower carpets. Send a call out for creatives in your parish community to come together to create these Catholic displays.

Resource
Revisit the Prayers for Adoration articulated in the Triduum section of the *Festive Faith Winter Ordinary Time, Lent, and Triduum Companion* at www. HisGirlSunday.com/FestiveFaith.

HOME ENTHRONEMENT OF THE SACRED HEART OF JESUS

NINETEEN DAYS AFTER PENTECOST

THE STORY

Most Catholics have probably seen an image of the Sacred Heart of Jesus. This symbol, although created in various artistic styles and in various mediums, is essentially a heart wrapped in thorns. A heart, the universal symbol for love, pierced with thorns is a profound depiction of Christ's undying love for the Church and the self-sacrificing nature with which he offers us redemption. According to St. Margaret Mary Alacoque, the thorns in the image of the Sacred Heart represent the sins that we commit, which prick the heart of Jesus. In images of the Sacred Heart that show the whole person of Jesus we usually see his pierced heart depicted with an outpouring of his blood that nourishes and gives life to us all. The significance of this should call to mind the Blessed Sacrament, our spiritual sustenance. Images of the Sacred Heart of Jesus usually also show flames—a biblical symbol of divinity but also an expression of passionate and all-consuming love. The Church highly values this devotion to the Sacred Heart as a way of fighting off the evils of the world and emboldening us in faith, morals, and piety. We can always take refuge in the heart of our Savior, who will not forsake us.

We have St. Margaret Mary Alacoque to thank for revitalizing the devotion to the Sacred Heart. She was born to a prosperous French family in 1647, and as a little girl she loved spending time with them as well as with her godmother. Sadly, her father died of pneumonia early on in her life, and it left the family in a very difficult financial situation. As a result, she was sent to school with the Urbanist Sisters of Charolles. She adored life at the convent and was even able to make her First Communion early. However, Margaret had to go home after she became very sick, and she was bedridden for about four years. After some time for healing, she led a fairly normal life as a teenager but received a vision after coming home from a dance one evening. The vision was of Christ being scourged, which she interpreted as her having betrayed Jesus for worldly pleasures. At that point she decided to enter the convent at only twenty-two years old. After a few years there she had a series of visions, which continued for a year and a half or so. The core message of these visions was Jesus asking her to spread a devotion to his Sacred Heart. The explanations of her visions along with the twelve promises which Our Lord gave to St. Margaret Mary for those who honor the Sacred Heart, were not initially received well, but a priest by the name of Fr. Claude de la Columbiere, now a saint, wrote them down and helped her spread the devotion. Over time, Margaret Mary was able to lead her convent community to the Sacred Heart of Jesus in many ways. She died at the age of forty-three, after having once again become very sick.

In the late nineteenth century, Fr. Mateo Crawley-Boevey, SSCC, the founder of the Enthronement of the Sacred Heart in the Home, began his apostolate with the mission of transforming society by means of devotion to the Sacred Heart of Jesus. After joining the Congregation of the Sacred Hearts of Jesus and Mary in Chile, he lived among people suffering from great poverty and other injustice. With great affection and closeness to the heart of Jesus, Fr. Mateo set out to change the injustices he was witnessing all around him by sharing the promises of the Sacred Heart that had been revealed to St. Margaret Mary. In his wisdom Fr. Mateo knew that the only way to achieve large-scale change in the world was by inspiring the Catholic faith within each household. After reflecting on Jesus's twelve promises, he came up with a plan for each home to display an image of the Sacred Heart in a prominent place. In 1907, after visiting the apparition site of St. Margaret Mary, he submitted to Church officials in Rome a proposed outline for Enthronement of the Sacred Heart to be used in Catholic homes. In a private audience with Pope Pius X he was granted the encouragement and consent he needed to spread this devotional custom far and wide.

THE TRADITION

All Catholic households can be inspired to dedicate their homes to the Sacred Heart by participating in a special celebration wherein the Sacred Heart of Jesus is enthroned as ruler of the household. By doing this we are expressing public recognition of Christ's kingship over our lives and our household. We are intentionally inviting Christ to dwell with us and reign over our lives and our home. Of course, the Lord is with us always, but through the Home Enthronement of the Sacred Heart, we make the dedication of our homes to the Sacred Heart of Jesus visible to us and all those who enter our home. Everything that we do within our home is for his glory.

While it may not be easy to dedicate all our behaviors to God, a life of virtue must start within the safety of our homes. Just as Fr. Mateo desired to change society by transforming the hearts and homes of those around him, we can also act as a representation of God's love and mercy to those in our families and out in the world. St. John Paul II said, "The nuclear family that develops from marriage is the basic cell of society." The Catholic culture that we build in our homes will inevitably get carried out to those whom we encounter in our everyday lives. This should strike a sense of hope and responsibility into us as we seek holiness within these days of Ordinary Time.

To do this there is only one item that you must have, and that is an image of the Sacred Heart of Jesus. The official Order for Enthronement can be found in the *Roman Ritual* as the form of enthronement historically authorized by the Church. The ceremony instructs that it be hung up in a special place of honor within your home for all to see and pass by. You can also hang an image of the Immaculate Heart of Mary, but that is optional. It is recommended that the Home Enthronement Ceremony be done by the authority of a priest; however, in extraordinary cases a head of the household can lead an adaptation of the ceremony. In this case, the image of the Sacred Heart would need to be blessed by a priest beforehand. As you plan to have your home dedicated to the Sacred Heart, be sure to communicate your desire and arrange a time for a priest to come over. On the evening of our Home Enthronement of the Sacred Heart, we invited close friends, family, and our parish priest over for dinner and the ceremony. I made Coq au Vin, a traditional dish of stewed chicken in wine sauce that originated in Burgundy, France, where St. Margaret Mary was born.

I also took this opportunity to create a small home altar for my family to use, and it has been an ongoing gift. Whenever we need quiet time with space to read, pray, or sing hymns, we sit in front of our home altar, which lovingly displays two large images of the Sacred Heart of Jesus and the Immaculate Heart of Mary. You can create a simple home altar by adorning a small piece of furniture with a nice tablecloth, beeswax candles, sacred art and images, prayer resources, rosaries, and Catholic reading material.

Other liturgical days in the year when you might consider enthroning the Sacred Heart in your home, if not on the Feast of the Sacred Heart, are Christ the King, Corpus Christi, and the Feast of the Holy Family. The entire month of June is dedicated to the Sacred Heart of Jesus and might serve as another extended period of time for you to unpack this devotion.

The First Friday Devotion is another closely associated practice that is worth considering. In the promises revealed to St. Margaret Mary Alacoque, Jesus asked the faithful to "receive communion on first Fridays of each month for nine consecutive months."[3] Obtain the graces and blessings of this promise by going to Mass and receiving Holy Communion in a state of grace on each first Friday. Essentially, you are partaking in a prolonged novena, which is a form of prayer typically said for nine days but in this case is for nine months. Venerate and grow in intimacy with Jesus's heart, which pours out life and perfect love for you.

CARRYING ON THE TRADITION

AT HOME
Discern partaking in this Sacred Heart devotion. Purchase an image of the Sacred Heart, and display it in a prominent place within your domestic church. Have your parish priest come over to lead the celebration of Enthronement of the Sacred Heart of Jesus in your home.

Consider This
- Invite close friends and family members over to witness the blessing and devotion.
- Share a meal with those attending.
- Create a home altar in a place where you will regularly see and pass it.
- Increase your devotion by going to Mass on every first Friday of the month for nine months.
- Read the promises that Jesus shared with St. Margaret Mary Alacoque.

IN THE PARISH
Increase devotion to the Sacred Heart of Jesus by teaching your parishioners about the Home Enthronement of the Sacred Heart and supporting them in accomplishing this blessing.

Consider This
- Make Home Enthronement of the Sacred Heart materials available to your parishioners through your website and other communication methods.
- Encourage devotion to the Sacred Heart and Home Enthronement of the Sacred Heart with a homily or an announcement at Mass.
- Collaborate with a local Catholic store by sharing your desire to increase this devotion. In exchange for a small parish-wide discount on Sacred Heart images, you can promote their business in your bulletin or e-newsletter.
- Offer Mass on the first Friday of every month with materials for understanding the First Friday Novena.

Resource
Review the twelve promises of the Sacred Heart of Jesus found in the *Festive Faith Easter and Summer Ordinary Time Companion* at www.HisGirlSunday.com/FestiveFaith.

========= *A LIVING TRADITION* =========

I learned about the Home Enthronement of the Sacred Heart as a member of the Legion of Mary and was told that it was a ceremony to make the Sacred Heart of Jesus the king of one's home and heart. I heard that many great graces would come by fully participating in this devotion, and I knew that I wanted to do this. It was around 1996 when we had Msgr. Wearden and my sister's priest, Fr. Louis Villarreal, from Our Lady of Light in Anahuac, Texas, come for Thanksgiving dinner. They celebrated Mass in my home, and then we did the Home Enthronement ceremony. I carried it on at my next house because I want all the grace and protection we can get, but I also want Jesus and Mary to be the center of our homes and lives and to honor them and their Sacred and Immaculate Hearts. Today more than ever people need to honor Jesus and Mary as king and mother in their homes, especially when there is a prevalence of glorifying movie stars and athletes. It's also a great way to witness your faith to your family, friends, and all the guests that come to your home because they will see the pictures of the Sacred and Immaculate Hearts of Jesus and Mary hung in a place of honor.

Gina Bibb

ST. JOHN THE BAPTIST BONFIRES

JUNE 24

THE STORY

Three special birthdays appear on the liturgical calendar: those of Jesus, Mary, and St. John the Baptist. The Solemnity of the Nativity of St. John the Baptist, which we celebrate on June 24, is sometimes called the "summer Christmas" or the "summer nativity" because of John's close relationship to Jesus and the crucial role he played in the ministry of Jesus. This is one of the Church's oldest and most prominent feast days dating back to the fourth century as an established feast in the liturgical year. In many places it is customary on the eve of his birthday to celebrate with a great bonfire and outdoor feasts. The reason for having a bonfire is associated with the season, our Catholic theology, and the mission of St. John the Baptist. His feast day, June 24, falls within the summer solstice when, during pre-Christian times, pagan solstice fires and other festivities were common throughout Europe. Solstice customs were thought to keep demons away and bring good fortune for lovers. Early Christians adapted these bonfire celebrations to mark the nativity of John the Baptist, and from them grew new Christian devotions and festive customs.

At the time of the winter solstice, we celebrate the nativity of Jesus, the Christ, and daylight begins to increase in the northern hemisphere—where Christianity first took root. Then, at the summer solstice in late June, we celebrate the birth of John the Baptist, and the daylight hours begin to decrease. In the early centuries of Christianity, those who followed Christ began to see the bonfires of summer solstice celebrations as symbolic of St. John the Baptist, who pointed people to Christ, Light of the World. As fire destroys, Christ destroys sin. As fire brings light, Christ shattered the darkness. Zechariah, father of John the Baptist, prayed in his canticle that John had come "to shine on those who sit in darkness and death's shadow, to guide our feet into the path of peace" (Lk 1:79).

THE TRADITION

From the fourth century the heart of the tradition has remained the same, to gather around a blazing bonfire with fellow friends and family. Many do this with a simple backyard firepit and simple snacks. The diverse Body of Christ has added a variety of cultural cuisines and activities to this evening's gathering, from tamales and water fights in Mexico, to sweet beer in Latvia, to bread and cheese in England. You can continue in that same method by preparing your or your family's favorite meal and snacks. I decided to imitate English custom and began offering charcuterie boards at our St. John the Baptist bonfire parties. Swept up in the spirit of things, I bought some special bonfire sticks that change the color of the flames; it adds a bit of flare, and guests enjoy the touch of novelty. We also created a cricket-eating challenge for our adult friends in honor of St. John's time in the wilderness, when he ate locusts and honey. It was funny and strange, but it gave us memories that we still fondly reminisce about today. It might interest you to give your parish priest an invitation so that he can bless your bonfire and enjoy time with part of his parish family. When we did so, this blessed time with our parish priest, who is often so busy, granted us the opportunity to get to know one another and to tighten the bonds between parish life and home life.

CARRYING ON THE TRADITION

AT HOME
Host a bonfire birthday party for your friends and family.

Consider This
- Decorate with birthday-themed items since we are celebrating the nativity of St. John the Baptist.
- Offer snacks and sweets that use honey in honor of his time spent in the wilderness.
- Read about St. John the Baptist in scripture and his role in preparing a way for Jesus.
- Invite your parish priest so that he can bless your bonfire and share in communal time with your family.
- Share in a water-balloon fight to cool down if you live where late June is likely to be hot!

Enjoy a summer night outside together by organizing a parish-wide or ministry-group bonfire by setting up a couple of fire pits in an open outdoor area.

Consider This

- Share the tradition of the St. John the Baptist bonfire, and make the connection between fire, light, and St. John preparing a way for us to grow closer to Christ.
- Make s'mores together as a budget-friendly outdoor treat.
- Have the priest bless the fire and sing a Catholic hymn together.
- Provide supplies for other outdoor summer activities such as a blow-up movie screen showing a saint movie, bubbles, yard games, and footballs.

GRAPES FOR THE TRANSFIGURATION

AUGUST 6

THE STORY

The Transfiguration is considered one of five major events in the life of Christ. The others are his baptism, Crucifixion, Resurrection, and Ascension. You can find the account of the Transfiguration in all three synoptic gospels: Matthew 17:1–8; Mark 9:2–9; and Luke 9:28–36. This event serves as a precursor to his Passion, Death, and Resurrection. In the story we read that Jesus takes Peter, James, and John up to a high mountain, what tradition tells us is Mt. Tabor. While there he reveals his glory to them; his face shines, his clothes are dazzling white, and rays pour over his body. Jesus reveals to them the fullness of who he is, the Son of God. Initially, they are pleased to see the radiance of Jesus: "Lord, it is good that we are here" (Mt 17:4a). We then hear Moses and Elijah speak of Jesus's suffering and death, which is a foreshadowing of what is to come. Toward the end of this account, we hear God's voice claiming Jesus as his beloved Son. The disciples are immediately struck with fear at the sound of this, but Jesus walks to them and, with a simple touch, commands them to stand.

Throughout this passage we can see that Jesus is preparing his disciples for what is to come. He is encouraging and strengthening them so that their belief is reinforced and they can carry on with courage. The *Catechism* tells us that "the Transfiguration gives us a foretaste of Christ's glorious coming, when he 'will change our lowly body to be like his glorious body'" (*CCC*, 556). Through the Transfiguration we learn that our bodies will also be raised and glorified in heaven after Christ's Second Coming.

During the Transfiguration, Peter, James, and John notice that Moses and Elijah are there with Jesus. Why were they there too? In short, the presence of Moses and Elijah on either side of Jesus shows that Christ fulfills the Law, represented by Moses, and the prophets, represented by Elijah. In fact, many theologians will refer to Jesus as the New Moses, who brings the Law to completion. There are many parallels that elicit this title, such as the fact that the Transfiguration takes place not long after the miracle of the multiplication of the loaves and fishes. Like Jesus, Moses was able to feed the Israelites in the wilderness with miraculous bread, called manna. We can also recall when Moses came down Mount Sinai after seeing God and his face was radiant; many images also depict his hair being completely white.

The Eastern Church began celebrating the Feast of the Transfiguration in Jerusalem around the seventh century. It later spread to the Byzantine Empire in the ninth century. The Western Church eventually adopted this feast, around the tenth century, but it wasn't officially added to the liturgical calendar in the West until 1457. Only a few short years before this calendar addition, the great city of Constantinople had fallen to the invading Turkish armies after centuries of withstanding attacks. Amidst the turmoil, Pope Callixtus III adapted the preexisting tradition of praying at noon on Fridays in honor of Jesus's Passion, by encouraging everyone to pray three Hail Marys at noon coupled with ringing the midday bells for the success of Christian knights who were fighting against the Turks in the Battle of Belgrade. This midday prayer is a part of what we now formally know as the Angelus. Upon news of the victory over the Turkish armies in 1456, he commemorated the day by placing the Feast of the Transfiguration on August 6 as an offering of thanksgiving to God.

THE TRADITION

Traditionally the first grape harvest is blessed on the Feast of the Transfiguration. The ancient tradition of having grapes blessed has lived on in the Church since the fourth century. In fact, we have the oldest prayer for the blessing of fruit from the fourth-century manual of the Christian life, *Apostolic Constitutions*. We also have a Prayer of Thanksgiving for new fruits from St. Hyppolytus that dates from around the year 220. And from the Sixth Ecumenical Council (680–681) we have canon 28, which tells us that new wheat and grapes are to be blessed on this day.

Grapes have an obvious connection to the Eucharist, since they become wine, which in turn becomes Christ's Blood. Creation is transfigured into something new and brilliant, but it doesn't end there. When we partake in the Eucharist, we, too, are transfigured, as we become what we have received, the Body of Christ. Through this holy use of the grape harvest, and our reception of the Eucharist, Christ then transfigures the world. On this feast day, Jesus reveals to us through his own Transfiguration the splendor that we were made for and promises us a restoration of life.

Enjoy this day by taking grapes to your parish to be blessed by a priest. You might also consider serving grapes as a snack, making a meal with grapes, or relaxing with a glass of wine. Above all, try to go to Mass today and partake in the Blood of Christ, the most precious gift from the vine.

The Angelus is a Marian prayer that can be learned or begun as a daily practice today in honor of the efforts of Pope Callixtus (also called Callistus) who believed that the power of prayer could aid in the defense of Christianity against the Turks. Traditionally said at 6:00 a.m., noon, and 6:00 p.m., the Angelus is a prayer that calls to mind the Incarnation. The significance of praying three times a day is rooted in its connection to the number three, which is often associated with theological perfection in relation to the Trinity. Praying the Angelus at these times each day is meant to disrupt our daily routine by acknowledging God's presence in our lives and work. The Angelus welcomes God into our daily activities, just as Christ came into our world through the mystery of the Incarnation. Create the habit of praying the Angelus by setting an alarm on your phone so that you remember to pray. Invite your spouse, roommate, or children to do this with you so that everyone in the household is called to see Christ in their midst. Parishes that offer morning, noontime, and evening Masses can also implement this practice by praying the Angelus before Mass begins.

CARRYING ON THE TRADITION

AT HOME
Have your grapes blessed by a priest, and serve them with dinner or as a dessert today.

Consider This
- Share with your family the faith-filled connection between grapes and the Transfiguration.
- Pick one recipe that your family will enjoy that uses grapes.
- Pack grapes for workday or school lunches today.
- Since it is a feast day, try to go to Mass today.
- Set alarms on your phone to pray the Angelus at one or all of the prescribed times.

IN THE PARISH

Offer your parishioners a blessing of grapes, and share the meaningful connection that grapes have to the Transfiguration.

Consider This
- Prepare your parishioners in advance by letting them know about this custom and how your parish will participate in it through your social-media platforms and other communication channels.
- Discuss the topic of the Transfiguration in the various ministry settings that you provide.
- If your parish has a bell system, begin ringing the Angelus bells at 6:00 a.m., noon, and 6:00 p.m.
- Pray the Angelus before any Mass times that are close to those three times.

Resource
You can find the Angelus in the *Festive Faith Sundays and Essentials Companion* at www.HisGirlSunday.com/FestiveFaith.

BLESSING FLOWERS AND HERBS FOR THE ASSUMPTION OF MARY OR MARYMASS

AUGUST 15

THE STORY

We mark another harvest festival on August 15, the Feast of the Assumption of Mary in the West. In the Orthodox and Eastern Catholic Churches the feast is known as the Dormition of Mary. In both East and West the feast marks the earthly death of Mary and her being taken up into heaven, but details of these events vary slightly. From the *Directory of Popular Piety*, we learn that in many Germanic countries it is customary to bless herbs on this day in recognition that it is God who gives us sustenance, growth, and good fruits from the earth. While the origins of the practice may be traced to pre-Christian magic rites intended to harness the healing power of herbs and ward off malevolent spirits, it was eventually embraced by the faithful as a divine blessing from God. Herbs hold within them natural properties for healing and strengthening, a gift of God's good creation. Certain flowers, such as lavender, primrose, and marigolds, possess healing properties that God affectionately gives to us through the work of creation as we wait for the fulfillment of our eternal healing, unification with God and all the angels and saints in heaven. Flowers are also blessed on this day because there is a legend that made its way to us from the Patristic era, the period of the Church Fathers, which says that after Mary was assumed body and soul into heaven, her tomb was found flowering with roses and lilies. It is on this feast day that we accept the fruits of life, not only on earth, but in heaven.

Celebrating Mary on this harvest celebration day only furthers our understanding of the intimate connection that we humans enjoy with all of creation. On this feast we commemorate the Blessed Virgin Mary, who was conceived free from original sin and who was assumed or taken up, body and soul, into heaven. Mary's assumption is "the highest fruit of the redemption, and a supreme testimony to the breadth and efficacy of Christ's salvific work. [It] is a pledge of the future participation of the members of the mystical Body of Christ in the paschal glory of the Risen Christ."[4]

The Feast of the Assumption of Mary is a resounding affirmation of her singular role in the saving work of the Father in Jesus. It brings us hope, for we, too, will be raised body and soul into heaven one day. Mary is our model of this, and through her we can find hope and joy that God is faithful to his promises. In the liturgy she is often described in floral terms, such as a vine, a lily, or rosemary. Even as early as the seventh century we can find this language from St. Bede, who likened Mary to the white petals of a lily because of her purity. We celebrate Mary, therefore, through the gift and blessing of herbs and flowers that spring forth from the ground with newness of life.

THE TRADITION

A common tradition associated with this day is blessing herbs and flowers. In the days leading up to this feast, find a parish near you that is offering the blessing of herbs and flowers, or ask your parish priest if he will do this for your community. As you prepare, trim the herbs and flowers from your garden, or purchase them from a grocery store or farmer's market. You may then want to bundle small amounts together with ribbons or delicate string. These are known as "Assumption Bundles," a name that has been around since the ninth century. After gathering your herbs and flowers (in bundles or not), ask a priest to bless them. Set these items apart in your kitchen, using the herbs to cook dinner with, or make herbal teas to drink during your morning prayer time. Allow them to nourish your body and those of your family in thanksgiving for all that God has given to us. Even the seemingly little gifts of good herbs can be a doorway to a life of gratitude. With the same grateful disposition, you can display your blessed flowers on your dining-room table or on your home altar. Offer a Marian image or statue that is within your domestic church a little bundle of flowers. Keeping fresh flowers in front of Our Lady can help us remember her blossoming tomb and how her assumption holds the promise of heaven that God has made to us all.

You might also consider reaping the rewards of a Marian Garden. In the medieval Church, works of religious art depicted Mary with the infant Jesus sitting amid an enclosed garden of flowers. Mary's virtue played a significant role in the symbolic meaning behind each flower, and often these images were entitled "Mary's Garden." Various flowers and herbs hold different meanings, such as the lily for her purity, the violet for her humility, and roses for her glory.

Some plants are named directly after her, such as marigolds. You can find a full list of garden recommendations in the *Festive Faith Easter and Summer Ordinary Time Companion* at www.HisGirlSunday.com/FestiveFaith.

Placing an outdoor statue of Mary in the midst of a garden harkens back to those medieval works of art that depicted Mary sitting encircled by blooming flowers and herbs. Whether you have a large or small yard or you live in an apartment or townhome with no backyard at all, this can be done—if even in the smallest of planter boxes. Your kitchen windowsill might become a place for your Marian Garden. If you don't already have one, begin planting one of these gardens on the Feast of the Assumption or during the first couple of weeks in August in preparation for this feast. If you already have a garden, today would be the right time to trim off some flowers and herbs to be blessed at Mass.

CARRYING ON THE TRADITION

AT HOME
Plant, or tend to, your Marian Garden, and bring the herbs and flowers that you've grown to Mass today to be blessed.

Consider This
- If you can't grow your own Marian Garden or planter box of flowers and herbs, go to the store and purchase them for this special feast day.
- Make Assumption Bundles, herbs and flowers tied together with a ribbon or string, and give them to your friends, neighbors, and family members.
- Arrange flowers for Mary, and place them near an image of her in your home or at a favorite image of her in your parish church.
- Make special meals and drinks with your blessed herbs.

IN THE PARISH
Provide your congregation with the blessing of herbs and flowers at daily Mass or on the Sunday nearest the feast day.

Consider This
- Articulate what Mary's assumption should mean for us as we walk through Ordinary Time seeking virtue and relationship with God.
- Show or tell your parishioners how to make simple Assumption Bundles by tying flowers and herbs together with a ribbon or string, and encourage them to share the bundles with others.

- Invite a parish ministry or the faith-formation families to develop a Marian Garden on your parish grounds for prayer and reflection. If you already have one, organize volunteers to spruce it up in preparation for this feast day.

Resource
You can find a Marian Flower Garden Guide in the *Festive Faith Easter and Summer Ordinary Time Companion* at www.HisGirlSunday.com/FestiveFaith

===== *A LIVING TRADITION* =====

In the Byzantine tradition, we bless flowers and herbs on the Feast of the Dormition (called the Assumption in the West). I always remember as a little kid gathering up dandelions and other wildflowers from around the backyard to place them by the concrete statue of the Blessed Mother we had. Even as I grew older, it always made me happy to see that someone had placed flowers in front of a statue or icon of Mary, especially when the variety and/or arrangement made it clear that they were placed there by a little one. Now that I have four children of my own, and my wife grows a variety of flowers, we love putting together an arrangement in the summer to bring to church with us to place in front of the icon of the Theotokos of the Passion (aka Our Lady of Perpetual Help). On the Feast of the Dormition, it's almost like Mary "gives back" as the church is filled with different arrangements and bouquets that we take back home so that we can enjoy the beauty of these flowers as autumn approaches. I also think the symbolic value of blessing flowers as we commemorate Mary's entry into eternal life is very fitting. The flowers we have blessed usually wither and fade within a few days, a reminder of how fleeting earthly honor and glory can be. Yet, these flowers often come from plants that will grow and bloom again this year or next, reminding us, also, that death is only fleeting for the Christian.

One of the beautiful things about Christianity, especially Catholicism, is the constant reminder that the spiritual and material worlds are not opposed to each other. Our sins can estrange us from the right relationship we should have with God's creation, but God constantly calls us to remember that his creation is fundamentally good, just as he said in Genesis. This is why I love the various blessings throughout the Church year of ordinary objects that surround us all the time. Sometimes it is easy to ignore them, but the Church reminds us on a regular schedule to look around and appreciate God's many blessings. It's almost as if the Fathers of the Church, through all these centuries, are still reminding us to "stop and smell the roses"—quite literally in the case of blessing flowers at the Dormition.

In today's world we are often subjected to heavily edited and composed photography claiming to show *real* life. This extends from movies, television, and magazines to the social-media pictures on the phones in our pockets. So many filters and touch-ups are done, even of pictures purporting to show the beauty of the natural world, that it can be hard to remember the natural beauty of the world around us. True, some of the flowers we bring to church for blessing will be the product of years of selective breeding, domestication, and so on, but they were born of a process where people worked with the natural ingredients God provided and cooperated with nature to create something even more beautiful. This is a metaphor, if I'm not stretching too much, of the amazing things we can do when we restore a right relationship with the beautiful world around us that God created.

Deacon Nicholas Modelski

BIRTHDAY PARTY FOR MARY

SEPTEMBER 8

THE STORY

On September 8 we celebrate the birthday of Our Lady. It is liturgically fixed to this date because it comes nine months after the Feast of the Immaculate Conception, on December 8. The Immaculate Conception refers to the Catholic belief that Mary was conceived without original sin as the child of Sts. Joachim and Anne. This holy couple was infertile but had fervently prayed for a child when Anne received the promise that their child would play an integral role in salvation history. One early tradition says that an angel of the Lord told Anne, "The Lord has heard your prayer, and you shall conceive, and shall bring forth, and your seed shall be spoken of in all the world."[5]

The account of Mary's birthday isn't present in scripture, but the tradition of celebrating it on September 8 has been passed down through the living tradition of the Church. In an ancient, apocryphal text known as the *Protoevangelium of James*, believed to have been written around the second century, we are introduced to Anne and Joachim in their roles as parents, and we see the deliberate and attentive care they provided for Mary. Each family member is conscientiously striving to honor God, with a particular emphasis on the way they nurture and raise Mary. This work also describes how "Anne made a sanctuary" in Mary's room and "allowed nothing common or unclean on account of the special holiness of the child." We also read in this ancient text that in Mary's first year St. Joachim, "made a great feast, and invited the priests, and the scribes, and the elders, and all the people of Israel." He also brought her to the priests, who blessed her, saying, "O God of our fathers, bless this child, and give her an everlasting name to be named in all generations."[6] St. Joachim was the first to arrange a great feast, a birthday party, for her, and in that same excitement we can mirror his efforts today.

This feast day is particularly interesting because we don't usually see birthdays on the liturgical calendar, and as you read in the section on St. John the Baptist there are only three: those of Jesus (December 25), John the Baptist (June 24), and Mary (September 8). The Church began celebrating the nativity of Mary around the sixth century in the Eastern Church, and it became widely spread throughout the Western Church in the eighth and ninth centuries. The significance of this feast day was highlighted by Pope Innocent IV when he established the feast to be observed with an octave in 1254. The nativity of Mary retained its octave until the calendar reforms of Pope Pius XII in 1954. This feast day is sometimes known as Latter Marymass, since it comes after the Assumption, which was known as Marymass. Mary's birthday is another opportunity to recognize and venerate her role in Christ's saving mission.

THE TRADITION

Because this liturgical feast is a birthday, it's only fitting that we have a birthday party! Let's imitate St. Joachim and throw a great feast, inviting extended family, friends, coworkers, neighbors, and our local priests—anyone we think will benefit from this joyous celebration. Mary loves it most when we honor her through her Son, so try to go to Mass today if you can. In the evening, when everyone is home, celebrate with a party. Some have adjusted the date of the party, if it falls on a weeknight, to the following weekend so that the celebrations can be more vibrant, but you could always offer something simpler on the evening of September 8, with a larger gathering the following weekend. Try decorating with blue balloons, streamers, and party banners. Bake Mary a cake or cupcakes, and sing "Happy Birthday" to her. You can have children make fun birthday cards as an activity. Close your evening by praying a Marian prayer such as the Rosary or by singing a joyful Marian hymn. Parish communities can also do this by offering blue cupcakes during the hospitality time on the Sunday that follows Mary's birthday. Certain ministry groups might also find it enjoyable to throw Mary a birthday party and extend the invitation for others to join. However you choose to honor the birth of Mary, do it festively!

CARRYING ON THE TRADITION

AT HOME
Host a birthday party for Mary that brings the entire family together.

Consider This
- We all love our Blessed Mother, so extend the party with food and activities to include everyone in your household and perhaps your neighborhood.
- Decorate with blue party items, a color that represents Our Lady.
- If you don't throw a full party, serve cake or cupcakes with your dinner tonight and let everyone know that today is Mary's birthday. You can find Marian Cupcake Toppers in the *Festive Faith Easter and Summer Ordinary Time Companion* at www.HisGirlSunday.com/FestiveFaith
- Make birthday cards or banners for Mary.
- Honor Mary by saying a Rosary or singing a Marian hymn together.

IN THE PARISH
Invite your parish moms' group or children's faith-formation classes to throw a birthday party for Mary, and give them tips and support.

Consider This
- Have the children make birthday cards for the Blessed Mother.
- Decorate with blue and Marian-themed decorations.
- Invite your parish priest to come by just as St. Joachim asked his community's priests, scribes, and elders to join him in celebrating Mary's birth.
- Serve a birthday cake or blue cupcakes during hospitality time on the Sunday after Mary's birthday, and top them with Marian-themed cutouts.
- If you have a large group, arrange your cupcakes in the formation of a rosary.

Resource
Brainstorm ways to celebrate Mary's birthday with the party-planning list found in the *Festive Faith Easter and Summer Ordinary Time Companion* at www.HisGirlSunday.com/FestiveFaith.

MICHAELMAS BLACKBERRIES, FASTING, AND FEASTING

SEPTEMBER 29

THE STORY

The Feast of Sts. Michael, Gabriel, and Raphael, Archangels, is celebrated each year on September 29, and is widely known simply as Michaelmas. Devotion to St. Michael runs deep in the hearts of the faithful, and the number of ways that you can live this day liturgically are plentiful. This feast follows the fall Ember Days, adding a touch of celebration and marking the arrival of the autumn season. The Ember Days, now optional, were once regularly observed in four sets of three days, which correspond to the four natural seasons. These were celebrated in thanksgiving for the crops that help us to celebrate the sacraments. These, like Rogation Days, were linked to the blessings of the earth and were marked by prayer, fasting, and in September particularly, thanksgiving for the grape harvest which is needed to make the wine that is then consecrated to become the Precious Blood of Christ. If you'd like to learn more about the Ember Days, go to the *Festive Faith Rhythms of Fasting and Abstinence Companion* at www.HisGirlSunday.com/FestiveFaith.

St. Michael is one of the principal archangels who fought against Lucifer, the fallen angel, and cast him out of heaven. Up until the eighteenth century, the Feast of the Archangels was considered a holy day of obligation. Tradition tells us that St. Michael is always engaged in spiritual warfare on our behalf, most of the time with little awareness on our part. According to Christian tradition he has four offices: "to fight against Satan, to rescue the souls of the faithful from the power of the enemy, especially at the hour of death, to be the champion of God's people, and to call away from earth and bring men's souls to judgment."[7] St. Michael guards, protects, and leads us in achieving victory against the enemy and all his empty promises.

St. Francis of Assisi began the custom of St. Michael's Lent, a period of prayer and fasting that begins on August 15 and ends on the Feast of the Archangels. St. Michael's Lent is practiced much like the weeks of prayer, fasting, and penitence that we keep before Easter. Tradition holds that two years before St. Francis of Assisi died in October of 1226, he went away to Mount La Verna, where he fasted and prayed in honor of St. Michael the Archangel. It was during this time that he received the stigmata, the holy wounds of Jesus. St. Michael's Lent became popular among the Franciscans before widely falling out of practice. Many Catholics are interested in bringing back the tradition, which is intended to give attention to deepening our relationship with Jesus and St. Michael, who is our most powerful intercessor in fighting against spiritual enemies. While we often think that penance is reserved only for the traditional season of Lent, the liturgical year and the saints prompt us to regularly partake in this form of prayer. Fasting and feasting go hand in hand, and it is through both means that we can grow to live more closely to the divine life of Christ.

THE TRADITION

A clever Irish folktale relates that when Satan was kicked out of heaven he landed in a blackberry patch, and he returns every year to curse and spit on the fruit that he landed on. This makes the berries so sour that they cannot be picked after the Feast of St. Michael. This story intertwines beautifully with the agrarian cycle because blackberry season kicks off in May and generally winds down in September. Thus, one Michaelmas tradition is to bake blackberry desserts with the last of the season's berries and serve these at feast-day meals.

In a Scottish custom farmers would dig a triangular hole in the ground that represented St. Michael's shield so that they could better access the roots of carrots while harvesting them. I usually try to make honey-glazed carrots as a Michaelmas dinner side, since they also are nearing the end of their harvest season at this time. There are many wonderful carrot recipes to try, both savory and sweet.

The tradition of eating goose on Michaelmas comes from certain areas within the United Kingdom. In fact, some still refer to the Feast of St. Michael as "Goose Day." A couple of legends point to the possible origins of this tradition. The first tells us that when Queen Elizabeth I heard of the defeat of the Spanish Armada she was at dinner having goose. She saw the goose as a token of good luck and promised to have it on Michaelmas every year. This custom spread, and more people throughout the United Kingdom began doing this also. There is even a popular rhyme that states that those who eat goose will have good fortune. The other story explains that Michaelmas was celebrated about the time of year that farming debts were due, and those who were trying to persuade their landlords to leniency would have sought to convince them by offering them geese. This relates to the rhyme "he who eats goose on Michaelmas day; shan't money lack or debts pay."[8] Whatever the origin, goose is a traditional centerpiece of Michaelmas dinner. If that is too expensive or difficult to find today, you can always adapt by preparing a turkey or roasting a chicken. If you don't eat meat, plan and prepare a favorite meal, make some simple table decorations featuring geese, and tell the story of Queen Elizabeth I and the goose as you sit down to your festive dinner.

As the seasons change and the spring and summertime flowers die, the little pointed and colorful aster flower, also known as the Michaelmas Daisy, remains. It gets its name in honor of the angel who fought against evil, because this small yet brilliant flower seems to fight against the impending gloom, cold, and dark days of winter. It's in bloom all autumn and is therefore full of symbolism. Because it is difficult for me to find aster flowers where I am, I usually grab a happy bouquet of daisies to put on the dinner table for this feast day. This sweet rhyme tells us of the connection between these flowers and the Feast of St. Michael:

> *The Michaelmas Daisies, among dede weeds,*
> *Bloom for St. Michael's valorous deeds.*
> *And seems the last of flowers that stood,*
> *Till the feast of St. Simon and St. Jude.*[9]

Beginning August 15, keep St. Michael's Lent as a special time of prayer, fasting, and giving thanks for the goods of the earth, which are now coming to harvest. If you're not ready to engage in something so involved, you could pray the classic St. Michael Prayer, a St. Michael Chaplet, or a St. Michael Novena in the nine days leading up to Michaelmas. Pick and choose from the liturgical-living customs provided, and be encouraged to make this feast day your own. Always remember that we are never on our own against temptation and the evils that might come our way; take comfort in that by fostering an ongoing relationship with the angels.

CARRYING ON THE TRADITION

AT HOME
Bake a blackberry dessert to share this evening, and pray the St. Michael the Archangel Prayer before you enjoy it, perhaps with extended family or neighbors.

Consider This
- Share the Irish folktale about Lucifer and the blackberries with those who are eating your dessert.
- Extend this into a full meal with carrots and goose, or turkey or chicken.
- Decorate your home altar or dining-room table with Michaelmas Daisies or geese décor!
- Partake in St. Michael's Lent by planning ahead and finding someone who will join you in the discipline.
- Ask for St. Michael's intercession by developing an ongoing relationship with him and the other archangels.

IN THE PARISH

Pray the St. Michael the Archangel Prayer at the conclusion of every Mass, or endeavor to share St. Michael's Lent with your community by providing them with the story of St. Francis of Assisi.

Consider This
- Share the benefits of a relationship with St. Michael and the archangels.
- Communicate the dates and description for how to participate in St. Michael's Lent.
- Put together a resource guide with ways that parish households can celebrate St. Michael and the archangels at home.
- Request blackberry recipes and carrot recipes from your parishioners to share as a compilation in your bulletin or e-newsletter. This is a great way to involve the community in the traditions of this feast day.

Resource
Find a recipe for Blackberry Turnovers in the *Festive Faith Easter and Summer Ordinary Time Companion* at www.HisGirlSunday.com/FestiveFaith.

ALL HALLOWS' EVE, ALL SAINTS' DAY, AND ALL SOULS' DAY

OCTOBER 31–NOVEMBER 2

Before we delve into these three days of festivity with much liturgical and seasonal complexity, let's begin by grounding ourselves in the meaning of what was once a common name for this three-part celebration—Allhallowtide. During this liturgical triplet of days we are called to remember and celebrate the Communion of Saints, *communio sanctorum*. *All* refers to all the holy men and women that we honor over these three days, *hallow* means to sanctify or to make holy, and the suffix *-tide* is used to indicate that this is a specific period of time. This terminology orients our focus to the Church now living on earth, the Church in purgatory, and the Church in heaven. These three days mark times of transition in the lives of all the faithful, and it's no coincidence that they fall during a time when we see creation changing.

Here in the northern hemisphere, the natural world undergoes a little death as the leaves and land slowly move from summer to fall to winter. When we attend to this changing of the seasons, we are humbled by examining our mortality and reflecting on the lives of the great saints and souls who have gone before us in faith. This is where we get the other name for these three days, the Triduum of Death. While it may sound scary, neither this name nor these feasts are intended to be. Rather, these days are meant to foster exploration into the mystery of death and of the life to come after. Holding the idea of dying in our minds can cause sorrow, worry, and trepidation, but without acknowledging this reality we fall prey to living with too much self-reliance. It's easy to get swept up in our own personal lives, which can quickly lead us to overemphasize ourselves, our families, our schedule, our troubles, and our obligations. We not only become disunified from God and what he wants for us but can also find ourselves even more disconnected from our role in the Communion of Saints.

All Hallows' Eve (Halloween), All Saints' Day, and All Souls' Day disrupt our regular rhythm to ensure that we understand our total reliance upon God for everything, including, and ultimately, our salvation. There is no other way to heaven except through death, and it is at this juncture that we must explore with full humility our part in this season. We are meant to be saints, and that doesn't just happen—all good and worthy things take work. Remembering our death, the worst of all consequences of the Fall, is a reminder to try to avoid sin and cling to the life of the sacraments throughout our ordinary routines. "In whatever you do, remember your last days, and you will never sin" (Sir 7:36). The difficult and unavoidable truth is that we are only here for an unknown while. We do not know the time when we will die, just as we do not know when Christ will return. Like all the saints we have the same bittersweet end, which is to die so that one day we might rise again with Christ.

ALL HALLOWS' EVE COSTUMES AND DÉCOR
OCTOBER 31

THE STORY

Hallowe'en, or All Hallows' Eve, is the vigil of All Saints. Before 1955, this vigil was designated a day of penance, fasting, and abstinence to prepare for the upcoming feast day according to the 1917 Code of Canon Law. Fasting and penance on the vigil of major feasts was standard practice for centuries, as vigils have a different character than Masses of anticipation. The Vigil of All Saints had its own prayers and readings and was considered its own liturgical observance separate from the day of All Saints. In the current *Roman Missal*, there is no Mass for the vigil anymore. Instead, on October 31 the Masses in the evening are offered as Masses of anticipation and use the same prayers and readings that are used for the Feast of All Saints. With the vigil no longer in place, the penitential rules for All Hallows' Eve were also lifted. While you could still choose to observe Halloween as a penitential day, it is also a time to rejoice for those who have made it to their eternal reward while anticipating that of our own.

Separate from what you may have heard about any pagan stories, beliefs, or influence, Christians from the first to third centuries paved the way for this commemoration. In the days of the early Church, when martyrdom was the frightening reality and Christianity faced some of its harshest persecutions, the locals would honor those who had died for the faith in secret. Neighboring towns even began to transfer and divide relics among them so that everyone could participate in this common memorial. As the number of faithful departed grew, especially as the numbers of those martyred for the faith grew in the third and fourth centuries, this observance needed a more practical approach. From this effort developed a one-day observance of all Church martyrs. Around the seventh century, the one-day celebration was fixed on May 13 as Pope Boniface IV dedicated the Pantheon to the Virgin Mary and all Christian martyrs. Later this commemoration of the martyrs grew to include both saints and martyrs and moved to November 1. The initial change is credited to Pope Gregory III, who dedicated a chapel on this day in St. Peter's Basilica to revere all saints and martyrs. Pope Gregory IV further solidified and progressed this feast day by requesting that King Louis the Pious make this an honored day throughout the entire Holy Roman Empire.

Halloween has always been a Catholic day of remembrance and commemoration for those who have died in dedication to Christ. Celebrating Halloween as an isolated "holiday" lacks context and authentic meaning unless one comprehends its connection to All Saints and All Souls, along with having an appreciation of the history and heritage of the early Christian centuries. The current secular celebration of Halloween tilts toward what we know of pre-Christian and pagan practices. The festive expressions we see the most today—such as spooky, scary, and sadly, violent costuming, decorations, and activities—are not derived from our Catholic lineage but from tales of evil spirits and superstitions about the dead. As faith-filled disciples it is our responsibility to approach Halloween not as the pre-Christian people did, but as people of the Resurrection. We shouldn't run away from Halloween, or the debate that it causes, because it belongs to us! Instead, approach it with a sense of intrigue and curiosity for your faith that reinvigorates your customs. Look back into its history, see how the Church lived it out, and spread the holiness of the saints throughout the world.

THE TRADITION

Invite the start of Allhallowtide into your household or parish by befriending the saints through books, prayer, intercession, and fun activities. Especially within the United States where Halloween festivities are broadly celebrated, bring the blessing of witnessing your Catholic faith to your friends, family, and community. A new tradition of carving Catholic symbols into pumpkins is making its way to doorsteps around the United States. The light that pours forth from the candle placed in the pumpkin illuminates a holy and sacred symbol that stands as an image of faith for others to see. In the same way that the light of Christ guides us out of darkness, these unique pumpkins are a light in the dark autumn days to those who encounter your home.

Meaningful Halloween costumes are another exterior sign of the faith. Many individuals and families have sought to dress like the saints whom they admire as a way of bringing the roots of this vigil to the world. While you might not find these in your local store, you can piece them together in your efforts to live liturgically. And while a saint costume might not be your style from year to year, dressing as other worthy professions, characters, and role models could be another option in bringing about a positive message.

Decoration also holds our attention as stores fill up with ghosts, goblins, and monsters. Creatively adorn your domestic church with images of Catholic saints, Memento Mori skulls, and butterflies, which remind us of the Resurrection. Every Halloween, I put my collection of saint prayer cards to good use by creating a banner. I simply clip them onto a string using clothespins, and voila!

As more people are drawn away from trick-or-treating, Catholic parish trunk-or-treating has been found to be a great substitute. Several years ago, I collaborated with a parish in organizing and implementing a saint-themed trunk or treat. The number of people who attended was more than I'd hoped! Thousands of families came to enjoy Halloween in a joyful and religious environment. Even community members who were not from our parish and many who were not even Catholic came to participate with us because they knew their children would be safe and happy. Hospitality has a way of transcending potential barriers when we show the concern of Christ for others, and what better time than on a day when we join with the entire Communion of Saints? Together we not only look upward but we look outward. Our families are looking for a place to go, and the parish can be that second home for celebrating shared belief and understanding in community with one another.

CARRYING ON THE TRADITION

AT HOME
Inspire Catholic celebration for Halloween by explaining to your household where this feast comes from and choosing more faith-filled ways to dress up and decorate inspired by the Communion of Saints.

Consider This

- Carve pumpkins using Catholic Pumpkins Stencils that you can find in the *Festive Faith Easter and Summer Ordinary Time Companion* at www.HisGirlSunday.com/FestiveFaith.
- Dress up as the saints.
- Decorate with more faith-based symbols such as butterflies, saint images, and Memento Mori skulls.
- Make a saint banner with prayer cards, string, and clothespins.
- Go to Mass and ask for the intercession of the saints.

IN THE PARISH

Consider having a parish ministry group host an All Hallows' Eve trunk or treat where families can go to enjoy the festivities.

Consider This

- If you cannot hold this on All Hallows' Eve, try another weekend that is close to October 31.
- Inspire the faithful to remember that they are a part of the Communion of Saints and are called to seek holiness as they prepare themselves for heaven.
- Offer an Allhallowtide Catholic resource guide for celebrating All Hallows' Eve, All Saints' Day, and All Souls' Day with attainable ideas that people can do at home.
- Take opportunities to talk about some of the words and themes associated with these three days, such as Halloween, Allhallowtide, and the Triduum of Death, and what these three days ask of us.

ALL SAINTS' DAY PARTIES
NOVEMBER 1

THE STORY

The Solemnity of All Saints is a day on which we venerate the men and women who have made it to heaven and also ask their intercession for those of us still on earth. There is no mistaking that we love the saints! Their stories are our real-life motivation, their patronage inspires us to consider our own passions, and their extraordinary examples instill in us the belief that heaven is within our reach. Not all saints have been canonized by the Catholic Church; we believe that there are more souls in heaven than are mentioned in the liturgical calendar. In addition to celebrating one or two saints on any given day throughout the year, we have one day where everyone in heaven is honored. This is a solemnity and a holy day of obligation, which means that the best way to honor the saints is by being with them at Mass and imitating their lives of virtue. Mass is the highest imitation that we have of heaven on earth, and within its celebration the Communion of Saints is never closer. The cloud of witnesses dwell in the full glory of God, while we here on earth receive Christ into our very bodies through our reception of Holy Communion. Within every Mass, and on this day especially, we esteem and seek to imitate all of those who have lived through earthly trials with unwavering love and dedication for Christ and his Church.

THE TRADITION

Understandably most of the outward acknowledgment and celebratory hype for All Saints' Day probably happens on the day before, Halloween, but as the curiosity in and hunger for liturgical living and Catholic culture grows, so do our more intentional festivities. Enrich your own faith by reading a saint book or journaling about ways that you can emulate these holy men and women. Then begin your own tradition of throwing an All Saints' party. This occasion would give you the opportunity to unpack the lives of some of the canonized saints in our tradition. For your party you might offer a saint-costume contest, saint-inspired snacks that are tied to their patronage, and an explanation of today's solemnity. One year my husband and I hosted an adult saint party where we gathered our friends to play a challenging round of saint trivia. I didn't anticipate just how much laughter we would share as we learned more about the saints.

During this time many parishes are hosting fall festivals. This is the right time to weave in the Catholic origins of Halloween and integrate more faith-filled customs into your gathering. Many people from near and far come out for these events, so now is your time to captivate the hearts of the faithful by bonding them together over our shared Christian ancestry. Combine your usual festival booths with activities like a Catholic pumpkin-carving station, Catholic-inspired saint treats or games, and a saint-costume contest. Many parish festivals have raffles. Pull together saint-inspired raffle baskets based on where the saint lived or died or perhaps their patronage. I'm envisioning a really great music basket for St. Cecilia, and there are so many other great ideas! If your parish happens to be named after a saint, rebrand your typical fall festival to be cleverly called something after your patron. Many parishioners are not aware that there is a saint's relic within each parish church's altar, and I can assure you that nothing holds people's attention more than these eye-opening Catholic lessons and stories. There are endless saint tales and topics for you to delve into during formation classes, ministry meetings, and homilies. While you might not do all of the ideas mentioned, begin community-wide traditions by choosing a few. As parish participants it can be easy for us to get distracted by the low-hanging fruit of our work, but remember, the main purpose of the Church is the salvation of souls. We are here to help encourage sainthood, so let's reorient our efforts to the overarching mission that Christ handed off to us.

CARRYING ON THE TRADITION

AT HOME
Bring the saints alive today in a way that you, your family, and your friends enjoy celebrating. Allow creativity to flow, host a party, or consider the other options below to get you started.

Consider This
- Throw a saint-themed party with snacks, games, costumes, and party decorations.
- Read a book about your favorite saint, listen to a story about him or her, and in some way get to know the saint better.
- Spend time reflecting and praying about your own journey toward heaven. Consider the virtues in which you are strong and weak, and invite the friendship of a saint to help you. Set small and attainable goals for your growth in holiness.
- Ask your children to befriend a saint. It could be their namesake, the saint whose feast day they were born on, or a patron saint of their favorite thing.

IN THE PARISH
Transform your October fall festival into an All Saints' Day festival, and extend more Mass times for everyone to meet their Mass obligation.

Consider This
- Craft another name for your fall festival that speaks to our Catholicism, All Saints' Day, or your parish patron saint.

- Offer a mix of typical fall-festival activities with saint-inspired experiences such as a costume contest, parade, snacks, raffle baskets, games, and a pumpkin-carving station.
- Provide more opportunities for Mass and Confession on holy days of obligation.
- Remind your parishioners that they are meant for sainthood, as some people have never been told that inspiring message before.
- Share saint-oriented details about your parish church such as information about the relic in your altar or the images in your stained-glass windows.

A LIVING TRADITION

All Saints' Day at our parish is a time for us to celebrate and give our children something to develop their understanding of the faith and build up our domestic churches as a family. Our parish's All Saints' Day festival consists of twenty to thirty booths, each based on a different saint's life. For example, we make monstrances with St. Clare, and we go on a scavenger hunt with St. Anthony. At each of these stations our children are given the opportunity to learn about a saint in an engaging and fun manner. These traditions are vital for our domestic churches and for faith formation. Having supportive parishes also helps with being able to celebrate and do activities in the community with other Catholic families. The All Saints' Day festival was not always huge at our parish. It started off very small; we just met at a playground with a bunch of kids and encouraged them to dress up. As it grew, we saw the need to keep this festival focused on the saints, so it did not become just another fall festival.

If you want to start celebrating All Saints' Day, start small by doing an activity: go to Mass, dress up as the saints, and explain to your children that today we celebrate the saints and tomorrow we pray for our families and the souls in purgatory. These are the memories that we want to nourish as parents! The family Rosary, which the month of October is dedicated to, and the All Saints' Day festival are memories and traditions that are intergenerational. I think about how amazing it will be to have my grandchildren dressing up as saints and praying a Rosary with me one day because it is the gift that I gave to my children that they will one day hand down to theirs.

Mariah Baker

ALL SOULS' DAY ALTARS AND CEMETERY VISITS

NOVEMBER 2

THE STORY

The faithful souls who are being purified in purgatory are celebrated on November 2 and throughout November. On this day, the Commemoration of All the Faithful Departed, or All Souls' Day, we remember and honor them for the lives that they lived in faith. The theological meaning behind this feast day is that, upon death, souls depart from the body and, if need be, they are made pure before entering heaven and receiving the beatific vision. Revelation 21:27 speaks of heaven in this way: "Nothing unclean will enter it." While we might not see the word *purgatory* in the Bible, we know that it means to purge, or to cleanse, and that this is necessary to being with Our Lord in the heavenly Jerusalem. We are encouraged to pray for these souls as they are being cleansed and freed from sin. The faithful on earth can assist them with prayer and sacrifice, especially offering Mass for them. We can pay tribute to our loved ones who have passed away by not only remembering them on All Souls' Day, Soulmas, but also demonstrating our connection with them as the Communion of Saints. By means of prayer and charity we demonstrate how we are all a part of the Body of Christ. The saints in heaven intercede for us, and we intercede for the souls in purgatory through prayer, fasting, and almsgiving.

From antiquity the Church has been consistent in praying for the souls of the faithful departed. In an early Church tradition of honoring their deceased brothers and sisters in Christ, the names of those who had passed would be placed on a diptych. Following that practice the Benedictine monasteries expanded the custom further by offering Mass and other celebrations to lift those souls up in prayer and offer on their behalf what might be lacking. These customs spread to other Catholic orders and eventually the entire Church. Credit is given to St. Odilo, an abbot of Cluny, who instituted November 2 as the universal date on which the faithful on earth would practice praying for the faithful departed. At every Mass we attend there is a particular moment of intercession for the souls in purgatory, but on this particular day and throughout November, we are to give prominent focus and rededication to these efforts.

THE TRADITION

Remember the faithful departed by putting up pictures of relatives who have passed away with a small tea light in front of each picture. By doing this, your family can keep the precious memories of your departed loved ones alive. Share fond stories of each person with your spouse, children, extended family, neighbors, and friends. Let everyone who enters your house this day and through the month know something of these dearly departed. Invite everyone who views your display to pray for those who have died. Keep this home altar addition up for all of November, since the entire month is dedicated to inspiring a deeper connection with the souls in purgatory. Praying for the dead, while a beneficial aid to our grieving process, can also meld us to the ancient tradition of praying for those who have gone before us, a practice that can be traced back to the Old Testament in the books of Maccabees. We pray for the dead as a way of offering consolation for those who are undergoing the painful purification process of purgatory with hope that it will help set them free to behold the beatific vision.

As difficult as it may be, this is an ideal time to visit the cemetery of a family member who has passed, and if not today, then at some point within the month of November. Read from scripture while you are there, pray the Litany for the Holy Souls, which you can easily find online, and bring a bouquet to freshen up the gravesite. Taking care of a departed loved one's resting place pulls our families closer together by maintaining a connection with our ancestors, as well as paving a way forward for us in unity with them.

In Mexican tradition, you can find deeply ingrained cultural offerings on November 2, *Día de los Muertos*, or the Day of the Dead. While November 2 forms the primary day of festivity, the Days of the Dead are commonly celebrated from Halloween through All Souls' Day. All Souls' Altars, known as *ofrendas*, or offerings, are another well-known practice born out of pre-Christian tradition. The motivation for constructing these altars, complete with food and refreshments, was to welcome the souls of one's deceased family members home on this day. While we do not believe that souls return to earth needing refreshments, Catholics have reclaimed this tradition as a festive practice to commemorate those who have died. Catholic *ofrendas* are created as colorful altars or displays in homes and in parishes. Within the home you might find a one-tier table or stand that is brightly decorated with *papel picado*, pecked-paper, flowers such as marigolds, candles, tablecloths, banners, a crucifix, images of saints and deceased loved ones, and some favorite belongings of deceased loved ones. All these things would be on a parish *ofrenda*, too, but on a larger scale. To accommodate the amount of pictures you will receive from the congregation, the parish will need to adapt this household custom by creating a three-tier display. Each tier can be explained as being symbolic of that which we celebrate during Allhallowtide, the Communion of Saints: the Church in heaven, the Church in purgatory, and the Church here on earth. All parishioners are invited to bring a picture of their deceased family member to display so the community can see the larger picture: that we are all linked together on our journey to heaven. As you are gathered together around your *ofrenda*, share stories of your beloved deceased to keep their memories and the grace of your relationships with them alive.

 A traditional prayer that we pray for the poor souls in purgatory is called the *Requiem Aeternam*. Also known as the Eternal Rest Prayer, it is commonly recited when Catholics learn that someone has died, on All Souls' Day, and throughout the month of November. The prayer goes like this: "Eternal rest grant to them, O Lord, and let perpetual light shine upon them. May the souls of the faithful departed, through the mercy of God, rest in peace. Amen." Many Catholics also pray the second part of this prayer when concluding their Grace before Meals prayer just before eating. This little tradition is a way to keep the dead of our families close to our hearts, especially during mealtime when everyone is together and their absence can be the most prominent. Although we can no longer eat with those beloved individuals as we once did, because of our common belonging to the Communion of Saints, they remain in a profound way with us always. By extending our prayers toward the souls of the faithful departed, we make the goal of being at the eternal feast in heaven present within our households.

 In Ireland and England during the Middle Ages, peasants and children known as "soulers" would travel from door to door, singing and praying for the souls of the deceased members of each household who had passed in the previous year. In exchange for praying for the dead, the children would ask for a soul cake. Some believe that this is the earliest version of what we now call trick-or-treating. Soul cakes are simple, spiced round cake with a cross marked on the top, similar to the way we marked the top of our hot cross bun, to show their association with prayer and alms. Italian culture also has a similar Day of the Dead baking tradition called *Ossi dei Morti* or "Bones of the Dead." Keep this baking tradition alive with your family or friends by making these easy cakes in honor of those who have gone before you in faith. You can say or sing this little rhyme while you make a cross on each little cake: "A soul-cake! A soul-cake! Have mercy on all Christen Souls, for a soul-cake!"[10]

CARRYING ON THE TRADITION

AT HOME
Visit and pray at the graves of your beloved deceased, bake soul cakes, or construct an All Souls' Altar or *ofrenda* to honor those who have died in Christ.

Consider This
- Bring fresh flowers and the necessary items needed to clean off the tombstone.
- Print or memorize the *Requiem Aeternam* or Eternal Rest Prayer to say with others or on your own.
- Bake soul cakes, or *Ossi Dei Morti*, to enjoy before family prayer time or to share with family, neighbors, and friends.
- Set up a small *ofrenda*, an altar for your beloved deceased, with the items listed in the section above.

IN THE PARISH
Display a three-tier *ofrenda* or All Souls' Altar in the narthex of your parish church to honor the faithful departed members of your parish. Adopt the custom of using a parish Book of the Names of the Dead.

Consider This
- Invite parishioners to bring one or two small images of people who have passed away in their household or family.
- Explain what this All Souls' Altar tradition means and why it is set up on this day and throughout November.
- Decorate the All Souls' Altar with the recommended items from the section above, such as brightly colored tablecloths, flowers, candles, and sacramentals.
- Invite parishioners to pray for the souls of the faithful departed in front of your parish-wide All Souls' Altar.
- Purchase and make easily accessible a Book of the Names of the Dead in your church. Provide ample explanation about this tradition in all your parish communications, and weave it into homilies. Invite parishioners to write in the book the names of their loved ones who have died. All

parishioners can then pray for these departed loved ones throughout the rest of November.

Resource
Use the Prayer for Visiting a Grave found in the *Festive Faith Easter and Summer Ordinary Time Companion* at www.HisGirlSunday.com/FestiveFaith. The Eternal Rest Prayer can be found in the *Festive Faith Sundays and Essentials Companion* at the same link.

NOTES

INTRODUCTION

1. Pope Pius XI, *Quas Primas*, December 11, 1925, no. 21, https://www.vatican.va/content/pius-xi/en/encyclicals/documents/hf_p-xi_enc_11121925_quas-primas.html#:~:text=21.,of%20the%20Kingship%20of%20Christ.

2. Quoted in Philip Kosloski, "St. Therese Repeated This Phrase Whenever She Was Lonely," Aleteia, September 27, 2022, https://aleteia.org/2022/09/27/st-therese-repeated-this-phrase-whenever-she-was-lonely.

ADVENT

1. St. John Paul II, General Audience, December 18, 2002, https://www.vatican.va/content/john-paul-ii/en/audiences/2002/documents/hf_jp-ii_aud_20021218.html#:~:text=We%20will%20pray%20that%20all,of%20the%20mystery%20of%20Christmas.

2. Maria Augusta Trapp, *Around the Year with the Trapp Family* (Manchester, NH: Sophia Institute, 2018), 6.

3. KidsGerman, "Advent Advent Ein Lichtlein Brennt," YouTube, December 21, 2022, video 3:11, https://youtu.be/1qDpUyFz3ek?si=_axk50UyXXpXyhsu.

4. Celine Fook, "Celebrating Christmas in France, Britain, and Poland!," Our Lady of Perpetual Succour, December 15, 2017, https://olps.sg/celebrating-christmas-france-britain-and-poland-1496.

CHRISTMAS

1. Thomas Celano, *The First Life of Saint Francis of Assisi* (Radnor, PA: Triangle, 2000), part 1, chapter 30, section 84.

2. Congregation for Divine Worship, *Directory on Popular Piety and the Liturgy*, December 2001, 111, https://www.vatican.va/roman_curia/congregations/ccdds/documents/rc_con_ccdds_doc_20020513_vers-direttorio_en.html.

3. Henry van Dyke, "The First Christmas Tree," https://americanliterature.com/author/henry-van-dyke/short-story/the-first-christmas-tree; originally published as "The Oak of Geismar," *Scribner's Magazine*, vol. 10, 1891, 686.

4. "Traditional Blessing of Wine on the Feast of St. John," Mater Dei Parish, December 26, 2016, https://materdeiparish.com/2016/12/blessing-wine-feast-st-john-tuesday-december-27th.

5. Pope Paul VI, *Marialis Cultus*, February 2, 1974, https://www.vatican.va/content/paul-vi/en/apost_exhortations/documents/hf_p-vi_exh_19740202_marialis-cultus.html.

WINTER ORDINARY TIME

1. United States Conference of Catholic Bishops, "Ordinary Time," accessed March 21, 2024, https://www.usccb.org/prayer-worship/liturgical-year/ordinary-time.

2. *Butler's Lives of the Fathers, Martyrs, and Other Saints*, ed. Rev. F. C. Husenbeth, vol. 1 (Great Falls, MT: St. Bonaventure Publications, 1997), 332.

3. Geoffrey Chaucer, *The Parliament of Fowles* (The Perfect Library, 2015), Kindle edition.

4. Francis X. Weiser, *The Handbook of Christian Feasts and Customs: The Year of the Lord in Liturgy and Folklore* (New York: Harcourt, Brace and World, 1958), 165.

LENT

1. United States Conference of Catholic Bishops, "Fast and Abstinence," accessed March 27, 2024, https://www.usccb.org/prayer-and-worship/liturgical-year-and-calendar/lent/catholic-information-on-lenten-fast-and-abstinence.

2. St. Patrick, *The Confession of Saint Patrick* (New York: Bantam Doubleday Dell, 1998), section 23.

3. Dom Prosper Gueranger, OSB, *The Liturgical Year: Passiontide and Holy Week*, vol. 6, trans. Dom Laurence Shepherd, OSB (Great Falls, Montana: St. Bonaventure Publications, 2000), 1.

4. Fr. Edward McNamara, "Covering of Crosses and Images in Lent," EWTN, March 8, 2005, https://www.ewtn.com/catholicism/library/covering-of-crosses-and-images-in-lent-4938.

5. *Missale Romanum* (International Commission on English in the Liturgy Corporation, 2010), 256.

6. Congregation for Divine Worship, *Directory on Popular Piety and the Liturgy*, December 2001, 139, https://www.vatican.va/roman_curia/congregations/ccdds/documents/rc_con_ccdds_doc_20020513_vers-direttorio_en.html.

7. Pius Parsch, *The Church's Year of Grace* (Collegeville, MN: Liturgical Press, 1964), 300.

8. Parsch, *Church's Year of Grace*, 303.

THE PASCHAL TRIDUUM

1. Dom Gaspar Lefebvre, *Saint Andrew Daily Missal* (St. Paul, MN: E. M. Lohmann, 1952), 824.

2. Herbert Thurston, "Pachal Candle," *Catholic Encyclopedia* (New York: The Gilmary Society, 1907–12), https://www.catholic.com/encyclopedia/paschal-candle.

3. United States Conference of Catholic Bishops, "The Roman Missal and the Easter Vigil," accessed March 21, 2024, https://www.usccb.org/prayer-and-worship/liturgical-year-and-calendar/triduum/roman-missal-and-the-easter-vigil.

4. United States Conference of Catholic Bishops, "The Roman Missal and the Easter Vigil."

EASTERTIDE

1. Pius Parsch, *The Church's Year of Grace* (Collegeville, MN: Liturgical Press, 1964), 244–245.

2. St. John Paul II, Angelus, November 30, 1986, https://www.vatican.va/content/john-paul-ii/en/angelus/1986/documents/hf_jp-ii_ang_19861130.html.

SUMMER ORDINARY TIME

1. United States Conference of Catholic Bishops, "Ordinary Time," accessed March 21, 2024, https://www.usccb.org/prayer-worship/liturgical-year/ordinary-time.

2. Pope Benedict XVI, "Homily on the Solemnity of Corpus Christi," June 7, 2007, https://www.vatican.va/content/benedictxvi/en/homilies/2007/documents/hf_ben-xvi_hom_20070607_corpus-christi.html.

3. St. Margaret Mary Alacoque, "12 Promises of the Sacred Heart of Jesus," EWTN, 1996, https://www.ewtn.com/catholicism/library/12-promises-of-the-sacred-heart-13683.

4. Congregation for Divine Worship, *Directory on Popular Piety and the Liturgy*, December 2001, 180, https://www.vatican.va/roman_curia/congregations/ccdds/documents/rc_con_ccdds_doc_20020513_vers-direttorio_en.html.

5. *Protoevangelium of James*, New Advent, accessed March 26, 2024, https://www.newadvent.org/fathers/0847.htm.

6. *Protoevangelium of James.*

7. F. Holweck, "St. Michael the Archangel," *The Catholic Encyclopedia* (New York: Robert Appleton Company, 1911), http://www.newadvent.org/cathen/10275b.htm.

8. Jeremy Butterfield, "Autumn Traditions and Their Lexicon," *Collins Dictionary*, September 27, 2022, https://blog.collinsdictionary.com/language-lovers/autumn-traditions-and-their-lexicon.

9. Michael Foley, "Michaelmas Day and Its Customs," New Liturgical Movement, September 29, 2021, https://www.newliturgicalmovement.org/2021/09/michaelmas-day-and-its-customs.html.

10. John Aubrey, *Remaines of Gentilisme and Judaisme, 1686–87*, ed. James Britten (London: The Folklore Society, 1880), 23.

WORKS REFERENCED

"Acts of John (Apocryphal)." New Advent, accessed March 27, 2024, http://www.newadvent.org/fathers/0827.htm.

Aubrey, John. *Remaines of Gentilisme and Judaisme, 1686–87*. Edited by James Britten. London: The Folklore Society, 1880.

Benedict XVI. "Homily on the Solemnity of Corpus Christi," June 7, 2007. https://www.vatican.va/content/benedict-xvi/en/homilies/2007/documents/hf_ben-xvi_hom_20070607_corpus-christi.html.

Bridge, James. "Acts of the Martyrs." *The Catholic Encyclopedia*. Vol. 9. New York: Robert Appleton Company, 1910. http://www.newadvent.org/cathen/09742b.htm.

Brown, Raphael. *The Little Flowers of St. Francis*. New York: Image Books, 1958.

Butler's Lives of the Fathers, Martyrs, and Other Saints. 4 vols. Edited by Rev. F. C. Husenbeth. Great Falls, MT: St. Bonaventure Publications, 1997.

Butterfield, Jeremy. "Autumn Traditions and Their Lexicon." *Collins Dictionary*, September 27, 2022. https://blog.collinsdictionary.com/language-lovers/autumn-traditions-and-their-lexicon.

Catechism of the Catholic Church. New York: Crown Publishing Group, 1995.

Celano, Thomas. *The First Life of Saint Francis of Assisi*. Radnor, PA: Triangle, 2000.

Chaucer, Geoffrey. *The Parliament of Fowles*. Kindle edition. The Perfect Library, 2015.

Collins, Joseph B. and Raphael Collins. *The Roman Martyrology*. Third Edition. Loreto Publications, 2014.

Congregation for Divine Worship. *Directory on Popular Piety and the Liturgy*, December 2001. https://www.vatican.va/roman_curia/congregations/ccdds/documents/rc_con_ccdds_doc_20020513_vers-direttorio_en.html

Coriden, James A., Thomas J. Green, and Donald E. Heintschel. *The Code of Canon Law: A Text and Commentary*. New York: Paulist Press. 1985.

Cottrau, Teodoro. *Santa Lucia*. 1849.

de Voragine, Jacobus. *The Golden Legend: Readings on the Saints*. Princeton, NJ: Princeton University Press, 2012.

Foley, Michael. "Michaelmas Day and Its Customs." New Liturgical Movement, September 29, 2021. https://www.newliturgicalmovement.org/2021/09/michaelmas-day-and-its-customs.html.

Fook, Celine. "Celebrating Christmas in France, Britain, and Poland!" Our Lady of Perpetual Succour, December 15, 2017. https://olps.sg/celebrating-christmas-france-britain-and-poland-1496.

Gray, Mark. "Eucharistic Beliefs: A National Survey of Adult Catholics." CARA, September 2023. https://static1.squarespace.com/static/629c7d00b33f845b6435b6a-b/t/6513358329f868492a786ea6/1695757700925/EucharistPollSeptember23.pdf.

Guéranger, Dom Prosper, OSB. *The Liturgical Year: Passiontide and Holy Week*. Vol. 6. Translated by Dom Laurence Shepherd, O.S.B. Great Falls, MT: St. Bonaventure Publications, 2000.

Holweck, F. "St. Michael the Archangel." *The Catholic Encyclopedia*. New York: Robert Appleton Company, 1911. http://www.newadvent.org/cathen/10275b.htm

Holy Bible. Douay-Rheims Version. Baltimore: John Murphy, 1914.

International Commission on English in the Liturgy. *Book of Blessings*. Totowa, NJ: Catholic Book Publishing, 1989.

John Paul II. Angelus, November 30, 1986. https://www.vatican.va/content/john-paul-ii/en/angelus/1986/documents/hf_jp-ii_ang_19861130.html.

John Paul II. Angelus, February 1, 2004. https://www.vatican.va/content/john-paul-ii/en/angelus/2004/documents/hf_jp-ii_ang_20040201.pdf.

John Paul II. *Dies Domini*, May 31, 1998. https://www.vatican.va/content/john- paul-ii/en/apost_letters/1998/documents/hf_jp-ii_apl_05071998_dies-domini.html.

John Paul II. General Audience, December 18, 2002. https://www.vatican.va/content/john-paul-ii/en/audiences/2002/documents/hf_jp-ii_aud_20021218.html.

KidsGerman. "Advent Advent Ein Lichtlein Brennt." YouTube, December 21, 2022. Video 3:11. https://youtu.be/1qDpUyFz3ek?si=_axk50UyXXpXyhsu.

Lefebvre, Dom Gaspar. *Saint Andrew Daily Missal*. St. Paul, MN: E. M. Lohmann, 1952.

Liturgical Institute. "The Meaning of Liturgy." YouTube, November 1, 2015. Video 3:11. https://youtu.be/6g-zSAgnxxk?si=SGeFY-6tEfxTRAPU.

Margaret Mary Alacoque. "12 Promises of the Sacred Heart of Jesus." EWTN, 1996. https://www.ewtn.com/catholicism/library/12-promises-of-the-sacred-heart-13683.

McClure, M. L. *The Pilgrimage of Etheria*. London: Society for Promoting Christian Knowledge, 1919.

McNamara, Fr. Edward. "Covering of Crosses and Images in Lent." EWTN, March 8, 2005. https://www.ewtn.com/catholicism/library/covering-of-crosses-and-images-in-lent-4938.

Missale Romanum. International Commission on English in the Liturgy Corporation, 2010.

Palafox, Jose. "In the Name of Heaven, I Ask You . . . the Litany to Request a Posada Is Complete!" Musica en Mexico, December 19, 2022. https://musicaenmexico.com.mx/musica-mexicana/en-el-nombre-del-cielo-os-pido-la-letania-de-las-posadas-completa/.

Parsch, Pius. *The Church's Year of Grace*. Collegeville, MN: Liturgical Press, 1964.

Patrick. *The Confession of Saint Patrick*. New York: Bantam Doubleday Dell, 1998.

Paul VI. *Marialis Cultus*, February 2, 1974. https://www.vatican.va/content/paul-vi/en/apost_exhortations/documents/hf_p-vi_exh_19740202_marialis-cultus.html.

Pieper, Josef. *In Tune with the World: A Theory of Festivity*. New York: Harcourt, Brace and World, 1963.

Pieper, Josef. *Leisure: The Basis of Culture*. San Francisco: Ignatius Press, 2009.

The Protoevangelium of James. New Advent, accessed March 26, 2024. https://www.newadvent.org/fathers/0847.htm.

Rituale Romanum. Milwaukee, WI: Bruce Publishing, 1964.

Thurston, Herbert. "Paschal Candle." *Catholic Encyclopedia*. New York: The Gilmary Society, 1907–12. Available online at https://www.catholic.com/encyclopedia/paschal-candle.

"Traditional Blessing of Wine on the Feast of St. John." Mater Dei Parish, December 26, 2016, https://materdeiparish.com/2016/12/blessing-wine-feast-st-john-tuesday-december-27th.

Trapp, Maria Augusta. *Around the Year with the Trapp Family*. New York: Pantheon, 1955.

United States Conference of Catholic Bishops. "Fast and Abstinence," accessed March 27, 2024. https://www.usccb.org/prayer-and-worship/liturgical-year-and-calendar/lent/catholic-information-on-lenten-fast-and-abstinence.

United States Conference of Catholic Bishops. "Ordinary Time," accessed March 21, 2024. https://www.usccb.org/prayer-worship/liturgical-year/ordinary-time.

United States Conference of Catholic Bishops. "The Roman Missal and the Easter Vigil," accessed March 27, 2024. https://www.usccb.org/prayer-and-worship/liturgical-year-and-calendar/triduum/roman-missal-and-the-easter-vigil.

van Dyke, Henry. "The First Christmas Tree," https://americanliterature.com/author/henry-van-dyke/short-story/the-first-christmas-tree; originally published as "The Oak of Geismar," *Scribner's Magazine*, vol. 10, 1891, 686.

Weiser, Francis X. *The Handbook of Christian Feasts and Customs: The Year of the Lord in Liturgy and Folklore*. New York: Harcourt, Brace and World, 1958.

INDEX OF MENTIONED TRADITIONS AND PRAYERS

FESTIVE FAITH

STEFFANI AQUILA is the founder of Liturgy Culture & Kitchen by His Girl Sunday, an online space inspiring Catholic culture and liturgical living in the home and parish. She is the director of communications and marketing at the University of St. Thomas in Houston.

Aquila has extensive experience in parish ministry, holding titles including director of liturgical life at the Co-Cathedral of the Sacred Heart in Houston, associate director of youth ministry, and communications director. She also has experience working in Catholic high schools as a dean and an honors-level theology teacher.

Aquila earned a bachelor of arts degree in education with a minor in theology from the University of St. Thomas in Houston and a master of arts degree in theological studies from St. Mary's Seminary.

She lives with her husband in Houston, Texas.

Website: www.hisgirlsunday.com

AVE

AVE MARIA PRESS

Founded in 1865, Ave Maria Press,
a ministry of the Congregation of
Holy Cross, is a Catholic publishing
company that serves the spiritual and
formative needs of the Church and its
schools, institutions, and ministers;
Christian individuals and families; and
others seeking spiritual nourishment.

For a complete listing of titles from

Ave Maria Press

Sorin Books

Forest of Peace

Christian Classics

visit www.avemariapress.com

AVE MARIA PRESS
Notre Dame, IN
A Ministry of the United States Province of Holy Cross